YEMEN IN THE SHADOW OF TRANSITION

STACEY PHILBRICK YADAV

Yemen in the Shadow of Transition

Pursuing Justice Amid War

OXFORD
UNIVERSITY PRESS

Oxford University Press is a department of the
University of Oxford. It furthers the University's objective
of excellence in research, scholarship, and education
by publishing worldwide.

Oxford New York

Auckland   Cape Town   Dar es Salaam   Hong Kong   Karachi
Kuala Lumpur   Madrid   Melbourne   Mexico City   Nairobi
New Delhi   Shanghai   Taipei   Toronto

With offices in

Argentina   Austria   Brazil   Chile   Czech Republic   France   Greece
Guatemala   Hungary   Italy   Japan   Poland   Portugal   Singapore
South Korea   Switzerland   Thailand   Turkey   Ukraine   Vietnam

Oxford is a registered trade mark of Oxford University Press
in the UK and certain other countries.

Published in the United States of America by
Oxford University Press
198 Madison Avenue, New York, NY 10016

Library of Congress Cataloging-in-Publication Data is available

ISBN: 9780197678367

Printed in the United Kingdom
by Bell and Bain Ltd, Glasgow

CONTENTS

PREFACE
IN MEMORIAM

Memorials come in all shapes and sizes. The one I visit the most often hangs to the left of my desk in an office on the campus of a small liberal arts college in upstate New York. It is a collection of photographs, pamphlets, lapel pins, cartoon illustrations, and even a pocket calendar. Each of these pieces is a commemoration. Some of the people remembered on this bulletin board were friends and mentors, people who shaped my thinking and being in the world. Some of them were people I interviewed or met when doing field research. Some were known to me only through the ways they were memorialized by others. They were journalists, trade unionists, politicians, and fellow academics. All of them were and no longer are. Each one was murdered.

This memorial space is important to me in two ways. Intellectually, some of my first fieldwork observations in Yemen and Lebanon involved events or ceremonies linked to the commemoration of assassinations. Trying to better understand politics in both settings has always been in some way tied to a reckoning with political violence and its aftermath. As Yemen has moved from authoritarian rule to transitional disorder to devastating war, political violence has been a throughline. The language of "shadows" that frames several chapters of this book is meant to capture some measure of the lasting darkness of this violence.

This commemorative space is also important to me on a more personal level. When I attended a candlelight vigil in Beirut at the site of the bomb that killed a Lebanese writer in June 2005, I did so mostly as an ethnographer but also as a person whose nerves were shaken by the percussive blast of his car exploding while I sat at my desk blocks away. This assassination was one of several political killings in Beirut that spring, and I gradually developed the need to participate in shared rituals not simply as an observer but as someone living in proximity to violence.

I was in Cairo a few months later when a friend called from Beirut to share news of another assassination, this time of a newspaper publisher whom she knew I had interviewed. My friend remembered me complaining that it had been a difficult and frustrating interview; indeed, neither the publisher nor the exhibit he sponsored, which commemorated the assassination of former Prime Minister Rafiq al-Hariri, are characterized in flattering terms in my first book. I keep an image of this publisher on the bulletin board as well, to remind me that I do not need to like or admire someone's politics in order to object to the injustice of their murder or the absence of accountability for it.

Alongside these reminders, the memorial also commemorates a painful personal loss. In November 2014, I opened my Facebook to pictures of a dear friend and mentor shot dead on his walk home from work in Sana'a and left in the street to die. It is not an exaggeration to say that his loss – the fact of it and the mediated circumstances through which I learned of it and have repeatedly re-witnessed it – have changed my way in the world. He had an abiding belief that justice could be pursued through the deliberative development of overlapping consensus. He worked for this in his scholarship, in his teaching, and in his political practice. As the theoretical argument laid out in Chapter 2 explains, this book is informed by that perspective and advances the same normative aim.

I do not have a picture of this friend and mentor on my bulletin board. I have almost no photos from my field research in Yemen, which is something I sorely regret. I only have one picture from across the decade that I knew him, a terrible, out-of-focus snapshot of the two of us sitting in his *mafraj*. It was taken sometime in 2009, which I remember because of the context. I had been away from Sana'a for a while, and he had just finished catching me up on the most recent threats against his life, dismissing them with the sanguine humor of someone who knows he takes risks and knows he will keep taking them. Before I left that day, I asked someone to take our picture together. I look at it sometimes, tucked away in my desk, but whenever I do, it is immediately replaced in my mind's eye by the image of his death. I leave an empty space on the bulletin board to remind me of the limits of commemoration in the absence of justice.

INTRODUCTION
PURSUING JUSTICE AMID WAR

On November 17, 2021, Nadwa al-Dawsari, a noted Yemeni analyst and non-resident fellow at the Middle East Institute in Washington, DC, tweeted the following:

> I attend events, webinars, & meetings with #Yemen analysts & I walk out feeling so depressed, every bloody time. I call Yemenis who are on the ground doing great work & I am filled with hope that Yemen will be OK. Maybe not today or tomorrow but someday it will.[1]

Though we write from different positions and for somewhat different audiences, the decision to write this book and to write it in the way that I have is driven by a similar sentiment. Working over the past several years with Yemeni researchers and civil actors engaged in peacebuilding projects, I have been both awed and reassured. Awed because of the tremendous work that they are doing and risks they are taking to hold communities together, mitigate conflict, and lay ground for the kinds of post-conflict futures that they imagine. And reassured because, though the Yemen I knew best from my earlier research is no longer a reality, there is something in the determination of Yemeni civil actors that I recognize as part of a deep continuity. It is, in short, Yemenis who inspire, and the abstraction of Yemen that produces the kind of despondence al-Dawsari rightly describes.

1

Writing about post-conflict justice is challenging in the context of an ongoing war, a crushing humanitarian crisis, and a peace process that inspires little confidence. Yet without thinking about what comes next, there is real risk that conflict dynamics will get built into new institutions in ways that undermine the possibility of meaningful recovery, reconciliation, or justice. No decision about institutions in post-conflict societies is made only with the immediate challenges of reconstruction in mind. The design of post-conflict institutions and the pursuit of transitional justice unfolds against the backdrop of history and anticipation. The histories that count, the comparisons that decision-makers (or advisors) draw, and the consequences that various actors anticipate all shape the trajectory of post-conflict states, societies, and economies.

This book explores these themes through the lens of Yemeni justice demands over the period since the unification of North and South Yemen as a single state in 1990. I identify three different modes of engagement with justice claims—disengagement, strategic engagement, and substantive engagement—and explore the adoption of these different approaches under the regime of former President 'Ali 'Abdullah Saleh, during the transitional period that followed the 2011 uprising and, now, amid the current war. Past engagements with justice structure current practices and the kinds of just futures imagined by Yemen's civil actors. Genuinely sustainable and accountable institutions and social transformation in post-war Yemen will only be possible through substantive engagement with questions of justice, including a reckoning with past transitional projects. The central argument of the book is that decision-makers can and should take as a model the substantive engagement—or 'justice work'—being done today by Yemeni civil actors in local communities across the country. Rather than waiting for a national settlement from the top or brokered from outside, civil actors are already engaged in the enactment of justice projects in real time. However, their ability to scale these projects beyond the local will depend upon the adoption of a 'peace learning' approach that recognizes the central importance of civil action.[2]

Transitional Justice and the Capabilities Approach

There is a well-developed body of cross-regional research on transitional justice that argues for approaches to post-conflict justice that range from universalizing 'toolkits' and one-size-fits-all institutional arrangements to those that emphasize hyperlocal traditions of justice and mediation. Academic research on Yemen, meanwhile, has paid little attention to justice questions—as such. Instead, much of the scholarly literature has focused on describing the causes and consequences of encroaching authoritarianism under Saleh and sources of political disorder and disintegration following the 2011 uprising. This has been supplemented with policy-oriented analysis produced during the 2012–14 transitional period. Since the onset of the war, there has been comparatively little academic research, given the limitations on access and restrictions on funding.[3] Some work addressing Yemen in its regional context and in relation to global economic and geostrategic concerns has helped to outline the kinds of pressures and opportunities that may emerge for post-war reconstruction, but such work largely does not take up questions of transitional or post-conflict justice explicitly. This book seeks to bring these individual strands of research together, connected by empirical and normative claims about the central importance of justice work by civil actors.

In simple terms, I take justice work to comprise action taken to diagnose and/or address a wrong. While the state's justice system can certainly be a channel for justice work, so can systems of justice that are grounded in tribal, religious, or customary law. Justice work can also occur outside of such systems, in forms that range from the theatrical to the mundane. The former might be literally theatrical, as with *masrah al-haquqi* or 'rights theater' as it developed during the 2011 uprising, or figuratively so, as with choreographed performances of non-violent opposition to the legal immunity extended to former President Saleh during the transitional period. Justice work can also involve far more quotidian practices that identify a harm—for example, the systematic exclusion of a group from decision-making—and seek to remedy that harm through representation and practical expansions of effective citizenship.

Justice work is not necessarily non-violent; some narratives of injustice can be used to mobilize violent action. But as I explain below, the justice work with which this book is primarily concerned is the non-violent work of Yemen's civil actors. Civil action is a distinctive form of non-violent action that is intimately tied to both effective citizenship and to peacebuilding.

Given the difficulty of organizing under conditions of ongoing conflict, those who engage in justice work that includes practices like documentation, memorialization of victims, public art, and more take on considerable risk. Recent scholarship has focused attention on the work of such civil actors and sought to elaborate their distinct role in conflict de-escalation and peacebuilding, often via transitional justice mechanisms.[4] Civil actors are not simply 'civilians,' nor are they necessarily non-contentious. Civil actors advance claims that are non-eliminationist in their rhetoric and practice, distinguishing them from conflict actors and from other non-violent activists.[5] Their approach is premised on an exceptionally thin version of civility—mere civility—which Teresa Bejan describes as manifestly low standard.[6] According to Avant *et al.*, this thinness distinguishes mere civility from more encompassing versions of civility that 'either restrict what is said or require some level of agreement on which to base interactions,' and instead entails only 'peaceable actions that are respectful enough of basic human decency to keep a conversation going.'[7] The mere civility of civil actors is associated with de-escalation of violence insofar as it disrupts the 'exclusivity, polarization, radicalization, and evocation of enmity' that scholars in the fields of contentious politics and security studies associate with violence.[8]

Some transitional justice scholars (and many practitioners) take for granted the normative correctness of the liberal roots of transitional justice, yet people do not only or always talk about post-conflict justice in ways that reflect the field's liberal assumptions. Work with Yemeni civil actors over the past several years heightened my awareness of the ways in which both liberal and communitarian claims might coexist in justice projects. Rather than adopting a liberal frame that emphasizes the centrality of individual rights and juridical equality over all else, I have tried to make sense of their work within the tradition of the Capabilities Approach. Such an approach has recognizably liberal and communitarian components that make it particularly helpful for analyzing structural injustice insofar as it is focused on entrenched inequalities as they function as constraints on individual freedoms.[9] More often associated with the field of development, the emphasis of the Capabilities Approach on institutions and its normative concern with questions of justice also make it an appropriate lens through which to consider approaches to peacebuilding and post-conflict planning in divided societies. Doing so offers the possibility of an approach to justice that is recognizable to liberal transitional justice practitioners whose focus is typically on the rights of individuals, but also to more communitarian actors concerned with the rights of groups.

Very generally, such an approach endeavors to advance what Amartya Sen refers to as transpositional scrutiny on issues of common concern as a means of securing comparatively just outcomes in the absence of transcendent justice. What does this mean? Sen's emphasis on comparative justice is essential to thinking about post-conflict institutions because it does not presuppose the possibility of transcendently 'just' outcomes but rather suggests that diversely situated people can be brought together in ways that allow them to develop an overlapping consensus on the most just among a set of alternatives. As states rebuild and societies recover from war, the question of what individuals need in order to live the lives they envision—a question at the heart of the Capabilities Approach—is one that can only be determined through this kind of transpositional scrutiny. While these Capabilities-informed normative claims and their relationship to transitional or post-conflict justice will be the focus of the next chapter, its vocabulary and grammar underwrite the project as a whole.[10]

Beyond the normative plane, there is good empirical reason to be concerned with questions of justice in Yemen. Yemen's so-called 'transitional period' (2012–14) was a point at which several mechanisms from an increasingly normalized and globalized transitional justice toolbox were introduced for both strategic and substantive reasons. Dynamics developed during this period and in part through these mechanisms contributed to the war that began in 2015. Moreover, many grievances that surfaced in the context of Yemen's eleven-month uprising were left unresolved, and demands for accountability for earlier wrongs from across the Saleh era (and even before) were shunted aside. Poor post-conflict engagement with justice, in other words, has had real and violent consequences.

The exigencies of the current war have not displaced demands for justice so much as added to them and changed the ways in which Yemeni civil actors pursue their claims. The fragmented nature of the current conflict and the securitization of justice work have meant that many civil actors are pursuing justice today through work most often described as peacebuilding. They do so under diverse conditions, divided from one another, and in the absence of a political settlement. Yemenis are not waiting, in other words, for an agreement to be struck to pursue justice claims. Justice work that is happening now, however, is largely unregulated by and disconnected from any set of state institutions and is often poorly integrated into the UN-led diplomatic process; new institutions are being built and old institutions resuscitated in different parts of the country through a combination of local need and regional interest. Some projects are being financed by international organizations, some by donors, and others still by private investors, risking the possibility that conflict dynamics may be literally built in to Yemen's post-war infrastructure. Collectively, this means that it is not too early to be thinking about what comes after the war ends or what kinds of structures and practices can amplify the justice work that is already being done.

How This Book Came To Be

Shortly before the COVID-19 pandemic closed the campus where I teach in March 2020, my colleague, Kevin Dunn, asked if I would participate in a short film that he was making for the International Studies Association meeting. We sat down to film in the same week that I signed a contract to write this book. I mention these two together because the question around which the film was organized has stayed in my mind throughout the writing of this book, more than I anticipated it would. It informed choices that I made, interviews

I sought out, and a chunk of the argument I make in the last two chapters of the book, especially. The film poses a simple question to a group of students, scholars, and activists: 'what would the discipline look like if [international relations] assumed people actually mattered?'[11] In my own response, I turned to Wendy Pearlman's work on Syria, which I admire not only for the way it maps concepts as they emerge from her interlocutors' self-understanding but for the way that Pearlman conceptualizes narration as a central form of political agency.[12] I cited her normative call for researchers to both recognize and elicit this agency by inviting narration as a practical means of putting people first.

My answer to Dunn's framing question, which has informed my approach to this book, was shaped by my own position in four interconnected ways. The first is disciplinary. I have not often connected my own work to debates in the subfield of international relations (IR) so much as those in comparative politics in large part because I have found IR, at least as I encountered it as a graduate student and early career scholar, to be too distant from the kinds of meaning-making practices that most interest me.[13] The second is methodological, insofar as my response reflects a commitment to abduction and emphasis on meaning-mapping that is characteristic of interpretive methods and post-positivist epistemology. It was also shaped by my position as a professor, and specifically as a professor of undergraduate students; in the classroom, I have observed the role of storytelling in encouraging intellectual curiosity and openness but have also seen that stories do not need to be neat or linear to illuminate for others important social realities. Finally, as I elaborate below, my answer was shaped by the importance that narrative and narration have played in my own learning with and from Yemeni civil actors and the ways they understand their experiences of past, present, and future.

Rather than coming to Yemen as a case through which to engage an academic literature on transitional or post-conflict justice, I more inductively came to recognize the centrality of questions of justice through my work on Yemen and engagement with Yemenis over the course of many years.[14] This book draws on qualitative research conducted in Yemen and among Yemenis spanning a period of close to two decades; it is based on over 100 individual interviews, dozens of focus groups and small group discussions, and fieldnotes from events that span from 2004 to 2022. It includes participatory action research conducted in the context of collaborative work with Yemeni colleagues, which I outline below. The book reflects the epistemological commitments of work in the interpretive tradition, oriented toward an ethic of 'world disclosure' that seeks to make what at first appears puzzling less so.[15]

I initially began field research in Yemen in 2004 when working on a doctoral dissertation that became my first book, *Islamists and the State*. This occurred at a time when a number of political movements were coalescing to challenge the regime of President 'Ali 'Abdullah Saleh. Two of these movements—the Houthi movement, or Ansar Allah, and the Southern Movement, or Hirak—became increasingly significant, though they were not the core focus of my research at the time. I was interested primarily in understanding the dynamics of cross-ideological alliance formation through the emergence and formalization of the Joint Meeting Parties opposition alliance. The two extrapartisan movements were nonetheless an object of ongoing discussion among partisan actors and civil society activists. The regime's response to each movement, as well as the growing risk of militancy from Al Qaeda in the Arabian Peninsula after 2008, shaped the options faced by Yemen's political parties and civil society alike. Returning to interviews, fieldnotes, and texts from the 2000s and conducting follow-up interviews more recently with some of the same interlocutors has helped me to trace justice-related themes from this period. These materials have helped me reach backward—understanding legacies of the unification process and brief 1994 civil war, the relationship between religion and state, and other dynamics that shaped both the Hirak and the Houthi movement—and forward, to the 2011 uprising, the transitional period that followed, and the ongoing war.

During the tumultuous period that followed the uprising, I continued to conduct research on Yemen and with Yemenis, but that work began to take a different form. Working now from outside of the country, I interviewed Yemeni activists and political figures and attended meetings and internationally sponsored training workshops and dialogues hosted in Istanbul, Amman, Qatar, the UAE, and Oman, as well as London, Washington, DC, and New York. During this time, I also communicated individually and via social media with politically active Yemenis, but I do not rely heavily on social media postings or tweets as sources of data here. I have largely avoided the use of social media content in this book, except where the author is known to me personally and has explicitly consented to its use. That said, I am grateful for—if sometimes overwhelmed by—the volume of information, insight, and deliberation that social media has allowed, linking Yemenis, the broad Yemeni diaspora, and non-Yemeni interlocutors. It has informed the discussion of Yemeni knowledge-production at the end of the book, in particular.

Where social media and other forms of digital communication have been most significant is in helping me to become aware of changes that I knew I would struggle to capture through research at a distance. This was a driving force in the pivot toward participatory action research in 2019. During the transitional period and the earliest stages of the war, I was observing international institutional processes but was not participating directly in them. In 2019, however, I began to work directly with Yemeni researchers on collaborative research on peacebuilding, including work funded through international peacebuilding organizations and European and Yemeni research centers. This work—both the product and the process—has given me access to perspectives that deeply inform this book. Because the research generated by these projects is not mine alone, I cite it wherever I make direct reference to our findings. But it also informs the background that shaped the book as a whole, as well as some of my reflections on process-level features of international peacebuilding and the role of Yemeni civil actors in knowledge production.

A decade ago, Charli Carpenter helped to explain the logic of participatory action research to positivist skeptics in the wider discipline of political science through her reflections on studying issue non-emergence in the human rights field.[16] Asking why an issue of serious harm had not emerged on the international human rights agenda, Carpenter recalled being discouraged from studying the issue by positivist social scientists who worried that describing this non-emergence successfully would lead to greater attention to the non-emerged human rights issue in a way that undermined her ability to study (and publish on) the subject scientifically. In other words, her research might render her original research question obsolete. For Carpenter, however, that was part of the point. The decision to undertake work with the very human rights organizations she was studying was at least partially a normative one. She recalls that 'it seemed unethical to me to study a human rights non-issue without contributing to well-intentioned efforts to turn it into an issue.'[17] But it was also empirical. What may have been puzzling at the outset—why doesn't this issue seem to matter?—became less so once Carpenter herself began to work in the international organizational contexts through which agenda-setting occurred, even as that work also helped to move the issue that concerned her onto the agenda.

Carpenter's insights, as well as her own public grappling with issues of epistemology and ethics that are often minimized or obscured by more positivist political scientists, influenced my own decision to engage in collaborative peacebuilding research as action research. The first work of this sort that I undertook involved research on women and everyday peacebuilding in Yemen. This was part of a five-team study on the peacebuilding work of different groups of civil actors sponsored by the Bonn-based Center for Applied Research in Partnership with the Orient (CARPO) and funded by the German development agency Deutsche Gesellschaft für Internationale Zusammenarbeit. In 2019, I worked with Drs. Iman al-Gawfi and Bilkis al-Zabara, both professors at Sana'a University, to design and implement a series of interviews and focus group discussions in urban communities of Sana'a and Aden as well as peri-urban and rural peripheries in Sana'a governorate and Lahj. This gave us access to the perspectives of members of communities living under the practical jurisdiction of the Houthis (Ansar Allah), the internationally recognized Government of Yemen (GoY), and the Southern Transitional Council (STC), which is the parastatal inheritor of the Hirak movement. The focus of this research was to better understand how variation in the material and political conditions in each area shaped the forms of everyday peacebuilding that women were enacting in their communities, as well as to gauge what men and women in each community viewed as the challenges and opportunities presented by women's peacebuilding work.[18]

The second collaboration was carried out with Maged al-Kholidy and Yazeed al-Jeddawy from the Yemeni civil society organization, Youth Without Borders Organization for Development (YWBOD), based in Taiz. This project, which was funded by international peacebuilding organization Interpeace, involved mapping hundreds of civil society organizations (CSOs) engaged in peacebuilding work across thirteen governorates. Our team designed and conducted interviews and focus group discussions with the staff of peacebuilding CSOs under a diverse range of conflict conditions.[19] The aim of this internal report was to help Interpeace determine whether or where it might become more directly engaged in supporting peacebuilding programming in Yemen with local partner organizations. Interpeace and YWBOD have subsequently designed a program based on this report.

The most recent collaboration was with Rim Mugahed at the Sana'a Center for Strategic Studies, addressing the dual challenge of partisan women's inclusion in the peace process. Paired with a two-week training workshop for partisan women sponsored by the Sana'a Center and funded by the European Union, our project included observations of the workshop and interviews with women nominated by their parties to participate in this training. We explored the barriers that women experience within their political parties, and tensions that exist between partisan and independent women engaged in peacebuilding work at different scales. Our report was published in the fall of 2021, as I was completing the manuscript for this book.[20]

What it means to identify 'the local' and craft conditions of local ownership in international peacebuilding is a subject of a great deal of critical peacebuilding scholarship, as I explore in later chapters. Participating in the process as a contributing researcher and observing the language, meaning(s), and practices of peacebuilding practitioners has informed arguments throughout this book, particularly in terms of the relationship that I ultimately see between local peacebuilding and justice work versus international approaches to peace-brokering. The arguments I advance here are mine alone, however, and cannot be taken as a reflection of views held by any of my Yemeni colleagues, unless I expressly cite them.

My relationship to data generated by interviews and focus group discussions conducted through these collaborations is a complex one and has shaped how I have (and have not) used data from these collaborative projects in the book. While I helped to shape the research design in each case, contributed to the selection of interview and focus group participants and the organizations where observations were conducted, wrote interview questions, and participated in analysis of interview transcripts and notes, I was not present for most of the interviews for these collaborative projects. For this reason, I cite the written analysis of these projects—itself reliant on deliberations among team members in which I participated directly as we interpreted the data together. In my references, I distinguish between interviews that I conducted personally ('with author') and other interviews conducted as a part of these research collaborations.

As a graduate student, I learned somewhat painfully how the specific parameters of consent matter to our ethical engagement with research materials and interlocutors. I published a controversial statement by a member of a Yemeni opposition party—for which I had consent—in a context outside my dissertation; when it was subsequently reproduced in a Yemeni newspaper without my permission, it put the speaker in a difficult position. I have written about the fallout of this incident and its impact on my fieldwork ethics elsewhere, but the lasting lesson for me is that consent to identify an interlocutor should be renewed whenever research materials are being used in a new context.[21] This has not been possible with much of the older field material that I use in several chapters of this book, whether because interlocutors are not reachable, have died (or been killed), are in prison, and so on. Circumstances have changed so dramatically that what might once have been a safe statement may no longer be. With most interviews conducted since 2015, interlocutors were guaranteed anonymity but I have decided to retroactively anonymize all earlier interview data as well.

In reaching this decision, I sought the advice of respected conflict scholars and discussed the issue with my research partners and with staff at the organizations involved with these collaborative projects. Reaching such decisions with others is only one of the ways in which collaborative research can be practically and ethically challenging. However, I question the contention that collaborative research is intrinsically a form of structural violence.[22] There are undoubtedly better and worse ways of organizing collaboration, partnerships that work well and those that are exploitative. My aim in participating in research partnerships has been to expand my own understanding of the dynamics of ongoing conflict, peacebuilding, and justice work when professional and personal circumstances have made it impossible for me to travel to Yemen. My commitment has been to do so in a way that centers the questions and concerns of my Yemeni partners and to engage in processes that maximize their control over the research. The funding structure and project design on the CARPO and YWBOD collaborations, for example, meant that I was brought on as a third partner or consultant, capable of being outvoted on any decision of consequence or removed from the project by my Yemeni partners (this never happened, but it was important to me that it could have). Budgeting responsibility, as well, rested with my Yemeni partners. These structural features were designed to address some of the critiques of collaborative research, and I believe—or at least hope—that they facilitated less exploitative relationships than other models of joint research that exist.

While collaborative research has been vital to my understanding of local-level peacebuilding practices and diverse political and material circumstances across Yemen, it has also inspired me to learn more and think critically about international peacebuilding work in Yemen. In the last chapter of the book, especially, I supplement knowledge gained through these collaborations with my own discussions with staff at international peacebuilding and human rights organizations. And in making the argument that Yemeni researchers are themselves doing justice work as civil actors, I include some reflections by Yemeni colleagues working in the area of peacebuilding research itself.

Engaging (and Disengaging) with Justice Demands

Although this book works to historicize justice demands over the course of 30 years, its animating puzzle is more recent. Given that the National Dialogue Conference (NDC) appears to have failed as the centerpiece of the post-conflict transitional process following the 2011 Yemeni uprising, why does it have such a central place in the political imaginings of so many civil actors engaged in peacebuilding work today? I have been surprised by the frequency with which civil actors mention 'returning the NDC outcomes,' and the diverse meanings that they appear to attach to this idea. As I explain in Chapter 4, the NDC was both an instrument for and a site of deliberation over transitional justice. As an instrument of transitional justice, national dialogues seek to shift away from elite brokering and toward more inclusive processes in which participants are able to 'discover, learn, and transform relationships in order to address practical and structural problems in society.'[23] According to the terms of the Gulf Cooperation Council Initiative, the externally-brokered agreement designed to bring the 2011 Yemeni uprising to an end, Yemen's National Dialogue Conference was presented as such a structure but also as the primary mechanism through which Yemenis could design a more expansive transitional justice program for the future.

There is a delicate line between recognizing the regional character of a phenomenon and acknowledging the particularities of a specific context.[24] Yemen is unique, and Yemenis are aware of their neighborhood, as well. This was reflected in conversations with and observations of Yemeni activists in advance of the NDC, where comparisons with the experiences of other Middle Eastern and North African (MENA) contexts were prevalent. Talking with Yemenis and others about how different countries in the region navigated the transitional justice process before and after the 2011 uprisings informed the development of a typology of justice engagement that guides me throughout the book. I rely on this typology to compare and make sense of the interplay between both elite and popular demands for justice and regime responses, as they occur within and outside of the context of institutions. The typology includes three basic approaches to justice claims, which are detailed below.

Disengagement

Actors can be said to disengage from justice demands when they ignore and/or actively suppress critics and work to protect status quo features of systems against which these demands are articulated.

Strategic Engagement

Actors can be said to strategically engage justice demands where there are targeted efforts to address some justice demands as a means of upholding the system itself. Those justice demands that take aim at the perceived injustices of the regime are unlikely to be selected for strategic engagement, but less controversial claims—especially demand for 'inclusion'—may be adopted as a means of strategically managing dissent.

Substantive Engagement

Actors can be said to substantively engage justice demands where there are opportunities for transpositional scrutiny through which differently situated actors can express grievances and imagine more just alternatives alongside others. This allows for the development of overlapping consensus regarding injustice and enables actors to express solidarities that support remediation of injustices that may or may not affect them directly. Process-level features of shared deliberation and mutual recognition (even if only on a minimal basis) themselves contribute to expanding agency and therefore may also be said to substantively engage justice.

All three of these approaches have been at work in cases across the MENA region in different measure, as they have been elsewhere.[25] Lebanon, for example, is a case that typifies elite disengagement with core justice demands in its post-conflict context, where the confessional regime ignored or actively resisted the justice demands of people seeking an alternative to the sectarianized status quo. Lebanon's post-war political settlement left institutions largely unchanged, with only minor tweaks to the electoral and institutional logic of a confessional system that extended across colonial and post-colonial regimes.[26] The tremendous economic burden of reconstruction paired with institutions that remain embedded in and captured by the logic of confessionalism has meant that reconstruction helped to both figuratively and literally build sectarian inequalities into the state itself.[27] Lebanon transitioned to a post-conflict order but did so without explicitly addressing the war's injustices.[28] A post-conflict settlement built on indifference to justice demands has fueled three decades of protracted political paralysis and intermittent crisis, shaping successive rounds of contention. Civil actors have nonetheless undertaken justice work that challenges the sectarian framework and addresses the necrotizing harms of a civil war long past.[29]

The case of Morocco, by contrast, shows that even when transitional justice mechanisms are formally adopted, engagement with justice claims can be strategic and regime-preserving. When he took over from his father, Hassan II, King Mohammed VI introduced a limited transitional justice program designed to address the abuses of the decades-long 'Years of Lead' without undoing the monarchical regime itself. Though it follows a very different path than Lebanon, the truncated nature of Morocco's engagement suggests that its regime was strategic in responding to the justice demands of some. This mode of engagement provided restitution to many Moroccan citizens harmed by King Hassan II's policies and adopted an approach to reparations that recognized both individual and collective claims.[30] But it also indemnified most state actors, upheld important political red lines, and laid ground for ongoing forms of political contention in the years that followed.[31]

Tunisia's transitional justice program was broader and featured more substantive engagement with justice than any other in the MENA region.[32] Beginning in 2011, Tunisians employed multiple tools from an increasingly normalized and internationally supported toolkit and secured (if incompletely) some reparative justice for victims of the Ben 'Ali regime. But Tunisia's transitional justice program also unfolded in a political context that enabled elected officials to strip the project of much of its content even before the political changes that occurred in 2021. This suggests that substantive engagement may be necessary but insufficient to ensuring that justice demands are meaningfully addressed.[33]

In Yemen, all three forms of engagement have been evident at different moments (and in different combinations) across the three decades considered in this book. These same three decades align with the period in which transitional justice has become normalized and institutionalized on a global scale as a core component of liberal peacebuilding. Chapter 1 reviews the main instruments of transitional justice and traces their evolution and sedimentation. It offers an alternative way to think of post-conflict justice that might rely on some of the same tools and remain recognizable to liberal peacebuilders without adopting an exclusively liberal *telos*. This is where I elaborate on the value of the Capabilities Approach for considerations of justice and, in particular, for its ability to recognize communitarian claims and evaluate process-level features of transitional justice and peacebuilding.

Justice and Injustice Over Time

Having laid theoretical ground in Chapter 1, the next section of the book is devoted to tracing the claims and work of civil actors over Yemen's recent history, marked as it has been by different combinations of disengagement, strategic engagement, and substantive engagement with justice by different actors at different times. It is not organized as a chronological 'history of Yemen,' but explores contention that has occurred within and outside of formal institutions to identify how various engagements with justice have shaped conflict and civil action alike.

Chapter 2 focuses predominantly on the 'institutional story'— the dynamics of the 1990 unification of North and South Yemen, the introduction of an electoral regime to manage dissent, the brief 1994 civil war, and the consolidation of an increasingly narrow authoritarianism in the years that followed. This chapter pays special attention to the role of justice demands in driving the formation of the cross-ideological opposition alliance, the Joint Meeting Parties (JMP). Understanding the motives and limitations of this alliance, and its paradoxical role in closing off institutional avenues of contention by 2009, is central to interpreting the 2011 uprising, developments in the transitional period, and beyond. Moreover, JMP members were powerful beneficiaries of the Gulf Cooperation Council Initiative (GCCI) and have enjoyed privileged access to the UN-led diplomatic process as part of Yemen's internationally recognized government.

The partisan story is matched by an account in Chapter 3 of extrapartisan mobilization by the Houthi movement in the North and the Hirak in the South, tracing the antecedents of both movements to justice demands and regime responses in the 1990s and even earlier. If Chapter 2 shows how the regime adeptly pitted elements of the partisan opposition against each other to largely avoid justice demands, Chapter 3 shows the introduction of some limited and strategic engagements with justice, paired with extensive repression. While the two planes of partisan and extrapartisan analysis intersect in some ways, I address them in separate chapters in part because of the different roles played by parties and movements in Yemen's post-2011 political and armed conflicts. In both chapters, however, the primary emphasis is on the type of justice claims that movements and parties made and the way their claims were (or were not) engaged prior to the 2011 uprising.

Chapters 2 and 3 jointly introduce several of the core social, political, regional, and economic cleavages in Yemeni society. Drawing on academic literature, interviews, fieldnotes, and other primary materials, the aim of this section is to enable readers to map continuities and discontinuities in the justice claims made by different segments of Yemeni society over time; these not only informed the 2011 uprising and the transitional process but continue to shape justice work in the context of the current war.

Justice Demands and Justice Work

The final section of the book explores the relationship between justice demands and justice work over the decade extending from Yemen's uprising to 2022. Chapter 4 is the longest chapter and covers the shortest time period (2011–14), mapping the years that demonstrated the greatest substantive gains by Yemeni civil actors pursuing justice. These gains were offset by strategic engagement by transitional elites that undermined civil actors, as well as by armed conflicts that unfolded in several parts of the country as transitional justice mechanisms were being employed at the center. This chapter discusses the role of the National Dialogue Conference (NDC) and its Transitional Justice committee as well as parallel mechanisms that operated outside of the context of the NDC and sometimes pulled against it. It ends with a discussion of Houthi military advances in the North and the campaign against Ansar al-Shari'a in the South, showing how these campaigns also mobilized narratives of injustice alongside engagements at the center.

The last chapter asks where civil actors are in the context of the ongoing war. I detail four core interlocking conflict dynamics that are shaping the substantive aims and capacities for action among civil actors: fragmentation, securitization, polarization, and humanitarianization. Amid a formal peace process that has been largely unsuccessful, civil actors are navigating these dynamics without many opportunities to shape negotiations or ensure that their justice priorities are reflected in post-conflict planning. But fragmentation has also enabled the establishment of 'pieces of peace' or pockets of stability where justice claims are being pursued.[34]

Both within and outside of such pockets, civil actors are enacting justice projects in real time. Whereas one might make a justice demand, for example, regarding greater gender equality or women's representation in government, local peacebuilders are working directly with local councils to make this happen where it can, rather than waiting for an agreement from the top. Chapter 5 includes many examples of quotidian local-level peacebuilding that I argue should be read as connected to longstanding justice claims. Peacebuilding research also works as concurrent documentation and enactment of Yemeni agency. As this chapter and the conclusion show, for many Yemeni researchers, research itself has become a form of civil action and justice work insofar as it helps to represent those who might not otherwise be seen or recognized by formal processes.

The challenge remains, however, to connect this work with national or internationally supported efforts to build sustainable peace in Yemen. Civil actors repeatedly stress that they do not have the luxury of waiting for a small number of elites and conflict actors to negotiate an end to the war or initiate a transitional justice program before they begin to address the needs of their communities or repair the legacies of harm. Enacting justice projects in the present is a means of anticipating and contributing to a more just future among those who cannot afford to wait.

UNCOMPROMISING COMPROMISE
A CAPABILITIES APPROACH TO TRANSITIONAL JUSTICE

Transitional justice might seem an odd focus for a book on Yemen. The country's modern history has been marked by successive conflicts, largely unresolved, with only limited engagement with the justice demands of Yemeni society. In hindsight, the country's most significant engagement with transitional justice mechanisms—the National Dialogue Conference undertaken in 2013—appears to have been a failure, eclipsed by a devastating war and extensive rights violations, some of which likely constitute war crimes. While I still regard features of the NDC as a causal driver of the war itself, as I have learned more about Yemeni peacebuilding work during the war, the legacies of some justice work from this period have become clearer.[1] Insofar as it was oriented toward the lasting transformation of institutions, Yemen's limited engagement with transitional justice mechanisms and practices did indeed fail to meet expectations. Yet Yemenis' practical engagement in the imagining of more just futures through some of these same institutions and practices had a lasting impact on civil actors and the projects they are currently enacting to advance justice.

This chapter explores the relationship between transitional justice, as a set of practices normalized at the global level, and what I describe as justice work in the context of the war in Yemen. Transitional justice is a broad term that refers to a host of post-conflict institutional arrangements and practices designed to help repair the damage wrought by sustained conflict. It takes many forms and responds to different conflict conditions, ranging from interstate warfare, civil war, ethnic cleansing and genocide, femicide, sustained authoritarian rule, and more. Transitional justice is fundamentally concerned with violations of human rights and promotes, at a minimum, the restoration or recognition of those rights.[2] While the appropriate scope of transitional justice is widely contested, it can reach well beyond restoration of a *status quo ante* to consider inequalities and injustices that have served as drivers of conflict, guarding against its resumption. In this way, transitional justice connects to the objectives of peacebuilding.[3]

As an evolving practice, transitional justice practitioners and theorists have worked to limit the role of 'victor's justice' in post-conflict settings, and to institutionalize liberalism as a safeguard against the temptations of collective punishment. The centrality of the individual as the subject of rights and responsibilities is thus at the core of twentieth century transitional justice, facilitated by the liberal internationalism of the post-Cold War period. Having achieved what Ruti Teitel describes as a 'steady state,' the field is now reconsidering its core parameters in light of changes in the global order. The erosion of (an always incomplete) liberal consensus has posed a challenge to human rights advocates but presents an opportunity for transitional justice scholars and practitioners to increasingly take up questions of group rights and the state's responsibility to address structural inequalities and abuses.

As this chapter will argue, normative claims and practical tools for evaluation derived from the Capabilities Approach may offer some guidance through this period of reconsideration. The Capabilities Approach sits at the intersection of development economics and political philosophy, asking the basic question of what individuals need to live lives of dignity.[4] By centering the individual as the subject of rights, the Capabilities Approach is significantly congruent with principles of liberalism and should thus be recognizable and accessible to liberal advocates of transitional justice. At the same time, however, the Capabilities Approach takes account of the way in which structures and institutions, including social norms, shape the choices of individuals and the freedoms that they can practically exercise. It is therefore concerned with entrenched inequalities between groups and their intersections. This is what theorists describe as the communitarian content of the Capabilities Approach.

This chapter introduces transitional justice as a concept and situates its core practices and its institutionalization in a genealogy of late twentieth century liberalism. It then describes some of the questions posed by empirical and normative challenges to liberal consensus. Finally, the chapter shows how the Capabilities Approach can offer an alternative normative foundation that allows for concurrent analysis of structural inequalities and nonetheless continues to advance the individual as the subject of rights. This is, I will argue, a compromise that is uncompromising in its normative commitment to the individual but offers the possibility of a decolonial reconsideration of liberal peacebuilding that understands the individual as always situated and operating relationally within the context of both state and society.

What Is Transitional Justice?

Transitional justice is a term introduced by legal scholar Ruti Teitel in 1991 to refer to a range of practices and institutions that work address the damage caused by sustained conflict and abuse. In its earliest usage, it was applied specifically to post-conflict moments of 'transition' or regime change.[5] Over the subsequent three decades, it has been used far more broadly to refer to practices that seek to transform institutions and consolidate liberal rights-based legal and political regimes.'[6] Teitel and others ground the origin of transitional justice in the post-war trials at Nuremburg, but its consolidation as a field of inquiry and its institutionalization as a global norm in post-conflict reconstruction are more closely associated with the period following the collapse of the Soviet Union and an ascendent, if never uncontested, liberal international order.

Transitional justice practices comprise a range broad enough to include high-profile international tribunals, national dialogues, and truth commissions on one end of the spectrum, and theater installations, memorials, and street art that give voice to the unrepresented at the other end. The underlying logic can be retributive, restorative, and/or reparative. Retributive approaches emphasize legal accountability (primarily through trials and tribunals) as a kind of deterrent to future conflict. Processes of lustration and vetting may also be retributive in nature. These are administrative measures that bar wrong-doers from holding office or serving in the bureaucracy.[7] Other retributive administrative measures can include security sector and judicial reforms that bar wrongdoers from roles in the military, police, security services, or judiciary. Lustration and vetting can raise important questions of due process, especially when exclusions are based on broad categorical membership in groups or organizations rather than individual wrong-doing.[8] For this reason, there is considerable debate in the literature on transitional justice about 'how much' lustration is necessary to ensure accountability and when or how such measures can themselves contribute to conflict or constitute collective punishment.

Restorative approaches, meanwhile, focus less on perpetrators and instead emphasize restoring the dignity of harmed individuals to their position *status quo ante*. Restoring seized property, releasing political prisoners and expunging their records, rehiring those who were wrongfully expelled from positions, and other similar measures seek to address the immediate harms produced by conflict. Insofar as they rely on rear-looking assessments of harm or loss, restorative approaches must reckon with changes produced and entrenched by conflict. In cases where the spatial relocation of communities was a feature of conflict, this can be particularly fraught, as justifiably restoring the property rights of some may contribute to the displacement of others. Under such circumstances, careful attention should be paid to due process to avoid reigniting conflict, though this has not always been the case.[9]

Insofar as they are directed toward individuals only, restorative approaches do not always address structural inequalities that may have contributed to conflict conditions. Some scholarship on transitional justice distinguishes between primary and secondary forms of victimization and places particular emphasis on the primary victimhood of those who suffer 'grave or serious' violations of human rights recognized in the International Bill of Human Rights.[10] Research suggests that in some cases, victims of abuse reject reparations that simply restore them to the *status quo ante*, especially when the inequities of this status quo were themselves understood to be drivers of conflict.[11] More recently, the distinction between primary and secondary victimization has been challenged in a number of ways. Susan Waltz, for example, has introduced a typology of human rights claims beyond those fundamental rights. These include due process rights, dignity rights 'including rights to social welfare and ability to participate in the polity,' and restorative rights 'including the right to rehabilitation, civil status, and the right to know.'[12] Scholarship on gender and post-conflict justice has shown that the primary/secondary distinction is strained by social conditions that can shape the substantive freedoms of women and men in different ways. In societies in which men are expected to serve as primary breadwinners or where women have limited economic mobility, the wrongful imprisonment, disappearance, or execution of a husband is not a harm he alone experiences; it can produce forms of vulnerability and precarity for his wife that constitute a primary harm in their own right.[13]

Considerations such as these have moved the literature on transitional justice from restorative toward reparative approaches that are more capacious in scope and aim at broader post-conflict transformation through a process of societal reconciliation. In this context, reconciliation entails more than the 'absence of conflict and situations of "thin" or "negative" coexistence, requiring deeper changes to the underlying ways in which former enemies perceive one another and their relationships.'[14] Indeed, (re)conceptualizing the relationship between victim and perpetrator is one of the most challenging aspects of reparative approaches. In cases of civil war, this line may be particularly blurry; reparative approaches tend to take a structural view that allows victims to seek acknowledgement of harm while recognizing that all participants in society have been shaped by inequitable systems of power.[15]

In its earliest iterations and in many cases today, transitional justice work has accompanied a period of political change. Some of the most prominent examples have come in the aftermath of armed conflict and include efforts to prosecute war crimes and crimes against humanity, such as the trials at Nuremburg or the International Criminal Tribunal for the Former Yugoslavia. International tribunals, national trials, and hybrid judicial mechanisms that combine elements of each represent efforts to provide accountability and deter future violence. Other instruments of transitional justice follow periods of sustained contention and prolonged authoritarian rule, such as South Africa's Truth and Reconciliation Commission following the end of apartheid rule, Peru's Comisión de la Verdad y Reconciliación, Tunisia's Instance Vérité et Dignité, and many others. These are often, but not always, restorative or reparative in their approach. Truth commissions can serve several purposes concurrently; they may help to provide an authoritative account of past abuses, hold individuals and institutions responsible for those abuses, and deter future harms. They may also provide an essential evidentiary basis for reparations programs. Marking a break from a troubled past, such mechanisms are designed to be victim-centered and are charged with promoting reconciliation, even if this charge is not always fulfilled.[16]

Transitional justice can also play a powerful, if complicated, role during periods of conflict. Some instruments, such as legal amnesties, which many view as an obstacle to justice, may be viewed as instrumentally necessary to produce the conditions that allow for the broader transformations that transitional justice promotes.[17] At the same time, empirical analyses suggest that there is considerable indeterminacy in the relationship between peace and justice.[18] This owes in part to the fact that 'the threat of prosecutions may create an obstacle to former combatants laying down their weapons, or could lead those responsible for human rights violations to enact coups or take up arms once more.'[19]

Moreover, given that the majority of conflict occurs today on an intrastate basis, transitional justice work undertaken in the context of ongoing conflict is not typically enacted through national institutions since these institutions may not be functioning or may lack widely accepted legitimacy in some or all areas. Instead, transitional justice under conflict conditions is often pursued at the local level and/ or at the international level, working around the contested state.

Where people feel that they cannot wait for agreements to be brokered between conflict actors, civilians may undertake the work of peacebuilding and reconciliation even as fighting continues. This can introduce a tension between local peacebuilders and national-level peace brokers, as the case of Yemen highlights.[20]

As I explore in the next section, there is a better chance of activating what some view as the 'mutually reinforcing nature' of peace and justice when the normative assumptions that underwrite peacebuilding and post-conflict justice converge.[21] Under such conditions, peace and justice can be pursued concurrently not simply because of the presumed deterrent effect of accountability measures and punishment of perpetrators but also through the role that transitional justice mechanisms play in enabling transpositional scrutiny and producing 'an authoritative historical record of the conflict,' on the basis of which reparative measures might be taken and through which revisionist denial might be contained.[22]

Documentation is one area in which there is a significant role for transitional justice work during conflict, and an area in which local and international transitional justice practitioners sometimes coordinate. Documentation work is vital to judicial approaches to justice. In Syria, for example, documentation produced by local civil society organizations has enabled prosecutions of Syrian perpetrators to move forward in German and Swedish courts under the principle of universal jurisdiction and in the absence of any kind of negotiated agreement.[23] Critics of the judicialization of transitional justice argue that a focus on documentation during conflict may 'privilege retributive forms of justice in ways that are often not conducive to conflict resolution or political or societal reconciliation.'[24]

Sometimes documentation work is also undertaken as a form of 'preservative justice' in the service of a broader range of objectives beyond criminal justice. In such cases, documenters work to retain records that might otherwise be destroyed or take testimonies that might otherwise be lost in the context of ongoing conflict, helping to create a historical record that could be used in future legal processes but could also support non-judicial approaches to justice.[25] Moreover, even explicitly judicial approaches can also play an important role in peace-brokering. As I detail in Chapter 5, the United Nations Human

Rights Council's recommendation in 2020 that several parties to the war in Yemen be referred to the International Criminal Court—a genuinely empty threat for pragmatic reasons—nonetheless played some role in jumpstarting moribund negotiations. Documentation work by local Yemeni organizations that preserved records pertaining to abuses by conflict actors played a role in this process.

In some cases, the absence of a national-level effort to secure post-conflict justice, or perceived weaknesses or omissions in national or international approaches, leads citizens to undertake efforts at documentation or issue demands for accountability through more informal practices of transitional justice. These may draw on local conflict resolution mechanisms, for example, that do not rely on national or international courts, or may involve performative or symbolic acts that document harm via visual and performing arts, digital archiving, and so on.[26] In some settings, civil action that articulates justice demands may be regarded as complementary to national-level efforts at post-conflict accountability and reconciliation; in other contexts, they may be seen as a threat to the parameters of officially sanctioned post-conflict frameworks. As I explore in later chapters, Yemen is in the latter case, where formal institutional and activist approaches have sometimes been in tension. This was true during the 2012–14 transitional process following Yemen's popular uprising, and it is true today in terms of the international framework for peace negotiations advanced by the UN Special Envoy to the Secretary General for Yemen.

The work of activists promoting transitional justice through civil action should not be underestimated. The concept of mere civility does not require (or even suggest) that civil actors must abandon contentious claims or sacrifice the demands of justice. Indeed, civil action is not defined by any particular ideology or set of claims but instead by actors' behavior; its efficacy in disrupting violence rests on the 'logic of authority behind particular social identities (or types of actors) and their relative capacities.'[27] While the literature on transitional justice does not necessarily use this language of civil action explicitly, descriptions of the peacebuilding and reconciliatory work of transitional justice emphasize characteristics that align with the concept of mere civility. The projects of civil actors do not aim at the elimination of rivals but are oriented toward the transformation of systems that have excluded or marginalized sectors of society; in this sense, civil action can help address the antecedents of armed conflict by expanding effective citizenship.[28] It is peacebuilding and justice work concurrently.

As a final point, it is also worth noting that transitional justice mechanisms may be adopted in the absence of any meaningful change in political regime (i.e. without transition) or when regime elites seek a means to indemnify themselves or others. In these cases, the same mechanisms that might help to secure accountability and promote reconciliation under some conditions can perversely be used to serve regime purposes, offering the appearance of reform or legitimating a new leader as a 'reformer' within an existing regime structure. In these cases, the scope and mandate of transitional justice institutions provide key insights into the 'red lines' that remain intact, highlighting the questions that are not asked or the concerns (or subjects) that are not included. As the case of Yemen will show, exclusions that are built into nominally inclusive transitional justice institutions can also pose a risk to peace.

Transitional Justice and Liberalism

The equal dignity and rights of individuals is a *sine qua non* underwriting the enterprise of transitional justice as a normative (and norm-transformative) exercise. In its rear-facing dimensions, transitional justice seeks to hold accountable those individuals and institutions that violated the rights of whole classes of individuals through practices of political exclusion and abuse. As a forward-looking practice designed to produce more just outcomes, it works to build liberal equality where it may not have previously been the foundation for political (or other) rights or where such equality has been recognized but not upheld.

In its earliest iterations, the relationship between transitional justice as a set of post-conflict mechanisms and the broader idea of democratization was reasonably unquestioned. Today, however, as the teleological promise of democratization wears thin, the relationship between transitional justice and liberal democracy cannot be taken for granted. While transitional justice was once focused predominantly on developing the kind of rule-of-law viewed as necessary to democratization, today it is more often tied to peacebuilding and the expansion of human security. Some critical peacebuilding scholars have thus defined it as part of a 'global project' with ever-expanding scope for intervention.[29]

Critiques of the implicit (or sometimes explicit) liberalism of transitional justice come in different forms. One is less a critique of its normative liberalism per se than of the way anodyne legalism is used to mask liberal commitments that originate at the global level by presenting notions of rule-of-law as an unassailable technocratic good.[30] Such legalism is defended by Teitel, who sees international law, in particular, as offering 'continuity in the enforcement of equal protection and adherence to individual accountability…' not as a form of exceptional post-conflict justice but as a regularized component of a global liberal order.[31] To critics, this defense is precisely how legalism displaces politics.

Some also take substantive issue with the way transitional justice emphasizes political harm over social and economic harm. In other words, the liberalism of transitional justice is both insufficiently political for some and too narrowly political for others. Here, Lars Waldorf singles out the field's 'longstanding legalistic bias toward civil and political rights' and notes that legalism's 'violations approach does not easily lend itself to remedying structural inequalities and exclusions.'[32] While this weakness has been partially resolvable through articulations of economic and social rights as legally justiciable rights, doing so deepens the hold of legalism itself.[33] Advocates of restorative and reparative approaches to transitional justice have long called for a shift in emphasis from the punishment of perpetrators to addressing the needs of victims and survivors of abuse. In this vein, Waldorf argues that victim-centeredness offers a powerful rationale for addressing economic and social rights, given how often these are cited among victims' priorities.[34] He then identifies non-judicial mechanisms such as truth commissions and reparations programs as the most successful in addressing these needs.

Some decolonial critics also see transitional justice as part of a reconfigured relation of colonial domination. As the intellectual tradition in international relations from which transitional justice emerges, liberalism 'aspires to embed the progressive institutions of domestic politics—law, rights, justice, security, peace—within international politics' on the premise that without such embeddedness, the requisites of 'the good life' cannot be equitably shared.[35] Scholars like Robbie Shilliam map the way in which the field of international relations itself developed on the premise of a bifurcated international society characterized by 'interdependency for civilized powers, dependency for uncivilized peoples.'[36] Such a system offers no redemptive promise of access to the 'good life.' Instead, legalism and liberal peacebuilding deepen this relation of dependence and institutionalize it.

This idea of asymmetry and dependency is explicitly at the center of Abdullahi An-Naim's critique of what he describes as the 'neocolonial' logic of transitional justice. In the introduction to a special issue of the *International Journal of Transitional Justice* devoted to this subject, An-Naim questioned the enterprise as a whole, writing that 'the implied assumption of this field, it seems to me, is that the "developing" society under examination is in transition from the state of being A, which we know, to becoming B, which we can predict.'[37] Read as part of a teleological progression, such a formulation cements the dominance of those whose experiences give condition B its predicted content.

To the extent that this occurs without an adequate historicization of either condition A or B, it can constitute an approach to justice that deepens injustice. In a provocative critique of criminalization of nation-building violence—and, therefore, legalistic approaches to post-conflict justice—Mahmood Mamdani has introduced a category of shared survivorship as essential to a decolonial—and intentionally political—approach to justice:

> A single-minded focus on identifying perpetrators leaves undisturbed the logic of institutions that make nation-building violence thinkable and possible. Instead of identifying and punishing perpetrators, the political model attempts to overwrite the institutional context. All survivors—victims, perpetrators, beneficiaries, bystanders, exiles—are included in an expanded

political process and reformed political community. It is political reform, not criminal reform, that enables escape from nation-building violence.[38]

This cuts against the legalism of transitional justice and victim-centeredness at the same time. It may appear to collapse a distinction between victim and perpetrator in a way that could undermine victims' desire for accountability, but this is an uncharitable reading. By naming victim and perpetrator as co-survivors of a system of oppression, Mamdani does not suggest that the two categories are indistinguishable. His language merely suggests that those who enact violence and those against whom it is enacted may have had their identities shaped by the same structures of inequity.

Mamdani's challenge to legalism, however, is more substantial. By favoring a political over a criminal (read: legal) resolution, Mamdani and other advocates of reparative approaches reject the technocratic rule of experts in favor of a messier but more meaningful grappling with power in and through political institutions. In relying on the political as a space of shared agonism and deliberation, categories and divisions that have been made to appear natural and inevitable—and linked to conflict—can be historicized and reconsidered. The kinds of institutions that can support such a politics may look similar to liberal institutions, but their animating logic may not be so narrow.

The potential for a decolonial approach to transitional justice is exciting, but like most approaches to transitional justice, it is primarily concerned with what happens in the aftermath of conflict, as institutions are (re)built and societies pursue reconciliation. Work that is done to advance justice claims during conflict is rarely described as a component of transitional justice, even though it may rely on some similar techniques and share some normative aims. Instead, this kind of justice work is more likely to be described under the broad heading of peacebuilding.

Institutionalizing Liberal Peacebuilding Amid Eroding Consensus

Liberal peacebuilding can be distinguished from peacemaking (or peace-brokering, given its negotiated character) by the former's far more capacious scope and methods. Liberal peacebuilding includes a host of practices ranging from 'reintegrating former combatants into civilian society, and strengthening the rule of law through training, restructuring local police, and through judicial and penal reform ... improving respect for human rights through monitoring, education, and investigation of past and existing abuses, and providing technical assistance for democratic development like electoral assistance and support for free media, for example.'[39] Its congruence with mechanisms of transitional justice should be evident, as peacebuilding seeks to address (and redress) sources of conflict. This is very different from peacemaking, which is focused on brokering a cessation of conflict and most often narrowly engages with conflict actors and elites. Agreements that are brokered by peacemakers often bypass at least some of the important drivers of conflict and may even lay ground for future conflict by ignoring or dismissing justice claims, as later chapters will show.

What makes peacebuilding specifically liberal is the way in which it positions the individual as the subject of rights and privileges individual political and economic freedom.[40] The institutionalization of these liberal norms advanced with the end of the Cold War, in particular, and the rapid transformation of political and economic systems in many parts of the world.

It was in this context that transitional justice became increasingly institutionalized as a 'steady state' at the center of post-Cold War liberal peacebuilding, producing what Teitel described as 'ambivalent consequences.'[41] This was accomplished in part through the creation of permanent mechanisms, such as the International Criminal Court but also through a broader normalization whereby 'what was historically viewed as a legal phenomenon associated with extraordinary post-conflict conditions now increasingly appears to be a reflection of ordinary times.'[42] This normalization was hastened by the perceived complementarity between democratization, justice, and peacebuilding.[43]

Notably, this normalization and institutionalization co-occurred alongside a global decline in democracy and the emergence of seemingly stable 'grey zones' of non-democracy. In the 20 years since Thomas Carothers argued that the transition paradigm had outlived its intellectual usefulness and was misdirecting programming, the global project normalizing transitional justice and liberal peacebuilding has become progressively more institutionalized.[44] The International Center for Transitional Justice (established 2001), Interpeace (established 2000), and other international organizations coordinate with the United Nations and work directly with state and non-state actors to tie post-conflict accountability to political and institutional change. Meanwhile, the International Dialogue on Peacebuilding and Statebuilding (established 2008) has tied peacebuilding and efforts to address the root causes of conflict to the wider agenda of sustainable development. Its Stockholm Declaration (2016), in turn, guides the work of Interpeace, the International Center for Transitional Justice, and others.[45] The isomorphism of these institutions is consistent with a global project described by Dustin Sharp, who notes how the convergence of global governance has 'been largely palliative, intended to moderate some of the excesses of market fundamentalism and state-perpetrated physical violence without fundamentally transforming systems in ways that would do more than establish a minimum floor for decency.'[46]

The idea that by the 1990s or early 2000s there was a 'liberal consensus' is thus misleading. There was, instead, a particular kind of liberal institutional hegemony that helped to normalize transitional justice as a component of peacebuilding and post-conflict reconstruction. This institutionalization developed, however, precisely as liberalism itself was being questioned and reconfigured, both through the erosion of US hegemony and European unity and through decolonial and other critiques of liberalism that call on advocates of liberal peacebuilding (and other liberal projects) to reconsider its universalizing impulse and broaden its scope.[47]

An Uncompromising Compromise

The Capabilities Approach offers a way forward through this shifting terrain. Considered by its proponents to be a normative framework through which 'to judge situations and inform social and political action so as to enable people to live well in a shared natural environment,' the Capabilities Approach is most widely recognized in the field of development as a critique of narrowly economic measurements of well-being.[48] However, I see in it a normative foundation for thinking about post-conflict justice in a way that resolves some of the challenges of anchoring justice to liberalism in a normatively plural or not-exclusively-liberal context. I refer to the Capabilities Approach as an uncompromising compromise insofar as it offers a way to think about justice that is not exclusively wedded to the traditions of political liberalism but remains grounded in a core commitment to the individual as political subject. This means that it should be recognizable to advocates of liberal peacebuilding even as it simultaneously makes possible serious consideration of the kinds of entrenched inequalities and social injustices that drive conflict and pose a challenge to peacebuilding and post-conflict reconciliation between groups.

The liberal content of the Capabilities Approach is unassailable. As Martha Nussbaum explains, it is an approach that evaluates the justice of a state of affairs by taking 'each person as an end, asking not just about the total or average well-being but about the opportunities available to each person.'[49] Centering the individual, the Capabilities Approach places paramount evaluative focus on the question of choice.

> It is focused on choice or freedom, holding that the crucial good societies should be promoting for their people is a set of opportunities, or substantial freedoms, which people then may or may not exercise in action. The choice is theirs. It thus commits itself to respect for people's powers of self-definition.[50]

As Amartya Sen elaborates, the core criterion of evaluation in the Capabilities Approach determines 'a person's capability to do things he or she has reason to value.'[51] This emphasis on the role of reason—and particularly Sen's focus on public reason—is important to understanding the kinds of institutions that are consistent with the Capabilities Approach.[52] Both the centering of the individual and the foregrounding of choice appear recognizably liberal. The Capabilities Approach does not presuppose—or advocate for—a uniform distribution of social goods or outcomes, but rather an equal distribution of opportunities for meaningful choice, distinguishing between 'capabilities' (or the real ability to reason through and act on one's choices) and 'achievements' or 'functionings' of individuals.[53] Indeed, in Sen's words, this approach marks 'a serious departure from concentrating on the means of living the actual opportunities of living,' which requires attention to questions of inequality that stem from or can be exacerbated by conflict.[54]

The Capabilities Approach also advances core communitarian commitments and accounts for obligations between individuals living in shared society. If its commitment to the individual is firm, it is also (and equally) 'concerned with entrenched social injustice and inequality, especially capability failures that are the result of discrimination and marginalization,' the eradication of which Nussbaum, at least, describes as an obligation of government.[55] Capabilities are understood here to mean 'not just abilities residing inside a person but also the freedoms and opportunities created by a combination of personal abilities and the political, social, and economic environment.'[56] These, of course, are deeply shaped by others in society and by institutions that organize and regulate their interactions and place them within the scope of normative evaluation.

Capabilities Approach theorists both recognize the value of group membership and identity and understand groups as fundamentally comprised of individuals. For this reason, Nussbaum argues that 'capabilities belong first and foremost to individual persons and only derivatively to groups.'[57] Sen recognizes the role that group belonging or identity may have on individuals' choices or valuations, but warns against the risks of reductionism. Viewing individuals 'merely as a member of just one particular group would be a major denial of the freedom of each person to decide how exactly to see himself or herself.'[58] In *Identity and Violence*, he connects such solitarist views of belonging to violence:

> Given our inescapably plural identities, we have to decide on the relative importance of our different associations and affiliations in any particular context. Central to leading a human life, therefore, are the responsibilities of choice and reasoning. In contrast, violence is promoted by the cultivation of a sense of inevitability about some allegedly unique—often belligerent—

identity that we are supposed to have and which apparently makes extensive demands on us... The imposition of an allegedly unique identity is often a crucial component of the 'martial art' of fomenting sectarian confrontation.[59]

It is not difficult to observe such reductionism in the context of ongoing conflicts like the one in Yemen. What is harder is imagining a way out of the trap of solitarism, as even 'inclusive' approaches to peace often adopt solitarist logics of representation, as I discuss in Chapter 5. For Capabilities Approach theorists, the converse of destiny is choice; institutions and practices that encourage and enable choice—in this case, choice about how to prioritize among our plural identities in a particular context—can help to erode the sense of inevitability that drives violence. Scholarship on ethnic conflict identifies the institutionalization of ethnic or sectarian difference as a core driver of violence.[60] It stands to reason, then, that de-institutionalizing difference as the foundation of rights would play an important role in post-conflict reconciliation in divided societies.

In this way, the Capabilities Approach can be seen as addressing the context of inter-group conflict without abandoning a commitment to the individual as the core component of any group. At the same time, the individual's right to belong to and value membership in groups is also recognized by Capabilities Approach theorists as a basic political entitlement whereby 'the person is respected as a social being.'[61] The intersection of the individual and the collective is made clearest is in the way Capabilities Approach theorists conceptualize agency.

While agency is viewed as a property of individuals, it is recognized as relationally and institutionally produced. Drawing on the work of Gustavo Pereira, Séverine Deneulin has developed a useful typology describing the socially constituted bases of agency. She grounds individual agency in the extent of each person's self-trust, self-respect, and self-esteem, where each of the three emerges from a different kind of social relationship. Self-trust refers to a person's 'need to be recognized for who they are so they are able to understand their own needs' and is built through intimate and family relationships. Self-respect, by contrast, addresses individuals' need to be 'recognized as equal subjects of rights so they are able to understand themselves as deserving equal treatment,' and is therefore the most explicitly concerned with state institutions. The last, self-esteem, is constituted through social relationships in the community, reflecting the individual's need to be 'recognized for their achievements so they are able to understand themselves as having talents and are able to contribute to the life of society.'[62] What is particularly significant about this typology is the way in which it centers the individual while simultaneously insisting on that individual's relational position to and constitution through others in society.

The Capabilities Approach is 'resolutely pluralist with regard to value,' meaning that the substantive choices made by individuals and the values they pursue are not significant in evaluating the justice of a state of affairs.[63] This can make the approach particularly appropriate for thinking about institutional arrangements that can support reconciliation in divided societies. It is through substantive opportunities to deliberate over issues of shared concern and engage in transpositional scrutiny that solidarity is cultivated, as 'people take an interest, through public discussion, in each other's predicaments,' in ways that support reconciliation.[64] While some political scientists might read Capabilities Approach theorists' occasional elision of the distinction between society and government as a problem, I regard this as appropriate to the complex challenges of peacebuilding and transitional justice where state institutions have themselves been contested or destroyed. Reconciliatory work seeks to address social ruptures and also to lay the foundation for the rebuilding of state institutions. The disruptive effects of conflict can leave some ideas, some entrenched inequalities, and some forms of institutional exclusion on the table for reexamination.

One important issue on which Capabilities Approach theorists do not agree, however, is the status of justice itself. Indeed, Amartya Sen and Martha Nussbaum, as two of the tradition's most prominent thinkers, are starkly at odds on whether justice is itself attainable. Nussbaum advances a partial theory of justice that establishes minimum thresholds of central capabilities that just governments should ensure for individuals.[65] Sen argues that any transcendent notion of justice is unattainable in a polyglot world in which comprehensive doctrines will not be shared, but that injustice can be reduced without agreement on the content of justice if there are conditions that allow public reasoning about injustice.[66] Deneulin appears to agree with Sen but nevertheless argues for establishing justice as 'the ethical horizon of public reasoning processes and decisions.'[67]

Setting justice as an ethical horizon is consistent with Sen's contention that agreement over the substantive content of justice is unnecessary to the practical struggle against agreed-upon injustices. Ameliorating injustice can occur when people with diverse underlying commitments (but a shared interest in pursuing justice) agree that a given state of affairs is unjust and work to eliminate or reduce that injustice. The basis on which actors conclude that this state of affairs is unjust does not need to be shared for them to work against it. This is also deeply resonant with Abdullahi An-Naim's understanding of overlapping consensus as central to decolonial indigenous formations of justice.[68] Taken together, these theorists inform my approach to understanding justice work throughout the book. Justice work need not advance a particular agreed-upon meaning of justice but needs only to set justice as its ethical horizon and make a claim to set something right.

Liberal institutions remain important as a practical means of managing difference among those with varied understandings of justice, without sacrificing the commitment to difference that both Sen and An-Naim value. This leads to the final uncompromising feature I see in the Capabilities Approach compromise: its central focus on political freedom. It is through free deliberation that overlapping consensus on what is unjust can be identified. Of the ten incommensurable and non-substitutable 'central capabilities' that Nussbaum's partial theory of justice identifies, it is noteworthy that she singles out two as 'architectonic' insofar as they 'organize and pervade the others.'[69] One of these is the capability of affiliation, which she defines as:

(a) being able to live with and toward others, to recognize and show concern for other human beings, to engage in various forms of social interaction; to be able to imagine the situation of another. (Protecting this capability means protecting institutions that constitute and nourish such forms of affiliation, and also protecting the freedom of assembly and political speech.) (b) having the social bases of self-respect and nonhumiliation; being able to be treated as a dignified being whose worth is equal to that of others. This entails provisions of non-discrimination on the basis of race, sex, sexual orientation, ethnicity, caste, religion, national origin.[70]

This is quite obviously a capacious concept that underwrites many core features of liberal democracy, but its value for my purposes lies in the forms of justice work it makes recognizable. Justice work occurring under conditions of war can expands these freedoms—often in hyperlocal contexts and in the absence of a political settlement from the center—and serve as an essential enabling condition for longer-term transformations of the sort that are the object of transitional justice and peacebuilding.

For Sen, opportunities for meaningful 'transpositional scrutiny' on issues of public concern offer the only way to identify the kind of plural grounding necessary to address injustice. Safeguarding the right to affiliation and creating conditions in which such a right might reasonably be exercised are thus instrumental to encouraging the kind of deliberation that makes reparative post-conflict justice possible. But these conditions do not require a negotiated agreement or a breakthrough in the formal peace process. They can be—and are being—enacted from below through acts of everyday peacebuilding.

While the Capabilities Approach has not yet been widely applied in discussions of transitional justice or peacebuilding, I am not the only one to see promise in their fusion. Lars Waldorf, for example, argues that victim-centered responsiveness to the actual priorities of affected communities 'would be a capabilities approach to transitional justice,' though he leaves this claim otherwise underelaborated.[71] Lauren Balasco's concept of 'reparative development' is more explicitly indebted to the Capabilities Approach in its consideration of 'lost life opportunities' of individuals as the focus of post-conflict reparations.[72] She also fuses the liberal and communitarian components of the tradition as well, writing:

We need to see [reparations] as part of a forward-looking programme that puts the reparation of lost life opportunities at the centre of their concerns. In addition, we need to recognise that while conflict harmed individuals, these individuals were embedded in communities. The harm committed to individuals has communal consequences that are equally in need of reparation.[73]

Work like Waldorf's and Balasco's contributes to a Capabilities Approach to peacebuilding and post-conflict justice, as I hope this book will. From a normative standpoint, my aim is to advance this approach through an examination of the past, present, and future of justice work in Yemen. The Capabilities Approach offers a way to conceptualize justice work—or, more aptly, work to remediate injustice—in both conflict and post-conflict contexts in ways that restore (or create anew) the rights of individuals *and* address the systematic structural inequities between groups that threaten peace and human security. One advantage that it offers over existing victim-centered approaches to transitional justice is the explicit emphasis that the Capabilities Approach places on identifying and expanding sources of agency. In the chapters that follow, I will work to use this normative framework to map engagement (and disengagement) with justice demands and evaluate justice work that is occurring under conflict conditions, sketching out the possibilities that a Capabilities-focused approach can offer in the absence of a liberal consensus.

2

THE SHADOW OF UNIFICATION
ELECTORAL CONSOLIDATION OF
AUTHORITARIAN UNITY

When to 'start the story' in an account of injustice or conflict is never an uncomplicated decision. This chapter focuses predominantly on political developments from the unification of North and South Yemen in 1990 through the postponement of the 2009 elections—in other words, the rise and fall of Yemen's electoral regime. This occurred alongside a set of developments outside of formal institutions, which is the subject of the next chapter. Taken together, they map a set of grievances and justice demands that were met with disengagement and, at times, strategic engagement by political elites. The pre-war regime's deferrals of Yemenis' justice demands remain something that peacebuilders and peace-brokers alike must address as they enact projects to address Yemen's present and future.

Over the course of two decades, the 'unity regime' of President 'Ali 'Abdullah Saleh reckoned with the inherited legacies of past conflict injustices that predated the unification of North and South Yemen in 1990. The regime adopted an approach that silenced most justice demands and strategically engaged others, shaping the trajectory of partisan politics, the engagement of the political parties with other important social forces, and ultimately, the development of powerful forms of violent and non-violent mobilization outside of the partisan context. These extrapartisan movements shaped and were shaped by the decisions of Yemen's political parties. The Southern Movement's origins lay in unaddressed conflict injustices, some tied to political parties, and the nature of the regime's engagement with Southern justice demands over the 2000s fueled the movement's growing secessionism. The Houthi insurgency that developed in the 2000s likewise originated in a set of justice demands at least partially related to political parties. Each movement eventually mounted a challenge to both regime and state, as discussed in Chapter 4. In both cases, the impact of regime action, the positions of Yemen's political parties, and the practices of the movements themselves had a significant impact on life opportunities for whole categories of Yemeni citizens in ways that fuel ongoing contention and shape the justice work of civil actors.

When I first traveled to Yemen in 2004, the brief 1994 civil war between Northern and Southern forces had been over for a decade, but factors that drove that conflict and practices that its outcome enabled continued to shape political events and the interpretations that Yemenis gave to them. The regime of President 'Ali 'Abdullah Saleh was by then consolidating increasingly authoritarian power not despite of but through Yemen's electoral institutions. The Joint Meeting Parties opposition alliance was coming to center stage, but distrust between its two largest members—the Yemeni Congregation for Reform, or Islah, and the Yemeni Socialist Party—clearly extended back to the events that both preceded and stemmed from the 1994 war.

There were sincere people committed to a joint opposition and the preservation or expansion of Yemeni democracy, no doubt. Some paid a very high price for that commitment. But there were many more who seemed to view the Joint Meeting Parties (JMP) as, at best, a tactical alliance and survival strategy for Yemen's embattled parties. For Islah, the JMP and its procedural reform agenda was a buffer against the regime's efforts to tie (all) Islamism to extremism and to bolster its position as a partner in the context of the United States' counterterrorism objectives. For the Yemeni Socialist Party (YSP), the alliance was a lifeline, a guarantee of national political relevance at a time when its organization had been hollowed out following the 1994 war. For reasons that I detail in this chapter, these parties and their smaller partners in the JMP could only coalesce around a narrow agenda of procedural reform. It was a platform that satisfied few, provoked many, and left the JMP's most committed leaders to face the dual challenge of taking on the Saleh regime and facing critics among their own core constituents. As multiparty competition and coordination became central to increasingly authoritarian governance in the 2000s, the opposition's failures thus directed citizens to pursue their justice demands outside of formal political institutions, well before the uprising of 2011.

Two States, One Society?

The Republic of Yemen formally came into being on May 22, 1990, through a merger of the Yemen Arab Republic (YAR), or North Yemen, and its Southern counterpart, the People's Democratic Republic of Yemen (PDRY). While Yemen had long functioned as a discursive object in diverse political projects, Lisa Wedeen notes that practices of imagining unity did not displace but found 'expression in and overlap with other solidarities' that varied across space and time.[1] Historiography reflects the 'contingency of space as an effect of complexes of knowledge and power on both sides of the North-South border,' characterized by the 'the making and unmaking of particular spaces,' and the regimes that order them.[2] In this context, the creation of the Republic of Yemen in 1990 should be read as a novel act of state-making that drew upon plural social identities, institutional histories, and material conditions, not as the 'reunification' of a previously extant or singular political community.

While the mechanics of union were abrupt, as detailed below, unification was part of a broader process that responded to shifting conditions, accelerating over the course of the 1980s. Changes in global and regional politics, economic pressures on both states, and endemic, low-level, but nonetheless significant armed conflicts within the YAR and the PDRY and across their border shaped the process and the pace of unification. The balance of these factors differed for the YAR and the PDRY, but leaders of each state saw unification as potentially beneficial and sought terms that would advantage their own relative positions. At the popular level, the 'enduring popularity of notional Yemeni unity throughout this period was a conspicuous reflection of the weak legitimacy of both the YAR and PDRY regimes.'[3] While there is some consensus that the South entered the union in a relatively weaker position than the North, interpretations of the scale and drivers of this imbalance differ.[4] What is important for the purposes of this chapter is a recognition that political dynamics in the ensuing decades—and indeed today—both reflect these differences of interpretation and contribute to them.

There were a number of important material characteristics of the two states that influenced calculations ahead of unification in 1990. South Yemen had better-developed infrastructure and a much greater share of proven natural resources, but only two percent of its land was cultivatable; despite state efforts to boost agricultural production, the PDRY remained highly dependent on food imports.[5] Both states were heavily reliant on remittance income and foreign assistance, but the PDRY's foreign debt burden—at 180% of GDP by 1987—was more than twice that of the YAR.[6] Important natural resources were identified on both sides of the border in the 1980s. Concessions for the development of these resources boosted revenues, but also debt, as each state borrowed against future anticipated earnings.[7]

While the North was 'plainly in the healthier position' on the eve of unification, it was not without significant challenges.[8] The YAR was home to the overwhelming majority of Yemen's agricultural resources, though donor-driven agricultural policies in the 1970s meant that much of this agricultural capacity was directed toward cash crop production by the 1980s.[9] With a population more than four times larger than the South, the YAR relied on imports for basic foodstuffs, contributing to a serious imbalance of payments. The North Yemeni regime attempted to address this by imposing import restrictions and other austerity measures in 1983. The political consequences of these restrictions, however, contributed to regime consolidation more than anything else, as 'import quotas assigned by the government to specific businesses created new ways for corruptive behavior and exclusively benefited certain family clans, usually those with military ties.'[10] Those who suffered the greatest losses were small shopkeepers in provincial capitals like Taiz and Hodeidah.

Differences in Northern and Southern economies, however, have sometimes been overestimated, given the fact that both states engaged in major state-led development initiatives designed to reshape economy and society. As Sheila Carapico argued at the time, the German metaphor, which dominated commentary on the unification of the YAR and PDRY, was a strained one, given that 'disparities in the relative weight of private and public enterprise were far more subtle than the designations "capitalist" and "socialist" indicate.'[11] Indeed, the 1980s saw considerable centralization and protectionism in the North and some liberalization in the South.[12] While this meant the two states were in some respects 'heading in opposite directions,' it produced a kind of policy convergence toward the middle that facilitated the run-up to unification in 1990.[13] Among the first concrete steps toward unification was the elimination of customs duties along the North/South border to facilitate intra-Yemeni trade.[14]

Understandably, however, liberalization and the diversification of trade was a source of some internal political friction in the South. As a Marxist party-state, the PDRY had long been highly dependent on the Soviet Union and other Eastern bloc states to support its program of economic, social, and political transformation. Over the span of the PDRY's existence, Soviet assistance accounted for the largest share of foreign aid, followed distantly by China and other socialist states.[15] As the Soviets' own position shifted, the ruling YSP faced the prospect of a significant decrease in external support. This contributed to the leadership's efforts to diversify sources of foreign aid over the 1980s.[16] Overtures to the Gulf states were limited by the PDRY's political support for causes that alienated the conservative governments. But labor migration provided a powerful reason to pursue normalization with Gulf neighbors, given that remittance income contributed more than two-thirds of the PDRY's foreign exchange earnings.[17] Increasing engagement with the Gulf states—relationships that one European diplomat at the time described as 'correct, not cordial'—narrowed the gap between the foreign policy orientations of North and South Yemen in a way that facilitated the merger.[18]

Economic setbacks in the PDRY—both real, as with the fallout of disastrous flooding in 1982, and anticipated, as the Soviet Union became a less reliable source of support—contributed to the Southern leadership's interest in unification. Yet the specific terms of unity and what this would mean for socialism mattered. The YSP leadership was divided over the issue of support for the National Democratic Front (NDF), a guerilla group in the North, as well as the Yemeni People's Unity Party (YPUP), which was essentially a vanguard party functioning as a political wing of the YSP in North Yemen. Ending Southern support for the NDF was a consistent Northern demand and one that contributed to friction within the Southern leadership. After the NDF's final defeat in 1982, the YPUP was given greater scope to participate in North Yemeni political life, while it concurrently held one third of the seats in the PDRY's Central Committee and played a 'full role in policy discussions' on the YSP's politburo.[19] Trust between Northern and Southern socialists was limited, however, and some accused the YPUP of putting regionalism ahead of party.[20]

Internal divisions within the PDRY were exacerbated by President 'Ali Nasser Mohammed's economic and foreign policies. Liberalization was seen as narrowly benefitting partisans of 'Ali Nasser at the expense of others, and some new investments by Gulf states and others were eroding the socialist orientation of the state. By the middle of the decade, factions within the Politburo and the Central Committee had turned on one another and begun stockpiling arms ahead of an anticipated confrontation. It arrived on January 13, 1986, when several members of the PDRY leadership were killed by President 'Ali Nasser's security entourage as they convened a session of the Politburo. This resulted in 10 days of fighting in Aden, Lahj, and Abyan, ending with 'Ali Nasser's flight to the North with as many as 30,000 of his supporters.[21] He was replaced by 'Ali Salim al-Bidh, who worked quickly—but ultimately not entirely successfully—to reconsolidate the YSP and return to collective leadership. Though al-Bidh was a longstanding rival of 'Ali Nasser, their policies looked largely the same, though al-Bidh showed 'far greater care to avoid antagonism and with a gloss of older rhetoric...'[22]

If the 1980s were a period of disunity in the South, the same years saw considerable regime consolidation in the North, strengthening President Saleh's hand in the unification process. Having come to power in 1978, Saleh succeeded in eliminating the military threat from the NDF by June 1982. With this, the risk of unification by force—imposed by either side—diminished.[23] As he pursued cooperative agreements with the PDRY's 'Ali Nasser, Saleh concurrently moved to more closely manage political challenges in the North through new institutional apparatuses. The General People's Congress was introduced in 1983, making YAR society more legible to the regime without ceding the control that Saleh was building. This approach to representational politics—one that offers voice without decision-making—allowed the General People's Congress (GPC) to develop proto-parties—Nasserists, Ba'athists, and the Islamic Front—without introducing genuine partisan competition.

The idea that the YSP and the GPC were the 'ruling parties' of North and South Yemen and that unification brought them together in partisan competition is partially apocryphal insofar as neither organization was (only) a ruling party before unification. The YSP was the organizational head of a party-state, while the GPC was a populist and corporatist structure designed to aggregate and organize interests while limiting accountable governance. Carapico describes it as a 'quasi-party "mass" institution' that co-opted existing Local Development Association (LDA) institutions to extend the state downward.

> In 1982, 700 delegates … were elected to the GPC through the LDA election process; another 300 deputies were appointed by the president. The Mu'tamar [GPC], casting itself as the non-partisan, all-inclusive bearer of the banner of early nationalist, third-force, and cooperative conferences, unanimously approved a quasi-constitutional document called the National Pact (al-Mithaq al-Watani). The Mithaq called for a sort of representational consultation through non-partisan popular conferences as well as a parliament.[24]

Importantly, after constituting the GPC, LDA institutions were then transformed into local councils for cooperative development and responsibilities were delegated downward to them from a centralizing Ministry of Local Administration. They functioned to collect taxes, increase zakat, and pursue back payments—in other words, they became extractive institutions, rather than deliberative decision-making bodies. While this boosted government revenues, 'the enormous energy apparent until then in so many co-operatives withered into disillusion as state control expanded.'[25]

The consolidation of the Saleh regime occurred in part through centralizing institutions, but also through the reconfiguration of power within and through those institutions. This is reflected in the restaffing of the provincial bureaucracy. Reversing the decentralization and local development that had been hallmarks of YAR governance in the 1970s, by the mid-1980s, President Saleh had begun to appoint regional governors and administrators from among a narrow cohort of Northern elites. This meant that the midland and coastal provinces were disproportionately governed by people from outside of these regions. The differences were sometimes stark, with greater than 80 percent of senior positions in Sana'a province's bureaucracy administered by Sana'anis, whereas only 10 to 30 percent of the same positions were under indigenous leadership in the coastal and midland regions such as Hodeidah, Taiz, or Ibb.[26]

Though North Yemen was in a stronger economic position than its Southern counterpart, the YAR was still running a budget deficit of 30% of GDP by the mid-1980s and was heavily reliant on remittance income in a way that left it politically vulnerable. With over $1 billion USD per year in remittances and more Yemeni workers migrating abroad than male workers employed at home, it is difficult to overstate the extent to which North Yemen's economy was tied to—dependent on—the economies of its Gulf neighbors.[27] Saudi Arabia was thus rightfully described at the time as 'the main point of reference for YAR foreign policy.'[28] The political vulnerability of Yemeni reliance on remittance income became unavoidably clear when over a million migrant workers were repatriated from the Gulf to a newly unified Yemen in 1991, as discussed below.[29]

Like South Yemen, the North also sought ways of diversifying its sources of foreign aid and, by extension, realigning its foreign policy.

Unlike South Yemen, however, which was signaling a new openness to the Gulf states, North Yemen pursued a closer relationship to Iraq through the creation of the Arab Cooperation Council in 1989—a move that one historian described as moving North Yemen to 'top table' in regional diplomacy.[30] Rather than seeking influence only or predominantly through central state institutions, the Saudis themselves countered this sign of North Yemen's increasingly independent foreign policy by accelerating direct payments to North Yemeni tribal figures

By the eve of unification, the motives of the two regimes differed, but policies converged on unification. The PDRY regime could see little path forward economically, and 'tried to wrap itself in the legitimizing rhetoric of unification.'[31] The North was seeking to cement a larger role at the regional level. Unifying territory and resources could help both sides. A draft constitution was agreed between the two Presidents in late 1989, and a referendum was scheduled for November 1990. Travel restrictions were lifted between the two states, and Yemenis began to make wide use of this new freedom.[32] The decision to preemptively advance the timeline on unification and cancel the referendum stemmed from growing domestic opposition in North Yemen and the efforts of some prominent figures to undermine the project.[33] Some Southern leaders—notably Haidar Abu Bakr al-Attas and Salim Salih Muhammad—pressed for confederation over union. Conservative Northern clerics who were concerned about provisions of the constitutional draft threatened to derail the whole project. While much would eventually be said about the use of democratic institutions as a mechanism for managing unification, it is important to note that while unification was widely popular at a conceptual level, its specific form was ultimately brought about through the executive fiat of two men.[34]

Unification and the March to War

The actual process of unification was both sudden and incomplete. It was sudden in that the advanced timeline meant that the two states' institutions were merged without much prior coordination beyond the rhetorical level. It was incomplete because the merger more or less hobbled together two existing sets of institutions rather than constructing something new. The Sana'a Agreement signed by Saleh and al-Bidh on April 22, 1990, established a 30-month transitional period for the integration of institutions. At the executive level, a five-member Presidential Council was elected by a joint session of the two states' councils (the Consultative Council in the North and the Supreme People's Council in the South) and this five-member group selected Saleh and al-Bidh as President and Vice-President, respectively.[35] The transitional parliament would simply fuse the members of the two chambers and add 31 members appointed by decree of the Presidential Council. In these ways, unification was a 'formal partnership between sovereign entities, rather than the true integration of political structures and institutions.'[36] A date was set for parliamentary elections at the end of the transitional period in November 1992, and the interim parliament's primary function would be to approve legislation introduced by the Presidential Council.[37] While the Presidential Council tipped in favor of the GPC, the YSP's al-Attas, who little more than two years earlier had argued at the Central Committee that unity was at least a decade away, balanced things out as Prime Minister at the head of an unwieldy, thirty-nine member cabinet comprised of the pre-unification ministers of the two states.[38]

This additive, not integrative, approach to the merger is one of the primary reasons that Yemeni unification faltered in the brief 1994 civil war, the legacies of which have been long-lasting. Former Ambassador Muhammad al-Qubati described the 'half for me, half for you' system of powersharing as having a negative and lasting effect on institutions in North and South alike.[39] Both President and Vice President, for example, had 'an equal and independent budget and enjoyed presidential power in decisions and appointments in their respective [geographic] areas.'[40] As Maysaa Shuja al-Deen has argued, the presidential council did reflect some genuine power sharing 'in the sense that Saleh did not exercise absolute authority,' but the budgetary and military non-integration made it easier for the two 'Alis 'to ultimately resort to military force to settle their political disputes.'[41]

Despite this limited integration, democratic institutions laid out in the unity constitution reflected Yemen's plural reality and were a pragmatic means of managing difference—two states, each with a great deal of regional and other forms of subnational variation, could more easily come together if there were an institutional means of giving voice to that pluralism. At the same time, efforts at political centralization were a part of both states' recent histories and both leaders' political goals.

As one Adeni activist put it, this meant that the new Republic of Yemen faced the challenge of establishing democracy premised on a 'culture of human rights' but in a changing ideological environment in which 'everyone has a different idea—or no idea—what [that] means.'[42] Ideological trends that had developed within the GPC umbrella now became independent political parties. Indeed, more than forty new parties were established between unification and the first round of elections in 1993. One of the effects of this was to reveal the GPC itself as a non-ideological party of power. As one women's right activist later remarked, after groups like the Baath or the Nasserists left the GPC to establish their own parties, those who remained were only 'people who want positions of influence, access to government resources.'[43] While many GPC members certainly spoke less cynically in the language of development or progress, it is true that as ideologically defined groups broke with the GPC to establish new parties, it was hard to see what the remainder represented.

The most significant of the new parties—electorally and otherwise—was certainly the Yemeni Congregation for Reform, or Islah. Developing out of the Islamic Front faction within the GPC, it brought together a disparate group of Muslim Brothers, *salafis*, and socially conservative businessmen, many of whom had ties to North Yemen's tribal elite.[44] Even in the South, however, where Islah was up against decades of official state secularism, the party found some support. In the run-up to the first elections in 1993, as the Socialists faced a grim campaign of political assassinations, they underestimated the appeal and the organizational efficacy of Islah and appeared caught off guard by the Islamists' second-place finish in the elections.

Critics of Islah regarded the new party as little more than a conservative wing of the GPC, and even GPC members sometimes acknowledged this view, arguing that 'al-Islah could never have become a party without the support of President 'Ali 'Abdullah Saleh.'[45] According to one Southern critic, even prior to its establishment as a party, Islahi leaders as individuals and as part of the Islamic Front had 'tasted power' within the GPC umbrella and did not want to function as an opposition party with limited prerogatives. Many therefore viewed Islah as 'part of the GPC strategy against the YSP.'[46] There was some logic to this interpretation; at a minimum, it was difficult to deny that the 1993 elections showed that the YSP—and arguably the South—had lost political ground through the electoral process.

One obvious counter, of course, is that the North was also home to an overwhelming majority of the Yemeni population, and any expectation on the part of the YSP that it would have an equal share of power beyond the interim phase misread the significance of demography. As former British Ambassador Noel Brehony observed, the YSP's share of the vote was 'about the same in percentage terms as [the South's] contribution to Yemen's population and GDP.'[47]

The YSP made more gains in governorates of former North Yemen than the GPC or Islah made in the South, however, which cemented the party's role as the primary voice for Southern regional interests. That said, the GPC was also able to capitalize on recent internal factionalization in the PDRY and pick up partisans of the displaced 'Ali Nasser; it won three seats and averaged 12% of the vote across the six southern governorates, while the YSP averaged 11% across governorates of the former North. Islah, which won no seats in the South, still managed 17% of the vote in Hadramawt and an average of 7% of seats across the six southern governorates, suggesting that its platform appealed more than the winner-takes-all electoral system might reflect in seat share.[48] Most importantly, Islah and the YSP were within one point of each other in their share of the national vote.

Amid the proliferation of new parties, the 1993 elections also featured an unexpectedly large number of independents. This led to realignments before and after the polls that further fueled suspicions of Northern coordination. As historian Paul Dresch notes:

> In several places GPC and Islah ceded place one to the other, and vast numbers of independent candidates coalesced, realigned and suddenly withdrew in patterns specific to each constituency but producing a result in which GPC managers had confidence before the process started.[49]

Observers at the time suggested that some independents appeared to run in order to negotiate conditions for their timely withdrawal. Others ran as independents because the parties to which they belonged had not nominated them or because civil servants could not have partisan affiliation.[50] Overall, independents secured a greater share of the total vote than either Islah or the YSP, though this was muted somewhat by the formula through which seats were allocated. While much attention has rightly been paid to Islah's sixty-two seats, independent candidates won fifty seats in the new parliament to the YSP's fifty-four, contributing significantly to the YSP's relative defeat.[51]

The 1993 elections surfaced an important division within the YSP that would continue to dog the party throughout the Saleh years—its leaders were divided over not just how but whether to function as part of the political opposition. Some party leaders, including Jarallah Omar, former leader of the YPUP and eventual architect of the JMP opposition coalition, felt that the YSP should campaign by distinguishing itself from the GPC. Others, including Ahmed Yassin Nu'man, who would go on to lead the party and would eventually join the transitional government after Saleh's departure from office in 2011, argued instead for close electoral coordination with the GPC. At the time, Prime Minister Haydar Al Attas described these two groups as functioning 'almost as two different parties.'[52]

Lack of institutional integration was particularly significant within the military. Neither the Sana'a Agreement nor the constitution that was ratified in 1991 spoke to the issue of military integration, only describing the establishment of a National Defense Council, with the President as its head. Rather than integrate the two militaries, Northern and Southern units continued to be locally staffed. In the run-up to the war, newspapers published lists of senior officers that showed that Northern units were narrowly recruited from the

President's Sanhan tribe, whereas Southern units were dominated by officers from Radfan and Dhale, among them those who had helped to defeat 'Ali Nasser's forces in 1986. The narrowness of military recruitment and its relationship to political factions in the North and South not only facilitated the non-integration of Northern and Southern units, but also sparked some intra-regional rivalries with those who were outside of the leadership cliques.[53] In the North, 'unstated realignments of troops were made,' that brought many units under the coordination of 'Ali Muhsin al-Ahmar, commander of the 1st Armored Brigade and a complicated then-ally of President Saleh.[54]

Saleh and al-Bidh, meanwhile, functioned more like two presidents than a unified presidential administration and 'the two 'Alis' rarely appeared together in the years after unification. In the summer of 1993, al-Bid made an unauthorized visit to (and was received by) the American Vice-President, Al Gore, after which he did not return to Sana'a. Instead, he retreated to Aden and issued an eighteen-point declaration outlining Southern demands.[55] This rapidly escalated into a tit-for-tat exchange in the fall of 1993 in what was then described as an 'acrimonious "war of declarations.'"[56]

A constitutional crisis developed over the delayed election of a new Presidential council. The outcome of the parliamentary elections and the terms of the Sana'a Agreement meant that it fell to Yemen's newly constituted parliament to elect a replacement for the five-member presidential council. After several months of delay, the October 1993 election process showcased the power of an incipient Northern alliance. Saleh was reelected with 93% of the votes cast, whereas al-Bidh earned only 61%, putting him in third place and theoretically blocking his reappointment as Vice President.[57] Adding insult to injury, Islahi cleric 'Abd al-Majid al-Zindani—a previous opponent of both unification and the constitution—secured only four fewer votes than al-Bidh, highlighting the roughly equal standing of the YSP and Islah. Despite al-Bidh's poor showing, Saleh nominated him as Vice President. Islah's Speaker of Parliament, Shaykh 'Abdullah bin Hussain al-Ahmar, likewise interceded to ensure that a second member of the YSP would serve on the Presidential Council, though Salim Saleh Muhammed had not met the necessary vote threshold.[58] In sum, a powersharing executive that afforded the YSP the same share of power—even the same offices—as it held before the elections was constituted, but only by virtue of the intercession of top figures in Yemen's informal Northern coalition. Al-Bidh sent his apologies to parliament, but did not attend the swearing in ceremony—'for reasons that you know about'—thus denying the country a constitutionally vested executive.[59]

While the elections and their aftermath had been significant in deteriorating the relationship between and among elites from the two former states and the three main parties, the liberalization of the associational sector and the media that accompanied unification provided an important counter. Newspapers—both partisan and independent—flourished and the associational sector expanded dramatically in the years between unification and the 1994 civil war. Moreover, many—though certainly not all—associations adopted transparent and accountable internal mechanisms: leadership elections, published policy programs, and so on.[60] As elite-level decisions, misaligned expectations, and incomplete institutional integration moved the country toward war, a politically engaged Yemeni society attempted to stem the disintegration.

Constitutional crisis turned to war, but not without the sustained efforts of Yemeni society to protect the pluralism that had accompanied unification and to leverage it in support of the new system. As the two 'Alis issued their rival declarations, an indigenously developed National Dialogue Committee of Political Forces was organized to deliberate over the respective demands, with representatives of the three parties of the ruling coalition and a range of other important intellectuals, opposition figures, and independents. Describing itself as a 'good group of Yemen's sons' who were committed to 'the principle of pluralism within the framework of unity,'[61] they met for several months before agreeing to a set of reforms to address the core drivers of the conflict. The most significant of these included:

> ...delineation and limitation of presidential and vice-presidential power; depoliticization, merger and redeployment of military and security forces, starting with the removal of checkpoints from

cities and highways; administrative and financial decentralization to elected local governments, starting with development budgets…and comprehensive list of other reforms.[62]

This Document of Pledge and Accord was signed in Amman on February 20, 1994, more than a month after its basic terms were agreed. As Carapico notes of the delay, 'small wonder that the two leaderships [of the YSP and GPC] were loathe to sign a document that would, if implemented, force them to give up direct control of their armies, their purse strings, and their cronies.'[63] Elite reluctance was met with popular pressure for the accord, however, reflected in the media and in the streets. As armed clashes unfolded between the two militaries and their irregular allies, civil actors from Yemen's unions, syndicates, and other civic organizations initiated sit-ins across provincial capitals throughout the country to demand the implementation of the accord, some extending for days at a time.[64]

When it finally arrived, then, the 1994 civil war was short in duration and largely—though importantly, not exclusively—limited to conflict between two militaries that had never successfully merged. On a political level, one striking characteristic of the conflict was the way in which both unity and democracy had become general frames accessible to Northern and Southern forces alike. In breaking with the regime, Al-Bidh did not claim to reinstate the PDRY, but declared instead a short-lived Democratic Republic of Yemen, which was offered not as a secessionist Southern state but as 'an alternative regime for [all] Yemen.' YSP leaders deliberately brought in members of important Southern families who had been alienated by the PDRY, and government ministers who left the Yemeni government to join the alternative union retained the same portfolios to which they had been appointed on the basis of Yemen's 1993 electoral outcome.[65] These moves reinscribed the now-popular notion of a single democratic state, even as they appeared to pull against it.

The war was nonetheless rapidly settled through the military defeat of the Southern forces; the fighting lasted from April 27—one year to the day after the 1993 elections—to July 7, when Aden fell and was subsequently sacked by a combination of Northern forces and Islamist irregulars. Over the course of these six weeks, however, a few things became clearer. One was that Southern political elites could not rely on the level of armed support that they enjoyed in Aden outside of it; several Southern tribes had allowed Northern forces to pass through their areas unchallenged. Another was that the Saudis and other Gulf states who had opposed unification were willing to put their thumb on the scale by offering support for the Southern war effort but not Southern victory.

In the immediate aftermath of the conflict, the Saleh regime moved to consolidate its power quickly. Somewhat surprisingly, the war was followed by only a handful of trials; al-Bidh and his closest allies were tried for treason in absentia, although their sentences were later dropped. Most participants in the fighting were covered by a broad general amnesty. Critically, this benefitted Northern irregulars and produced little by way of accountability for acts of extrajudicial violence, theft, land expropriation, or other war-related grievances.

Saleh focused primarily on the political isolation of his adversaries and promotion of his allies. Amending the constitution to eliminate the joint executive, he took on expanded powers as president. Former Presidential Council member 'Abd al-Aziz 'Abd al-Ghani assumed the role of Prime Minister, with a cabinet of twenty-six ministers, of whom all but one were members of the GPC or Islah.[66] An important ally of 'Ali Nasser from Abyan, Abd Rabbuh Mansur Hadi, was promoted to Defense Minister during the war and became Vice President thereafter.[67] Islah, for its part, secured leadership of seven ministries and the Vice PM post, and achieved its objective of amending Article 3 of the constitution to elevate shari'a from the main source to the source of all national legislation.

The YSP was not formally dissolved, but the Southern bureaucracy was substantially restaffed by those linked to 'Ali Nasser and / or those demonstrably loyal to the GPC.[68] Though they were not charged with crimes because of the amnesty, Southern military officers were nonetheless disarmed and discharged, losing their pension benefits. They 'sat at home collecting half-pay with no benefits, while northern soldiers and policemen took control of southern lands.'[69] Generally, analysts noted 'insufficient integration of political leaders from the former south Yemen into government structures,' and regional grievances hardened in the face of perceived injustices.[70]

Political discourse shifted in the North and South. As 'talk of decentralization and federalism was replaced among Northerners by sterner terms of unity (*wahdah*) against secession (*infisal*),' Southerners spoke of 'internal colonialism' and 'annexation.'[71] Some Adenis would later describe the war and its aftermath as a war of northern aggression. Indeed, in interviews and focus groups in Aden, self-conscious invocation of language from the United States' civil war—including the process of reconstruction—was often invoked by means of analogy, with particular emphasis on Islah's role in the Islamization and 'retribalization' of the South framed as 'carpetbagging.'[72] Some took a more nuanced view that attributed the appeal of Islah and the Islamization of the South to a kind of reaction to the 'the single party state in the South' and lack of internal democracy in the PDRY.[73] But no one denied that a lot had changed.

Regime Consolidation, 1997–2003

The political and military defeat of the YSP made relationships between Yemen's parties more complicated. After the war, Islah served in a coalition government with the GPC. As one party MP explained, this was a 'path to influence' by which Islahis hoped they could play a role in decision-making without being held accountable for governance failures.[74] Soon, however, its deputies found that they could no longer exert much influence on the ruling party, and began to express concern about growing government corruption. Moreover, Islahi MPs complained that they were used by the GPC to make decisions appear more consultative than they genuinely were. One MP recounted that parliamentary committees were often 'sent back to vote again and again until the vote comes out "right."'[75] By 1995, several Islahi members of the cabinet had resigned, arguing that they were 'unable to do their jobs and were prevented from taking steps to reduce corruption within their ministries.'[76] Islah's sharply declining political influence was a subject of some reflection inside the party, where some members felt that 'their biggest mistake was to try to implement reforms too quickly, particularly in challenging corruption.'[77] By 1997, the government was exclusively composed of members of the ruling party.[78]

The YSP, meanwhile, boycotted the 1997 elections in protest against its marginalization, the seizure of party resources, and the exile of its leadership. The decision was reached after weeks of deliberation, and the Central Committee took a divisive and close internal vote on the decision, with only 64% in favor of boycott.[79] Without the socialists, Islah was no longer what President Saleh had described as a 'card to play against the YSP' and Islah's utility as part of the ruling coalition declined as well.[80] Islah saw a drop in its number of seats from sixty-six to fifty-three. Given the structure of Yemen's single-member district system, the popular vote reflected a smaller gap between the parties than these seat changes suggest, but the GPC's parliamentary majority—224 seats out of 301—was now large enough to amend the constitution unilaterally.

This is precisely what President Saleh called on the GPC to do following his own reelection in 1999. The amendments he brought forward in August 2000 promised to extend the terms of the existing parliament and the presidency itself.[81] In 2001, the amendments to the constitution were approved by a popular referendum, as required by the constitution. The question asking voters to approve the amendments was tied to local council elections which again affirmed a substantial GPC majority, with Islah in second place. While the YSP fared adequately in some Southern governorates, it did not perform well in Aden, where the ruling party concentrated its efforts. Elections themselves had become a powerful instrument for regime consolidation and became a core instrument of a system by which 'parliament extends patronage to a large section of local elites and gives them a stake in the political system without offering them sufficient power to alter it.'[82] Unsurprisingly, the regularization of elections was praised 'more by outside observers than by Yemeni monitors themselves.'[83]

Without any meaningful institutional check on the ruling party or the consolidation of the Saleh regime, the terrain of rights abuses shifted in some notable ways. On the one hand, the government took admirable measures to crack down on the presence of 'private prisons' operating throughout the country. These facilities—

sometimes in the context of local justice traditions associated with the tribal system and sometimes as instruments of bribery or ransom—functioned in parts of the former North and South.[84] At the same time, the centralization of security and criminal justice was tied to an increasingly authoritarian state with little transparency or civilian oversight. The YSP became a particular target of regime lawfare, whereby rules regulating meetings, associations, and other public gatherings were used to curtail the activities of YSP members. While the YSP was not formally banned, its members were arrested, for attending party conferences or for publishing materials that were alleged to question the unity framework for example. When the Central Committee reinstated exiled members in 2000, including some who had been tried and sentenced in absentia for treason, a parliamentary committee was established (by the GPC) to explore the formal dissolution of the party.[85]

As the only sizable party aside from the GPC, Islah played an ambivalent role during this period of regime consolidation. A member of one of Yemen's smaller opposition parties remarked, 'in the 1990s, Islah cooperated with the GPC against the YSP, but learned that if you play *taktik* with one who is stronger than you, you will lose.'[86] After striking a deal to support Saleh's first campaign for direct election as president in 1999—a move which was internally divisive among Islahis—the party began working with Yemen's smaller parties on a joint program to address corruption, challenge the dominance of the ruling party, and restore the kind of competitive politics that had seemed possible a decade earlier.[87] The alliance took the name of the Joint Meeting Parties, but is often described conversationally as simply *'al-Mushtarak.'*

The origins of the JMP alliance have been characterized differently by its participants, democracy promotion practitioners, and scholars. Leslie Campbell, for example, who served as director of the National Democratic Institute (NDI), has characterized it as a 'tactical party coalition,' and emphasized the NDI's role in convincing the YSP to remain engaged in partisan politics despite its leaders' deep reservations. Campbell, in fact, locates the formation of the alliance to the 'unlikely venue' of the Democratic National Convention in Los Angles in 2000, when the heads of the YSP and

Islah were invited guests.[88] Practitioner accounts from within the democracy promotion community disproportionately focus on the brokerage of deals between key actors. Other practitioner accounts and interviews with staff at the NDI, International Foundation for Electoral Systems (IFES), United Nations Development Programme, and other democracy promotion organizations in the early years of the JMP alliance similarly stress a 'brokerage' model that relies on agreements between key elites, typically facilitated by international organizations.

Scholarly accounts offer a range of more structural and ideational analyses. Some view the JMP as a 'defensive' move whereby 'the JMP has provided its smaller members with protection from the regime, and in return the smaller parties have added legitimacy to the JMP's rhetoric of political exclusion and have helped to provide evidence that Islah and the YSP—both previously in coalition with the GPC— have now defected from the regime.'[89] Others, by contrast, emphasize the ideological changes at work in both Islah and the YSP, as well as the influence of the smaller parties to the alliance, which played a role far greater than their electoral weight.[90] Both interpretations align at least in part with generational and social network analyses that emphasize the role of overlapping educational and professional networks among partisans in their 30s and 40s and their peers in the associational sector as central to the development of the JMP's reform agenda.[91] These accounts are not inconsistent with the idea that international organizations developed programs that brought party leaders together, but rely on different understandings of Yemeni agency.

The generational dimension was particularly clear in the setting of *qat* chews and other collective fora in the JMP's early years. Older members of the various member parties exhibited more comfort with one another (despite their often substantial differences of view), and younger, mid-level cohorts—the people who actually ran the party offices, wrote for the papers, and so on—would similarly sit together at *qat* chews, eat meals together, or split taxis to or from events.[92] The quotidian work of the mid-level professionals, as well as their social bonds, cannot be overestimated. My fieldnotes from the time are full of seating maps and notes about who introduced me to whom and how they knew each other; these crossed partisan lines as often as they adhered to them and were often located in shared educational experiences and/or shared regional origins, categories which themselves overlap.

Many of my observations related to these generational cohorts come from the daily practice of chewing *qat*—a practice that is partially constitutive of the 'politics of deliberation' central to Yemeni public life. Lisa Wedeen has extensively theorized the role of the *qat* chew, identifying four distinct ways in which chewing *qat* should be viewed as substantively political:

> First, during some *qat* chews, actual policy decisions get made…
> Second, people make avid use of *qat* chews to share information about political events and to discuss their significance in public…
> Third, these gatherings provide an occasion for negotiating power relationships between elites and constituents in which elites are held responsible and are required to be responsible to the needs of participants by guaranteeing goods and services or by advocating on behalf of the village, electoral district, or local group. Fourth and relatedly, the 'public' of the *qat* chew is also a lived forum for political self-fashioning, an occasion for cultivating what Arendt (1958) called the 'human capacity for action'—the ability to begin anew through words and deeds, to think in unanticipated ways about recent events, to make sense of their multiple meanings with others, and to take pleasure in the dynamism of specifically agonistic encounters.[93]

My experience chewing *qat* with many members of the JMP in the 2000s included observations of each of these functions. Moreover, because of the networked element I describe above, it was often through qat chews that overlapping consensus between member parties of the JMP (and its limits) could be mapped out. The co-participation of party members, journalists, civil society organization (CSO) staff, and more, allowed not only for multi-perspectival deliberation and efforts at persuasion—Wedeen's agonistic encounters, Sen's transpositional scrutiny—but also allowed for the transmission of these messages to the pages of Yemeni newspapers, the programs of local CSOs, and the priorities of some international organizations and donor agencies—and vice versa. It was not unusual for me to read in the paper about something I had heard discussed at a chew in the days prior, or for someone to bring a news article or policy report to a chew to discuss with others. Staff from NDI, IFES, United Nations Development Programme, and any number of proliferating 'governance' programs participated in some of these deliberations; my notes do not indicate that they enjoyed any special status but do record exchanges in which they were explicitly challenged by interlocutors This is a part of why I am skeptical of practitioner accounts like Campbell's that narrate the emergence of the JMP as a function of external organizations providing the 'key assistance and advice.' They, too, were understood as actors with a stake in the Saleh regime's 'reform agenda' and its strategic use of multiparty elections to consolidate power.[94]

There was not enough time or trust for the member parties of the incipient JMP to run a joint slate of candidates in the 2003 election; instead, they ran individual campaigns but pledged 'to not compete against other JMP members—either directly or indirectly,' though the parties only effectively coordinated this approach in about one third of the districts.[95] Despite seeing an increase in voter participation and women's participation, in particular, these elections were the least free—and, it turns out, the last—parliamentary elections in Yemen since unification in 1990. The GPC walked away from the polls with 79% of the seats in parliament; Islah saw a loss of nineteen seats, and all JMP member parties together held only 20% of the newly elected chamber. The number of independents shrunk to only fourteen, but ten of these declared for the GPC after the election.

Not unexpectedly, in the years following the election, concerns with regime corruption escalated, as did the regime's efforts to suppress its critics. This played a powerful role in JMP cohesion, and was reflected by increased media scrutiny, the activism of civil society organizations, and their coordination with members of the parties in the emergent JMP alliance. External assessment of corruption does not entirely match Yemeni perceptions; the country's score on the Corruption Perception Index, for example, was nearly steady across the 2000s, indicating little change.[96] I have long struggled to make sense of popular database scores for political rights and freedoms in Yemen, which pick up little to no variation in the years after the 2003 elections. An overwhelming majority of my interlocutors described a political system that was closing, harassment of the media and opposition parties, and unchecked government corruption. In explaining its methodology, Freedom House, for example, explains that 'a score is typically changed only if there has been a real-world development during the year that warrants a decline or improvement (e.g., a crackdown on the media, the country's first free and fair elections), though gradual changes in conditions—in the absence of a signal event—are occasionally registered in the scores.'[97] It was not until 2010, when the electoral system had effectively ceased to function and violent conflict shaped North and South that Freedom House adjusted its scores.[98]

The relationship between corruption, repression, and opposition politics was highlighted by a prominent case that occurred in 2005. It was a member of Islah who first showed me a page in *al-Wasat* listing the names of Yemeni students who had been awarded scholarships to foreign universities and congratulating them on this accomplishment. As we read through the names, he listed out each student's familial relationship to members of the regime's inner circle. I found it interesting, but my field notes indicate that I thought he might have been exaggerating when he described *al-Wasat's* publication of this list as a critique of growing corruption. A couple of days later, I got a late-night call from someone who I knew to be friends with the editor of *al-Wasat*. He explained that the editor, Jamal 'Amer, had just been taken from his home to a hilltop outside Sana'a, where he was beaten and threatened—because he had published this list of names.[99] Before 'Amer was released, he was reportedly told not to tell anyone about the beating unless he wanted his family to face the same fate. I expected that I would not hear about this publicly, so I was surprised to soon see his beaten face on the front of several newspapers associated with the opposition. As the editor of a different paper explained, publicizing the attack was a perverse way of protecting 'Amer from future violence by amplifying his name-recognition, especially through his inclusion in English-language press.[100] In 2006, 'Amer was awarded the International Press Freedom Award by the Committee to Protect Journalists. He used his speech as an opportunity to criticize the lack of accountability for crimes committed by 'corrupt shaykhs, politicians, and military officials,' and the impunity this encouraged. This kind of triangulation between parties, journalists, and human rights organizations was a hallmark of efforts to resist regime encroachment as they developed after the 2003 elections.[101]

An more direct effect of the regime's electoral consolidation was a further deterioration of the role of parliament in decision-making, already limited by the 2001 constitutional amendments. Sarah Phillips noted at the time that 'the regime has undermined the parliament's constitutional right of oversight, and the parliament has not, as an institution, vigorously demanded these rights to be upheld.'[102] Indeed, one opposition MP complained that so many MPs would skip sessions that there were rarely more than 40% of MPs present at any given time and that parliament regularly functioned without quorum.[103]

Challenging the president in a direct election in 2006 afforded the opposition an opportunity to focus its efforts and hammer out enough differences to field a single candidate. Agreeing on independent Hadrami technocrat Faisal bin Shamlan, the JMP member parties chose someone with a record of government service before and after unification. As a member of the PDRY's Supreme People's Council, bin Shamlan was acceptable to the YSP and Southern partisans. Because he supported unity in 1994 and served in both the cabinet and the parliament as an independent, it was difficult for Saleh to dismiss him as a secessionist. His clean reputation was central to his appeal to many alliance members. One story that circulated at the time recounted that when he resigned his ministerial portfolio in 1995, 'he returned his ministry car before catching a taxi home.'[104]

While Saleh won reelection in 2006, the electoral campaign offered at least three important lessons. The first was that the opposition was, in fact, capable of working together, but that this occurred largely at the mid-level. Two of Islah's prominent figures—Shaykh 'Abd al-Majid al-Zindani and Shaykh 'Abdullah bin Hussein al-Ahmar—defected from bin Shamlan and supported Saleh. Two other figures—one Islahi and one Socialist—ran small and largely insignificant presidential campaigns without their parties' support. But the core of the member parties' leadership and much of the organizational capacity of Islah were turned to bin Shamlan's campaign and account for a finish that JMP members widely praised as a 'success' despite his loss.[105]

Second, it cemented the role of procedural reform as the core of the JMP agenda—for good or for ill. The area of overlapping consensus among the parties—and thus the content of the JMP's published 'Document of Reform' and bin Shamlan's campaign in 2006—focused on electoral and other procedural reforms. By speaking only about those procedural rights and freedoms on which they could agree, the JMP platform had an 'anodyne emptiness' and ran the risk of 'weakening all of the members by enforcing a sometimes bland uniformity.'[106] When I asked a member of the JMP about this, he explained:

> The more important objective of the JMP is determining how to organize the political field fairly. They don't discuss other programs (education, health, etc.) but simply how to establish an even field.[107]

References to issues of gender equality or the appropriate role of religion in public life—issues that were deeply divisive among member parties—were largely omitted from JMP discourse, while member parties continued to pursue their own objectives concurrently.[108]

Finally, the 2006 election highlighted that the opposition could make Saleh work harder. While bin Shamlan had little chance of winning the presidency, this was not the metric that many used in evaluating his campaign or the JMP's role. Instead, as one member of the alliance explained:

> After the elections, it became easier to talk critically about the president; the elections changed the rules of the game in Yemen toward a focus on the rights of citizens. Having a viable second candidate with a different platform, unlike 1999, mattered a lot for the regime.[109]

More open dissent, however, was countered by demonstrably greater repression. By 2009, Human Rights Watch documented patterns of abuses and characterized a rights environment that had 'deteriorated markedly' since the presidential election.[110] At a *qat* chew early that year, a member of the JMP was blunt, arguing that since the election, the regime had been trying to impose *beit al-taa'* on the opposition. I explained that I was only familiar with this concept in the context of a much-debated proposal to legally require state officials to return 'disobedient wives' to their husbands by force; its proposal in 2000 had caused considerable stir and was staunchly opposed by the YSP and numerous civil rights organizations at the time.[111] Another member of the group affirmed that I had correctly understood the reference. It meant that 'the JMP is like a woman to the government,' he explained, with all that this implied.[112]

Repression of JMP parties was paired with efforts to court individual members away from the alliance, straining member parties from within.[113] Given the internal factionalization of both the YSP and Islah, this remained a significant fear for members of the parties who were helping to build a unified opposition. Whether and to what extent joint opposition was sustainable remained unclear. A Yemeni staffer at NDI who was working closely with the member parties at the time bluntly declared that the alliance was 'not a vehicle for future political advancement. It is a shield, for political protection. The parties find themselves in the same trench…'[114] This is why the JMP moved shortly after the 2006 election for serious reforms to the electoral system. They started early, knowing that it would take time (and pressure) to reform the electoral law before the next round of parliamentary elections in 2009. In particular, they were cognizant of the uneven playing field, and proposed a shift to a proportional representation system and equal access to security for all candidates and campaigns.[115]

A general commitment to reform the system was agreed by the ruling party and opposition in 2006, with EU facilitation, but little tangible progress followed. A draft law was submitted to parliament in August 2008, including many of the opposition's favored reforms. In what Islah's parliamentary spokesman described as 'a blow to the understanding reached among the parties,' the proposed reforms were voted down by the GPC supermajority.[116] In several interviews and group discussions about the failure of the agreed proposal, members of the opposition cited the President's decision to unilaterally announce his support for a 15% quota for women in the upcoming parliamentary elections as a deliberate wedge issue timed to derail the electoral reforms. While this was not included in the proposed reform, the close timing was confusing, and most people who mentioned this to me—men and women, from the GPC and the JMP member parties—argued that muddying the issues was a way for the regime to pursue (or be seen to pursue) reforms that were important to external donors, while also guaranteeing the failure of the electoral reforms overall. Without reforms, particularly to the composition and independence of the Supreme Council on Elections and Referenda, JMP members worried that they would 'have to compete with the state (*al-dawla*), not the ruling party (*hizb al-hakim*)' in any subsequent election.[117]

By the winter of 2009, just months before parliamentary elections were slated to occur in April, JMP members were deeply divided over whether to move forward with an unreformed system or press for a delay. As a member of the ruling party explained, 'there are two views [on the elections] within the JMP. Those who think that there must be reforms before there can be elections, and those who see elections as the door to reforms.'[118] These positions did not fall strictly along party lines. Given that only Islah held a sizable number of seats in the 2003 parliament, many agreed that in the event of an opposition boycott, 'the biggest loser would be Islah, without question.'[119] As one independent journalist argued, 'the regime is pushing the JMP to call for the delay [in the elections], so that they [the regime] can give up responsibility for the issue. Neither side wants to be the one who calls for it first.'[120] Those who tilted toward a delay saw doing so as helping to save the electoral process, arguing 'we are not against elections, of course, but we hope to make them free.'[121]

Some members of the ruling GPC saw the problems facing the country but viewed elections as 'an opportunity to resolve these problems.'[122] Such statements seemed to minimize opposition concern that elections might serve (as they had in the recent past) to further consolidate the regime's hold on state resources and limit accountability. A close advisor to the president dismissed this worry, saying, 'we are not saying that there are no problems, but if we want to resolve all of these [procedural] issues first, we won't be able to hold the elections on time.'[123]

Some linked the issue of elections to the broader context of the 2008 global financial crisis and the likelihood of coming austerity. 'The ruling party would like either a long delay or very quick elections, since they can't control the consequences of [current] the international financial crisis.'[124] A member of the ruling party saw the president as constrained:

> President Saleh understands the quagmire he's in. The GPC itself wants elections, but Saleh is concerned also about Western opinion. But some are saying 'so what? So what if the West doesn't recognize our elections [as free and fair]?"' Both sides want a delay, but neither wants to be responsible for it.[125]

After several months of internal deliberation, on February 25, 2009, representatives of the parties announced that they had agreed to postpone the elections to April 2011. The postponement was tied to an agreement reportedly brokered by representatives of the EU and NDI that would include most of the JMP's priorities, including dramatic changes that would decentralize political power and adopt a parliamentary system with proportional representation.[126] Because these would require constitutional amendments, however, they would require time (as well as the support of the sitting parliament). The revised date for elections was set for April 27, 2011. As soon became clear, these elections would never come to pass.

Closing the Institutional Door

While a popular uprising was not something that I imagined at the time, my fieldnotes from 2008 and 2009 record important qualitative differences in the way people spoke about the regime and note my surprise at the bluntness and sense of urgency compared to the period before the 2006 presidential race. They record how openly people had begun to express grievances in spaces outside of the home or *qat* chews with friends, including in 'low trust' settings where they were in the presence of members of the ruling party or state security. This was despite ample evidence of government surveillance, efforts at intimidation, and growing restrictions on the press.[127]

One GPC member of parliament conceded the change, saying 'I'm with the GPC, but even I know that this isn't the GPC's country.'[128] This shift is largely attributable to the spiraling crises that are the subject of the next chapter. But these crises are not wholly separable from the partisan dynamics described here. The gradual consolidation of Saleh's authoritarian regime through electoral institutions is deeply imbricated with the extrapartisan forms of mobilization that co-occurred in the second half of the 2000s. The JMP's responses to the Houthi insurgency after 2004 and the Southern Movement by 2007 highlight the opposition's ineffectualness and help to explain why extrapartisan mobilization dominated Yemen's politics even before the popular uprising in 2011.

As one observer put it, 'the 2006 elections destroyed the idol' by challenging President Saleh directly for the first time.[129] But the notionally mutual decision to delay parliamentary elections destroyed something more, signaling that the door was closed to any genuine institutional challenge to the regime that Saleh had built. The JMP's participation in the agreement to delay the elections in 2009 was in many ways an abrogation of any responsibility to pursue the justice demands of Yemeni society through electoral means. It was a preemptive admission of defeat and one not easily forgotten.

A Capabilities Assessment

The events described in this chapter reflect official disengagement with justice demands under the unity regime, and erosion and suppression of institutions that could, at least theoretically, support transpositional scrutiny. Elections themselves—from the difference between expectations and outcome in 1993 to the manipulation of independents to the machinations over the eventual delay— became instruments of substantive injustice through which an increasingly narrow and unaccountable regime was consolidated. The mere existence of multiple political parties and some measure of press and associational sector freedom did not mean that Yemeni institutions offered a meaningful path through which to address past or present wrongs.

Opportunities for transpositional scrutiny and public reason are central to the development of overlapping consensus on the nature of injustice and the need for remedy. Such opportunities were initially expanded through the introduction of multiparty competition and the liberalization of media and associational sector restrictions, in particular. This played a role in enabling civil actors to undertake important initiatives to mediate conflict among elites, as with the Amman declaration, but were not enough to forestall violent conflict. As parliament struggled to maintain any meaningful independence in the aftermath of the 1994 conflict, opportunities for public deliberation in the media, through the syndicates, and in other public fora continued, but were critically disconnected from the workings of government. Partisan media and associational sector activism nonetheless continued to buoy efforts by Yemeni civil actors to name and identify in public the problems that they faced and to discuss potential solutions was an important form of justice work in this period, even if civil actors struggled in the face of barriers erected as a part of the Saleh regime's consolidation.

The events described in this chapter had a largely negative impact on the agency of Yemen's civil actors. In Deneulin's terms, opportunities for deliberation—especially among literate urban-dwellers, who were a minority of the population overall but a growing share of its youth—expanded means by which Yemenis were able to reason together in the formation of a conception of the good. But the uneven experience of rights was a major impediment to forms of agency tied to self-respect. All Yemenis experienced practical limitations on their civil and political rights stemming from the lack of judicial independence and the introduction of specialized courts. Some Yemenis also experienced more targeted limitations, given the asymmetries in access to legal institutions and entrenched inequalities that persisted across regions and among categories of citizens. When paired with the inefficacy of electoral institutions, it is little wonder that Yemenis turned to extrapartisan forms of mobilization through which to press their claims. As the next chapter shows, these extrapartisan claims were closely tied to perceived injustices unaddressed—or worsened—by the country's political parties.

THE SHADOW OF PAST SOVEREIGNTIES
EXTRAPARTISAN MOBILIZATION AND JUSTICE
DEMANDS THROUGH 2010

The declining efficacy of partisan politics outlined in the previous chapter occurred alongside the development of powerful forms of extrapartisan mobilization that challenged both the Saleh regime and, eventually, the foundations of the Yemeni state. Each movement relied in different ways on the shadow of past sovereignties, though neither was a straightforward restorationist movement. Unlike the reform-minded Joint Meeting Parties (JMP), extrapartisan movements mobilized around injustices related to cultural, religious, and economic rights more than political rights, though such distinctions can be overly rigid. The Houthi movement in the North and the Hirak, or Southern Movement, in the South emerged in response to dynamics of state-building, regime consolidation, and unaddressed justice demands, alongside the closing of institutional avenues of contention mapped in the previous chapter. Each expressed grievances that reflected the eroded status of earlier political orders, and articulated justice claims in a way that challenged the commitments of the regime as it was constituted under President Saleh.

The primary aim of this chapter is to map the terrain of justice claims that each movement articulated at its inception and the regime's responses to them as they dynamically shaped the violence of both state and non-state actors in the last decade of the Saleh regime. Historicizing the political projects of the Houthi movement and the Hirak captures shifts in dynamics of belonging over time. As this chapter will show, regime practices combined disengagement and some limited strategic engagement with justice demands to catalyze both movements; repression of non-violent contention pushed both extrapartisan movements in the direction of more radical demands and methods by the eve of the 2011 uprising.

Egalitarian Challenges and the Hereditary Elite in the North

Throughout the 1990s, much of the focus of the formal political parties remained on the relationship between North and South, and the rise (and fall) of Yemen's putative democratic opening. At the same time, however, subtle and not-so-subtle changes had been ongoing in Yemen's far north that were at least as significant but had a less obvious relationship to formal political institutions or elections. The development of the Houthi movement does not begin with the Houthi family itself and predates the armed conflict that developed in its name in Sa'ada in 2004 by at least two decades. Instead, it is grounded in a series of challenges to the status of North Yemen's hereditary elite, most especially the privileged position of the *sada*, or members of the Prophet Muhammed's family, *Ahl al-Bayt*.

Alongside its dramatic political shifts, the twentieth century in North Yemen was nonetheless a period in which 'distinctions of rank were endless and a great deal depended on descent.'[1] In this context, social status derived from 'descent'—or *nasab*—can index many dimensions of social identity, including region, membership in a tribe, proximity to the Prophet Muhammed, heritable access to religious training, occupational caste, gender, and more. Moreover, as this section discusses, the status of particular descent categories has varied as political regimes have changed.

Tribes or 'tribalism' are often seen as central to Yemeni politics, but these terms have a range of meanings. In different parts of Yemen, for example, one can distinguish between characteristics of tribal orders that are rooted in productive agriculture—where shaykhs function as landowners—and those whose wealth is tied to commerce or to their relationship to the state itself.[2] As much as descent, or *nasab*, has been and remains significant, individuals can also 'as linguists say, "shift register," and in the name of Islam or the nation or revolution, not tribalism, one can turn against immediate kin and neighbors.'[3] While tribal identity is a significant feature in Yemeni society, in other words, there is still variation in the pull of tribal membership for individuals.

While the overwhelming majority of Yemenis are Muslim, the religious landscape of the country is also substantially variegated. In the northernmost parts of the country, many are Zaydis, followers of a branch of Shi'i Islam that differs from the much larger and better-known Twelver branch; Zaydism includes a unique legal tradition more closely resembling the Shafa'i school of Sunni jurisprudence, which is the most popular Sunni tradition in Yemen. Sufism has been widely practiced in some parts of the country, though it has been under pressure from the growth of *salafism* over the past several decades, which is discussed at some length in sections that follow. There are also some Isma'ili Shi'a, a small community of Yemeni Jews, and an unknown number of Baha'i, although this last group is not legally recognized or enumerated.

Some religious distinctions intersect with descent-based categories and have played an important role in Yemeni political life. These include the privileged status of *sada* (singular *sayyid*), or descendants of the Prophet Muhammed through his daughter, Fatima. In Southern and Eastern parts of the country, which predominantly follow the Shafa'i *madhab*, *sada* did not claim specific political rights but have nonetheless enjoyed a privileged status. In the North, however, a Zaydi imamate was organized for close to a millennium on the principle that a governing imam could be recruited exclusively from among the *sada*, concentrating political power in North Yemen narrowly. In the Yemeni highlands, *sada* have traditionally enjoyed a symbiotic relationship to local tribes, who offer them protection in small towns or hilltop sanctuaries.[4] Non-*sada* categories are also significant. Qadis, or judges, are men of religious learning who are neither *sada* nor tribesmen, and who perform important legal functions for the community as a whole. This, as with other occupational categories of lesser status, is seen as a heritable role with caste-like properties. Powerful norms of endogamy helped to perpetuate stratification through the early republican period (and sometimes still do).

In 1962, a republican revolution sought to displace the Zaydi imamate; while the imamate had only functioned as a hereditary monarchy since the rule of Imam Yahya in 1948, it had for centuries been patterned on the expectation that the governing imam ought to be a descendent of the Prophet Muhammed through his daughter, Fatima, and her husband 'Ali Ibn Abi Talib. Beyond this, the Zaydi imamate was based on the principle of *khuruj*, which holds that the most righteous among eligible claimants to the position of imam is the one who can successfully command a following. Articulated in contrast to quietist alternatives that enjoin Muslims to obey an unjust ruler as a means of avoiding *fitna*, or chaos in the community of believers, the principle of *khuruj* is understood to enjoin resistance to an unjust ruler and to valorize rising to the call of the most righteous.[5] In practice, this principle was not always central to the selection of Zaydi imams, and it was certainly not central to the dynastic imamate that was overthrown by republicans in the 1962 revolution, but it remains an important and relevant principle with which Yemenis continue to contend.

The republican revolution of 1962 was followed by almost a decade of conflict in North Yemen, including the direct military engagement of Egyptian and Saudi forces in support of rival Yemeni factions. A new republican regime set in motion a series of changes in the structure and function of tribal authority in North Yemen that challenged the hereditary position of the *sada*, who had previously formed the political and administrative backbone of the imamate and occupied a privileged position in North Yemeni society. This was followed by a sustained campaign of evangelism by new *salafi* Muslims, intellectually and materially encouraged by their ties to Saudi Arabia, which further reshaped the religious, social, and political landscape of Yemen's northernmost regions in the 1980s and 1990s. While their projects differed, both republicanism and *salafi* evangelism expressed egalitarian challenges to the hierarchies that had ordered North Yemeni society for centuries.

These challenges took two principal forms. The republican challenge involved the elevation of alternative sources of power through the tribal system. This did not simply build upon a functioning tribal system but altered it. As shaykhs were drawn into state power as an alternative to *sada*, their relationship to both *sada* and to ordinary tribesmen and other members of society shifted. The republican regime's patronage system, particularly as President Saleh expanded it in the 1980s and 1990s, reworked this representational relationship by creating a cohort of 'republican shaykhs' who were offered political offices and access to economic privileges. Rather than representing the interests of their members, many moved to Sana'a and were seen as increasingly distant from the interests of their tribesman.[6]

The social advancement of these republican shaykhs was intimately tied to the declining position of the *sada* as a class during the early republican period. This reversal of fortune occurred along several planes concurrently. As a political loss, the dissolution of the imamate meant the end of hereditary rule by *sada* and, at least initially, the displacement of its existing elite.[7] It also had a range of material consequences. The practice of 'waqf-grabbing' or the seizure of lands that functioned as hereditary religious endowments eliminated a primary source of livelihood for many *sada*.[8] When paired with the increased profitability of agricultural production and trade in the North in the 1980s—trade that was now concentrated in the hands of newly empowered tribal shaykhs—the *sada*'s loss of privilege was both relative and absolute.

Socially, the recalibration of power also found expression in challenges to marriage practices that had long reproduced the system of social stratification under the imamate.[9] Steep inequalities were upheld through marriage rules that allowed a sayyid to marry a tribeman's daughter but not the reverse.[10] A range of lower-status hereditary groups had less mobility still, and the *muhamasheen* (also called *akhdam*, pejoratively) were almost fully endogamous.[11] So rigid were these status distinctions that low-status Yemenis would need to 'immigrate' to another region of Yemen in order to socially advance.[12] Northerners from low-status categories also numbered disproportionately among those who migrated to Saudi Arabia and elsewhere in the Gulf for work.[13] Efforts at 'passing' beyond one's station were considered violations to be adjudicated by Zaydi courts from at least the eighteenth century.[14]

Non-reciprocal marriage rules were premised on the principle of *kafa'ah fil-nasab*, or social equivalence between spouses.[15] As anthropologist Gabriele vom Bruck explains, non-reciprocal relations whereby tribesmen might marry their daughters to *sada* (but not the reverse) established broader relations of social dominance:

> On marriage a man assumes authority over his wife who is expected to be subservient to him. By virtue of being the primary wife-givers, non-'Alids symbolically became the 'brides' of the *sadah*.[16]

Given that women 'metonymically symbolize the identity of tribes and their collective liabilities,' the rules governing marriage are significant to power relations within tribes, among them, and in their relations with those outside of the tribal system, like the *sada*.[17] When and among whom marital bonds may be seen as unbuildable is a politically relevant source of grievance, a perceived injustice and source of marginalization. Republicanism destabilized existing practices, providing an authorizing logic by which newly empowered shaykhs might not only marry *sharifas* but even, in a remarkable reversal of power, might refuse them as a means of humiliating *sada* families.[18]

The leveling effect of republicanism was reflected in some intellectual developments among Zaydi scholars themselves, helping to further shift the landscape of religious identity in the North after the 1962 revolution. Most important among these was a reconsideration of the principle of *shart al-batnayn*, or the requirement that political leadership must come from among the descendants of Hassan or Hussayn, the two sons of Fatima and 'Ali Ibn Abi Talib, whom Shi'i Muslims regard as inheritors of the Prophet Muhammad. This principle, which was the basis of the *sada*'s claim to privileged political status under the imamate, was a clear target of republican statebuilders, who not only criticized it but also disallowed festivals commemorating the designation of 'Ali as successor to the Prophet and other practices emphasizing 'Alid descent.[19]

By the point of unification in 1990, some prominent Zaydi religious scholars, like the influential Majd al-Din al-Mu'ayyadi, had rejected *shart al-batnayn* as a principle, and had begun to reexamine other elements of the Zaydi Hadawi legal tradition that were seen as non-egalitarian.[20] Moreover, influential figures like Muhammad al-Mansur argued that elections could function as a call to follow the righteous, a contemporary form of *khuruj*, the obligatory challenge to an unjust ruler.[21] Najam Haider explains such reinterpretations:

> Recall that a qualified candidate establishes a new Imamate by summoning his followers to overthrow an oppressive state. In the new formulation, democracy allows a candidate to demonstrate his credentials and topple a repressive regime through a political campaign (da'wa) rather than military action.[22]

These changes suggest that the eventual Zaydi revival that developed in the 1990s was not only a response to *salafi* evangelism, discussed below, but also relied on normalization of and responses to republicanism.[23]

Indeed, it is important to note that neither the prohibitions on Zaydi festivals nor the intellectual repositioning of Zaydi clerics were a consequence of encounters with a 'Sunni state' or even a state in which Sunni Islamists held much institutional sway, since the weight of Islamist organizations like Islah developed later. Instead, it came through the encounter with republican officials who sought to stamp out hereditary privilege (or, at least, to reorient them away from the inherited privileges of the *sada* toward those of certain shaykhs). Many of the state's new officials were themselves of Zaydi background, attracted to republicanism as means of mobility in opposition to the narrow strictures of the old regime of *sada* privilege. These changes, then, help to locate the development of the subsequent Zaydi revival in its distinctly republican context, distinguishing it from earlier royalism, but also from sectarian reaction.

That said, the considerable expansion of evangelical *salafism* in the 1980s and 1990s also intensified claims against the *sada*, offering an alternative basis for fraternal equality and a rejection of hereditary rule. There is little question that the expansion of *salafism* in North Yemen was tied to material investments by Saudi interests, both public and private, as well as to the exposure to *salafi* interpretations that many Yemenis experienced when working in the Gulf states. At the same time, commentary that frames the tensions that developed in the North as an autochthonous conflict between an 'indigenous Zaydi Shi'i population and Sunni Salafi fundamentalists who have relocated to the area,' underestimate the power of local grievances against the injustices of *sada* privilege in North Yemeni society.[24] Evangelical *salafi* appeals were directed specifically to lower-status Zaydis from the North, promising 'a direct, unmediated to relationship to God and valorized fraternal, egalitarian bonds among male coreligionists.'[25] Ethnographic research suggests that support for *salafism* grew most among those who felt humiliated by descent-based exclusions grounded in Zaydi religious hierarchies and hierarchies within tribal society.

Tribal shaykhs—whether they had been 'humiliatingly rebuffed' when proposing marriage to *sharifahs* before the revolution or empowered to take them as second or third wives in its aftermath—still depended on heredity and strategic marriage alliances for their own positions and were thus somewhat ambivalent about the growth of a specifically anti-hereditary discourse in their communities.[26] Indeed, 'the shaykh's vision of the world was one in which the *sadah* and the *qaba'il* were equals, whereas farmers, craftsmen, and traders were inferior by virtue of their heredity and occupations.'[27] Among ordinary non-shaykhly Zaydi tribesmen and low-status non-tribesmen, however, the appeal of *salafi* egalitarianism resonated against diverse sources of social subordination.[28]

Some academic sources and Yemeni critics describe this evangelism in the North as Wahhabi.[29] This both acknowledges the material and ideological role of Saudi patronage of *salafi* evangelism and also obscures some important endogenous characteristics of the movement. In interactions with Yemeni interlocutors in the 2000s, the term Wahhabi was used as a polemical signifier of foreignness. Those personally aligned with the *salafi* movement usually described themselves as *salafi* or as *Ahl al-Sunna*, followers of the traditions of the Prophet Muhammad (perhaps also as a juxtaposition to *Ahl al-Bayt*, denoting the *sada*).[30] Some described themselves simply as 'Muslim.'

Those who used the term *Wahhabi* to describe others, by contrast, rarely missed an opportunity to explain that this was an ideology rooted in the Saudi experience and to suggest that it was incompatible with Yemeniness.[31] For example, the trope of foreignness and inauthenticity was often deployed in descriptions of the Islah party's most prominent *salafi* figure, 'Abd al-Majid al-Zindani. Rarely was his name mentioned without commentary characterizing the time he spent in Saudi Arabia as decisive to his political sensibilities, religious commitments, and bank account. Reflecting on the role of the *salafi* wing of Islah in fomenting conflict in the North, observers recalled that when al-Zindani returned from Saudi Arabia, he worked to expand the popular base of the party through *salafi* institutions while figures like Mohammed al-Yadoumi and Mohammed Qahtan, viewed as closer to the Brotherhood wing of the party, provided 'acceptable cover' in Sana'a.[32]

As Laurent Bonnefoy has argued, such narratives 'characterize the Salafis as feudal bondservants of Saudi Arabia,' and 'enemies who have infiltrated Yemen and who are thus completely illegitimate.'[33] Instead, he argues that important figures in *salafi* expansion—natal Zaydis, like Muqbil al-Wada'i, the movement's most influential leader by the 1990s—adopted *salafi* principles not in spite of being born Zaydi but at least in part because of their experience of discrimination.[34] Without denying the significant material and ideological role of Saudi patronage for Yemeni *salafi* institutions and individuals, this is why he and others have worked to identify the contours of a distinctly Yemeni *salafism* that is not derivative of the relations between states but reflects instead translocal forms of cultural embeddedness.[35] This understanding of an endogenous (but translocal) *salafism* is significant, insofar as it shapes how one understands the culture war that developed in the far North in the 1990s and eventually fed the Houthi insurgency after 2004.[36]

Whether and to what extent *salafis* are viewed as co-equally indigenous to North Yemen is of considerable significance to understanding rival justice claims. So are *salafi* polemics that seek to exogenize Zaydis. If one interprets *salafis* as 'immigrants' or as Saudi proxies, this elevates the status of Zaydi (and eventually Houthi) autochthonous claims and ignores the appeal of *salafi* egalitarianism offered in a republican context. Likewise, if *salafi* claims to Qahtani (Southern Arabian) indigeneity are taken to be authentically juxtaposed to the putatively foreign 'Adnani roots of the *sada*, the latter's belonging and claims may also be called into question.[37]

If shaykhly republicanism had been in some respects a critique of the *sada* by fellow Zaydis from among the tribal elite, *salafi* evangelicals took the issue further and repudiated Zaydism and Shi'ism more categorically. Zaydi fears of cultural obsolescence through evangelical *salafi* encroachment were evident from the earliest stages of the Zaydi revival movement, eventually called the Believing Youth, as it first developed in Sa'ada in the 1990s. One contemporaneous account described revivalists as defensive in tone, aiming to 'preserve Zaydism from the Wahhabi-Salafi onslaught and a continuing government policy of neglect and, at times, outright persecution.'[38] Both *salafi* repudiation of Zaydism and the Zaydi revivalism that countered it played a role in the sectarianization of political conflict in North Yemen, mobilizing rival claims of injustice.

Sectarianization and Rival Institutions in North Yemen

While it is quite popular today to impose upon Yemen a sectarian 'proxy war' interpretation that focuses on the roles of Saudi Arabia and Iran as patrons of Sunni and Shi'i clients, this is not how Yemeni interlocutors described conflict dynamics in the 2000s as the Houthi insurgency took shape. Nor did sectarian distinctions that make some sense today circulate in the same way for many researchers working in Yemen before then. For example, in her introduction to a 2016 collection of essays on Yemen written by various scholars over the course of several decades, Sheila Carapico observes that no one 'thought to mention [in earlier work] that Sana'a was predominantly Zaydi whereas both Taiz and the people in the southern regions were Shafa'i. We noted piety, but not denominational differences, which seemed utterly irrelevant…'[39]

By the time I started doing fieldwork in Yemen in 2004—the year that the Houthi insurgency began—sectarian distinctions were no longer irrelevant, but they had by no means the social force that they do today. While I would sometimes encounter claims that reflected what Lisa Wedeen has called '*madhab* essentialism' or denigrating stereotypes, such statements were often criticized by other Yemenis for the ways they obscured important 'contextual ways in which denominational categories matter, when they do.'[40] Indeed, unlike Lebanon, where interlocutors almost invariably made sure that I understood their sectarian background in our first interaction, Yemenis in the mid-2000s were far more likely to offer different identity markers. These might include the village where their family originated, the nearby city where they went to school, their tribal membership, or their party affiliations. I have notes from scores of interviews recording such details but they rarely mention sectarian affiliation as such.

The fact that sectarian difference stands out as such a relevant fault line in the conflict today should be read as a product of sectarianization, as a political process. Writing against what they view as the 'new orientalism' of sectarian essentialism, Nader Hashemi and Danny Postel describe sectarianization as 'a process shaped by political actors operating within specific contexts, pursuing political goals that involve popular mobilization around particular (religious) identity markers…' This processual concept is deployed against sectarianism, which 'tends to imply a static given, a transhistorical force—an enduring and immutable characteristic of the Arab Islamic world from the seventh century until today.'[41] The sectarianization of conflict in North Yemen (and now, perhaps, throughout the country) unfolded gradually, both through state institutions and outside of them.

Non-state institutions were central to the sectarianization process, insofar as they helped transform 'mildly constraining forms of affiliation into a more vigorous and active sense of urgency and commitment.'[42] The proliferation of *salafi* and Zaydi revivalist institutions can be read as a kind of material expression—and driver—of a culture war in North Yemen over what the republican state meant in the context of Yemen. If the state was committed to the equality of the republic's citizens, should this not mean that the state would provide equal protection for members of diverse groups? By contrast, if it was premised on the equality of individuals before God, should the state not provide the conditions that allow individuals to choose their paths to righteousness? The appeal of both *salafi* and Zaydi revivalist arguments rested in the internalization of the republican promise of equality and measured injustice against it.

Scientific institutes teaching a *salafi* curriculum consisting mainly of the 'religious sciences' of *fiqh* and *usul al-din* were built throughout the North beginning in the 1980s and extended elsewhere after unification, at their height teaching 13 percent of all Yemeni youth enrolled in schools. While religious education had previously been housed within the Ministry of Education and supervised by republican officials, a combination of funding from Saudi Arabia and from private donors allowed these new institutions to remain off the public roll and to operate outside of Ministry of Education oversight until 2001.[43] As Maysaa Shuja al-Deen has shown, such schools spent up to six times more per student than Yemen's public schools, and were often more accessible to families in remote areas than their public counterparts. As such, they constituted a powerful parallel education system. The two systems were linked, however, insofar as graduates of the religious schools could not qualify for admission to university, but could continue in teacher-training programs and then find posts teaching in state-run schools.[44]

The most significant of the scientific institutes—Dar al-Hadith—was built in Dammaj, just 7 km from Sa'ada city. In the heart of the Zaydi highlands, its location was described by Zaydi leaders there as 'a bit too close for comfort.'[45] The school was established by Muqbil al-Wada'i, whose personal biography mirrors wider developments, and its location is inseparable from his own history of perceived discrimination. Born an ordinary Zaydi tribesman, he argued that this socially subordinate position in North Yemeni society 'prevented him from having access to religious knowledge.'[46] Seeking to build on ad hoc studies that he had begun informally while working as a doorman in Saudi Arabia, al-Wada'i returned to Yemen shortly before the 1962 revolution and tried to study at the famous al-Hadi mosque but was 'stigmatized by the [Zaydi] 'ulama because of his tribal origin and he was disregarded by the *sada* "aristocrats."'[47] This drove him to return to Saudi Arabia to further his studies, highlighting the translocal dynamics at play in the sedimentation of a distinctly Yemeni *salafism*. He was both personally shaped by and helped to spread critiques of injustice common among those Yemeni to whom *salafi* evangelists directed their appeal.[48]

The institute that al-Wada'i eventually founded outside of Sa'ada in the early 1980s trained leaders of Yemen's emergent *salafi* movement, many of whom established schools of their own in other parts of the country throughout the 1990s. Islamist influence in the Ministry of Education, before and after unification, enabled this expansion to proceed unchecked.[49] In particular, Islah's participation in a powersharing government and its resistance to bringing the curricula of the scientific institutes under the supervision of the ministry was a core grievance that shaped the direction of the Zaydi revival. Dar al-Hadith remained a symbolic and material site of conflict with the partisans of the Believing Youth, the precursor to the Houthi movement.

The Believing Youth began with a series of supplementary summer camps or programs for Zaydi youth and eventually extended to include to a network of Scientific Schools (mirroring the *salafi* 'institutes'). Bernard Haykel traveled to Sa'ada in 1995 and observed that these schools represented 'the first attempt in Zaydi history to formalize the educational process into a set curriculum with standard textbooks.'[50] Schools were named for heroes of Zaydi history who had been persecuted on the basis of their faith. Summer camps, while less intellectually oriented, also advanced a similar cultural vision, reaching tens of thousands of Zaydi youth.

Through these parallel institutions, the North Yemeni culture war sedimented and the sectarianization process intensified at the same time that multiparty electoral politics were becoming institutionalized. Believing Youth institutions promoted a kind of communitarian Zaydism that was focused less on the hierarchal status of the *sada* than asserting a political right to cultural space for Zaydism and collective rights for Zaydis.[51] Indeed, one of the most prominent intellectual figures in the revival was Muhammad 'Izzan, a Razhi scholar who was not himself from a *sayyid* family.[52] As he and others promoted Zaydi cultural rights, *salafis* sought protection from the government for their right to evangelize. This competition for the youth of Sa'ada was an alternative plane of competition that existed outside of the sphere of partisan politics. In each case, adherents were making a justice demand directed toward the state itself and its republican promise of equality.

From Revival to Insurgency

The dynamics discussed above chart the sectarianization of North Yemen but also help to elucidate a range of justice claims (and counter claims) that underwrote political conflict in the 2000s and remain unresolved. The government's failure to regulate or supervise *salafi* Scientific Institutes was a major source of grievance among Zaydi citizens as a whole, not simply *sada*. The historical discrimination experienced by most Northerners (including many Zaydis) by *sada* was a rival source of sociocultural grievance. The republican dislocation of *sada* privileges amounted to a kind of counter-discrimination in the eyes of some, sometimes even described as akin to racism (*'unsuriyya*). All of this was tied up with the economic underdevelopment of the region—which was viewed by many as targeted, given Sa'ada's role as the last royalist holdout against the republican regime—and the political consolidation of the Saleh regime's patronage networks. Saleh's patronage of tribal shaykhs—including some who had embraced *salafism*, whether aligned with the General People's Congress (GPC) or Islah—and his use of electoral institutions to distribute patronage to shaykhs from both parties produced what many experienced as single-party rule by the time of Yemen's last parliamentary election in 2003.[53]

Shortly before these elections, the revival had split followers of Mohammed 'Izzan and those of Badr al-Din al-Houthi's son, Husayn, a former MP for the small Zaydi political party, al-Haqq. As the government moved toward closer cooperation with the United States in the context of its Global War on Terror, the anti-imperial and anti-American themes in al-Houthi's sermons and curricula became increasingly confrontational. After a particularly provocative rally of thousands of supporters at Sana'a's Grand Mosque in 2004, state security embarked on what became a months-long armed campaign to arrest and detain al-Houthi. He was ultimately killed in Sa'ada in September of that year. This brought to an end the first of what would ultimately be six rounds of armed warfare between Houthi insurgents, the Yemeni military and security forces, irregular militias and eventually Saudi forces, collectively described as the Sa'ada Wars (2004–2010).

Early waves of conflict were relatively contained and ended through a combination of negotiation, tribal mediation, and some measure of government concession, including the use of amnesties. As the conflict proceeded over successive rounds, however, the line between times of war and peace became blurrier.[54] Analysts have also described progressively greater brutality across successive waves of conflict, though the reasons offered for this vary, as discussed below. By the final round of the six Sa'ada wars in 2009–10, the military faced few political constraints. The decision to delay the elections, discussed in the previous chapter, left the regime politically unchecked, and within about six weeks of the delay, Yemeni forces launched 'Operation Scorched Earth,' in which as many as 40,000 troops were deployed in pursuit of a decisive military defeat.[55] Saudi forces were directly engaged in this campaign, as well, rendering the fighting even more asymmetric through a campaign of aerial bombardment and infusing the conflict with a regional geopolitical and sectarianized significance.

The brutality of the fighting and the role of irregular forces in the Sa'ada Wars are often casually attributed to the 'tribalization' of the conflict. This is misleading in at least two ways. First, the military itself was already closely imbricated with North Yemen's tribal system through the creation of a cadre of 'colonel shaykhs,' or tribal leaders whose political loyalty was rewarded with military appointments and other forms of regime patronage.[56] The distinction between 'officer' and 'tribesman' is thus too neat.[57] Second, and as significant, North Yemen's tribal system is itself predicated on the normative value of conflict de-escalation and offers considerable protections to non-combatants, meaning that the brutality that developed over the course of the war and the impact on civilian communities owed to the breakdown of tribal norms, which were increasingly violated by tribesmen themselves.[58] This breakdown did not owe to any single pressure, but Marieke Brandt attributes it at least in part to 'the presence of various sectarian elements in the fighting forces' and, eventually, to the profound asymmetries introduced by the military's increasing reliance on air power, whether its own or that of the Saudis.[59]

The Sa'ada Wars also occurred amid an almost unprecedented level of media blackout, meaning that a full account cannot be given.[60] Restrictions on media access to Sa'ada during the earliest rounds of conflict were a significant source of political mobilization among opposition journalists and even within the Journalists' Syndicate itself. I attended numerous meetings and public events at the Journalists' Syndicate in Sana'a and in branches in other cities where journalists with substantively different views of the conflict nonetheless viewed the media blackout as a perilous marker of authoritarian consolidation. While cellphone video was not yet a normalized part of the information landscape, my fieldnotes record instances in which journalists received (and shared with others, including me) urgent SMS messages from contacts in Sa'ada reporting details on the ground. Journalists were generally unable to verify many of these details, however, which gave regime-friendly media the opportunity to discredit journalists who tried to report on the insurgency or the military's response. The campaign for greater press freedom that developed by the end of the decade was not principally about the Sa'ada Wars or the Houthi conflict, but about efforts to report on a conflict of national significance.

Journalists were not alone in being denied access to Sa'ada during the conflict between Yemeni forces and Houthi militias. The weaponization of humanitarian assistance to civilians was another feature of the Sa'ada Wars and one that foreshadowed developments in the current conflict. Though it constituted a form of collective punishment, the Saleh regime denied humanitarian organizations access to affected communities in Sa'ada, leaving civilians to cope with the consequences of the fighting with little support.[61] Provocatively, international agencies were allowed to partner with the Islah Charitable Society (ICS) and make use of its existing distribution channels. One UNICEF staffer described government agencies as 'completely paralyzed' by the scale of the reconstruction challenge and explained that this was why international organizations shared operational costs with the ICS and delivered aid through its network of schools and health centers in Sa'ada. He noted that the

'Ali Saleh Foundation provided similar services, but UNICEF was reluctant to partner with it because Saleh's son-in-law, a security officer, served as the foundation's director and UNICEF perceived ICS as more neutral.[62]

The Islah Charitable Society, however, was far from neutral; though semi-autonomous from the Islah party, it was neither fully independent of the regime nor fully aligned with it. By the onset of the Sa'ada Wars, the ICS was one of only two non-governmental organizations with branch offices in each governorate, giving it a genuinely 'national' reach. This is one reason why the ICS was appointed by the Saleh regime in 2010 to represent Yemen in regional charitable fora. Close coordination between the ICS and the Ministry of Social and Labor Affairs made it something akin to a parastatal organization, even as its leadership was politically aligned with Islah, furthering the view that Islah was neither wholly with nor wholly against the regime. Its role in the humanitarian response in Sa'ada contributed to political distrust of Islah and narratives of government neglect concurrently.

The perception of ICS neutrality voiced by international aid workers was not widely shared among Yemen's political class, where such partnerships were characterized as opportunistic. The ambiguity of the relationship between Islah, the ISC, *salafis*, and the regime was compounded by the role of General 'Ali Muhsin al-Ahmar (more often just 'Ali Muhsin') in the armed campaign against the Houthis. As the commander of the 1st Armored Brigade, 'Ali Muhsin was directly responsible for the state's military response to the insurgency. Described as a 'figure of mythic proportions,' 'Ali Muhsin was at the time 'widely recognized as a controlling powerbroker at the very heart of the regime, and almost without exception he was mentioned in hushed and furtive tones.'[63] But 'Ali Muhsin was also widely recognized for his close relationship to *salafi* figures in Islah and outside of it, as well as his tribal ties to President Saleh. While not formally a member of Islah, 'Ali Muhsin's personal biography as the brother-in-law of Tariq al-Fadhli, veteran of the Afghan jihad, and their joint role in mobilizing *salafi* irregular militias in the 1994 war in the South contributed to 'Ali Muhsin's reputation, as did his purported financial patronage of *salafi* scientific institutes.[64] This support extended to al-Iman University, where Islah's preeminent *salafi* figure, Shaykh 'Abd al-Majid al-Zindani, served as rector. Delegating to 'Ali Muhsin the campaign against the Houthi insurgency unquestionably contributed to the sectarianization of the conflict in the North.

The role of Islah allies in the Sa'ada Wars contributed to some internal turmoil among party leaders in the early stages, especially among those most involved in the formation of the JMP.[65] By 2009, *salafi*-leaning members of the party, including al-Zindani, had become dissatisfied by the critical drift of the party since the formation of the JMP and joined with *salafis* who were more closely aligned with the GPC to create a new extrapartisan organization of culture warriors. This coalition, which found institutional expression as the Fadilah Group, contributed to harassment and extrajudicial violence against non-conformists in a bid to 'enjoin virtue and prohibit vice.'[66] These included women who did not adhere to the group's conservative interpretation of gender roles, Zaydis and other Shi'a and religious minorities, and even some Islahis who were deemed insufficiently mindful of their religious obligations. The mutual imbrication of 'Ali Muhsin, the Fadilah Group, the ICS and influential tribal shaykhs proved a powerful counterweight to the politically vacuous centrism of the 'JMPers' in Islah; the former contributed to the sectarianization of conflict with the Houthi movement, while the latter were unable (critics argued, unwilling) to stem it.

Members of Islah who were not aligned with the *salafi* wing did try to distance themselves from Fadilah and to frame its creation as a regime strategy to use Islahis to confront the Houthis. As one explained at the time:

> Islah has nothing to do with Fadilah. It is from the regime. It came into existence to challenge al-Houthi, and it was Saudi-engineered, with $150m being distributed not through the government but directly to private individuals, tribal shaykhs or religious clerics. At the first meeting about 'enjoining virtue and prohibiting vice,' only 15 people—the ones right around al-Zindani—knew what was going on, but the other 95 didn't understand why the group had been established at this specific time.[67]

Even still, in his effort to explain the limits of the Fadilah coalition, he presented a portrait in which Islahis were torn between pursuing sectarian objectives and challenging the regime:

> When the Fadilah Group issued a fatwa calling the Houthis *kufar* and saying that they were heretics, a large group of the [Islahi] *ulema* withdrew from Fadilah until the language was softened to only accuse them [the Houthis] of sedition. The regime was behind all this. Fadilah was the straw that broke the camel's back between those *salafis* who are with the regime and those who are not.[68]

The suggestion that the Fadilah Group was engineered by the ruling party was echoed even among Socialists. Wary of Islah's influence in the JMP, some nonetheless saw the formation of the extrapartisan group as 'having had a green light from the President in order to malign Islah, to say they are all terrorists, extremists.'[69] Members of the ruling party strenuously denied this; one prominent figure in the ruling party went so far as to boldly reject the group as having 'no basis, constitutionally, legally, or within the framework of shari'a.'[70]

No one in Yemen's political mainstream, it seemed, wanted to own the Fadilah Group, given its clear association with sectarianism and extrajudicial violence. It was, however, part of a multifaceted response to the Houthi insurgency that blurred the lines between ruling and opposition parties and between state and regime by combining military force, extrajudicial vigilantism, and powerful institutions for the dissemination of sectarian rhetoric.

Meanwhile, a short-lived agreement brokered by Qatar had promised the reconstruction of Sa'ada and an amnesty for combatants in exchange for partial Houthi demilitarization; it fell apart because it 'provided no specifics on how to reconstruct Sa'ada or arrange the exile of the senior Houthi leaders' and because, in the view of regime officials, 'the Qatari mediation efforts led the Houthis to believe they were equal to the state.'[71] Instead, new rounds of fighting had followed. The line between the fifth and sixth rounds of fighting were blurry, but the sixth is associated with the declaration of Operation Scorched Earth. The Saudi air force's bombardment of civilian areas was so severe that close to 60,000 people were driven from their homes in Sa'ada in the first two months of the campaign, amid a complete blockade of humanitarian resources. When aid was finally allowed in October 2009, it came across the Saudi border, not via Sana'a, underscoring the Yemeni state's abandonment of civilians in Sa'ada. One analyst describing the ceasefire in early 2010 concluded that 'it is likely that the current lull in violence will last longer than previous interludes, in large part due to mutual exhaustion. Nonetheless, because nothing has been done to resolve the grievances at the heart of the conflict, it is also likely that the fighting will resume.'[72] By the eve of the 2011 uprising, the Houthi movement had developed a powerful insurgent campaign unable to deliver a military victory in its own right but capable of contributing to popular demand for regime change.

When the last round of armed conflict in the Sa'ada Wars ended in 2010, the accumulated grievances and justice demands of citizens in the North extended well beyond those of the culture war phase prior to 2004, though they grew from its foundation. Indeed, if anything, the community that the Houthi movement sought to represent had grown through the government's campaign of destruction and its perceived partnership with those engaged in a cultural onslaught against Zaydi beliefs and practices. These unresolved grievances would fuel the movement's position in the 2011 uprising and many of its own brutal and destructive practices in the years that followed.

The Southern Movement

While the Houthi insurgency and other domestic political developments took much of the political focus in Yemen in the first half of the 2000s, justice demands also remained unaddressed and escalated in the South. The Yemeni Socialist Party (YSP) returned to electoral competition in 2003 after its 1997 boycott, but as a hollowed-out version of itself. Its representation at the national level was limited, as was its ability to effectively advocate on behalf of Southern interests through institutional channels. The party's primary significance in the 2000s was as a founding member of the JMP alliance. While the Yemeni Socialist Party did endeavor to advocate for Southern interests within the JMP, it was gradually displaced as a representative of Southern interests by the new Southern Movement, or Hirak, which emerged outside of the partisan sphere in 2007.

The Hirak developed as a response to the aftermath of the 1994 war and, to some extent, to changes produced by unification itself. Unlike the Houthi movement, its grievances were (and remain) predominantly economic and political, but sometimes extend to more cultural claims about the 'retribalization' or Islamization of the South through a campaign of Northern hegemony. As in the North, discussion of women and girls has been a symbolic site of struggle, where retribalization and Islamization were both seen as disproportionately targeting gender norms and social practices associated with the People's Democratic Republic of Yemen (PDRY). Yet at its core, the Southern Movement resists the displacement of Southern sovereignty and the inequality its supporters see as built into the unity framework. In the years before the 2011 uprising, its primary concerns were with what members viewed as the theft or misallocation of Southern resources and the military and security forces' repression of Southern people.[73] What they saw as the best remedy to this varied from deep decentralization to outright secession.

Political and economic grievances were (and remain) significantly entwined for the Hirak, as it was the political and military victory of the North in 1994 that enabled economic changes that were particularly significant in the South. Echoing the language of many Hirakis, Stephen Day recounts that 'in the weeks following the 1994 war, northern politicians, military officers, tribal sheikhs, and businessmen descended on southern cities, seeking to profit from the defeat of al-Beidh's army.'[74] This language captures the affective urgency that Hirakis (and even non-Hirakis) attach to the period following the war, though the Northern onslaught built upon some changes that had already been initiated well before the 1994 conflict.

Like many other countries, Yemen undertook a privatization campaign in the 1990s through which state-owned enterprises were sold or restructured. The effects of this privatization were starkest in the South. Part of this was to be expected, given the role of state-led development in the PDRY.[75] But the acceleration of privatization and its targeting of Southern enterprises after 1994 owes as well to the marginalization of the YSP and the effects of post-war looting and destruction. After the 1994 conflict, the Southern bureaucracy was restaffed, primarily with Southerners who were assumed to be loyal to the Saleh regime, including partisans of 'Ali Nasser who had aligned with the North during the fighting itself and who were predominantly from Abyan and Shabwa. It was these bureaucrats who oversaw the privatization process, and whom Hirakis associated with the spread of corruption in Southern institutions.[76]

Looting during and immediately after the war was destructive in its own right, but also had a knock-on effect on the privatization process. As Susanne Dahlgren recalls:

> In Aden, industrial enterprises were closed down because looting had left them unable to function and the employees, most of them women, were sent home with a state pension. The factories were then put up for sale. Some of them were simply turned into real estate, affording investors access to huge tracts of land. In actual terms, privatization meant idling Adeni industries and freeing up market share for producers located in the Northern industrial zones of Ta'iz, Hudayda, and Sana'a. After a few years, former factory workers in the south lost their pensions and joined the swelling ranks of the unemployed.[77]

Unemployment in the South was also compounded by an influx of new residents. Mass repatriation of Yemeni workers from the Gulf states flooded the labor market, and a staggering 56.5 percent of the Yemeni migrant workers expelled from the Gulf states in 1990 lacked housing upon their return.[78] This led to the creation of shantytowns and camps in the periphery of several Yemeni cities and strained already poor public services. Many of the internal migrants to Aden originated in the Tihama along the Red Sea coast and were interpreted (correctly or not) as *muhamasheen* and their resettlement framed as part of a strategy to impose Northern social norms and forms of stratification on the South. Resented as part of the Northern onslaught and colloquially described as 'the messengers of 'Ali 'Abdullah Saleh,' these newcomers often begged or performed menial services in the streets, rendering them a highly visible symbol of changes attributed to the North.[79]

At the other end of the spectrum, the unity government's return of property previously appropriated by the Marxist regime also accelerated the return of historically prominent Southern elites who had been exiled or left because of the policies of the PDRY. Land seizures occurred in rural and urban communities alike. Privatization of state farms and cooperatives often left farmworkers 'entirely without income,' and occurred through a range of mechanisms, in some cases restoring past expropriations, sometimes relying on forged deeds and, in some cases, simply turning land over to regime elites.[80] As Northerners came south, some moved directly into the homes of YSP members who had left the country during the fighting.[81] As Dahlgren observed of this time, 'as both the rich and the starving returned and with them came a rise in consumer prices, social origin started to matter again.'[82]

This notion of social origin—and its resurgent role in Southern life—figured in accounts of the retribalization of the South. So too did changing attitudes and practices related to gender. Southern rights activists clearly linked a decline in women's mobility, labor market participation, and educational rights to Northern incursion. Gender segregation gradually began to 'structure the town' in Aden, as the separation of the sexes was introduced through a combination of formal rules and informal harassment employed to shape public behavior.[83] Scholars are careful to note that this was not a reintroduction of prior cultural norms, since colonial era and rural forms of gender separation had followed different logics; it traced instead to the same *salafism* that was reshaping the North. Nor were changes produced only through harassment or vigilantism—ideas mattered. As important as force was 'the coming to the forefront of ideologies that favored traditional family-related role models for women and the curbing of women's "unnecessary" movement outside the home.'[84]

Whether associated with the effect of Islah's political expansion, tribal norms, or labor migration to the Gulf, shifting norms were broadly constructed as something exogenous to the South, and particularly foreign to Aden. Women who were adults at the point of unification routinely used the language of 'going backwards' to describe the effects of unification. Some Southern men, too, struggled to understand the choices of their own daughters a decade after the 1994 war. One middle-aged human rights activist, for example, was puzzled by his own daughter's decision to wear the niqab, or face veil, attributing it to the effects of Islah-promoted gender segregation in the schools—even elementary schools—introduced when she was small.[85]

There was some division among Southerners about whether to attribute these changes to unification, war, or Islamization—and where precisely to draw the line between them. Those who tended to blame the changes on Islamists and the influence of Islah often voiced support for the unity framework but hoped to see it reformed more equitably to protect Southern cultural distinctiveness. Others saw Islah as a part of a broader Northern incursion that had become institutionalized through state institutions after 1994. The YSP's 1997 electoral boycott, while understandable to many, was also interpreted as a kind of abandonment that left people looking elsewhere.

The Southern Movement was born and grew through an iterative series of protests and acts of suppression unique to the South but occurred as the Houthi insurgency was ongoing in the North and as the efficacy of Yemen's parliamentary opposition was eroding. While the substantive demands and methods of the Hirak and the Houthis differ, it is clear that the regime was concerned about how its conduct in Sa'ada would play in the eyes of its Southern critics. Without sharing any substantive sympathies, Houthi successes in an asymmetric contest with the Yemeni armed forces 'inspired southerners, who sensed the time was ripe for mass opposition to the regime.'[86] For this reason, government officials feared that concessions in the North might 'show weakness and a lack of state resolve' to regime challengers in the South.[87]

By May 2007, protests and sit-ins organized by former military officers from the South were attracting growing crowds. The regime's decision to use force against non-violent protesters likely reflected a desire to put a decisive end to Southern contention before it could become a second front. Protesters' responses, however, were markedly different than the Houthis' had been three years earlier. Rather than developing an armed insurgency, Hiraki protesters used innovative tools for organizing near-spontaneous non-violent protests in different locations, making it more difficult for the regime to anticipate or subvert their plans.

The army's response included a dramatic escalation of force that was out of proportion with the provocation; it was undoubtedly shaped by the concurrent insurgency in the North and the specter of secession from 1994. Using 'blockades of entire provinces… live ammunition against unarmed demonstrators, air raids upon entire cities, assassinations, and arbitrary detentions,' the regime unleashed a response far out of proportion to the movement's earliest demands.[88] This fueled the movement further, as it adopted horizontal organizing techniques that observers would later see in other parts of the region. Building the movement as a 'snake with a thousand heads' gave it core advantages in surviving regime repression. As one movement activist explained, 'authorities cannot stop it, as when local leaders are detained or go undercover, new ones replace them. It is the strength of the movement that it does not have a national leadership that can be liquidated.'[89]

Of course, the regime did try to subvert the movement through means other than physical repression, including attempts to regulate media coverage of the protests and their violent suppression by government forces. While this was part of the broader campaign against the independent media discussed above, longstanding Adeni paper *al-Ayyam* became a special target of regime attention. Fieldnotes from a *qat* chew with several of the paper's staff record harassment and interference before the formalization of the Hirak, including threats against the staff by people identified as *salafi* and presumed to be deployed by the regime. In the years that followed, critics of *al-Ayyam* made good on these threats through both legal and extralegal mechanisms, including vigilante violence.[90] In 1999, publisher Hisham Bashraheel had been convicted of 'instigating the spirit of separatism' and given a suspended sentence, while a court rejected the government's request to close the paper.[91] As an index of how much had changed as the Southern Movement crystalized, in 2009 government forces surrounded the paper's headquarters and compelled it to cease production in response to its coverage of military suppression of Hirak protests; tens of thousands of copies of the paper were interdicted at checkpoints in different parts of the country and burned.[92] Government forces fired on protesters, including members of the Journalists' Syndicate, who staged peaceful protests outside of the paper's headquarters in Aden.[93] Bashraheel and his sons were eventually tried in a specialized court on what the Committee to Protect Journalists called 'politicized criminal charges.'[94]

In part, the Hirak's growth and its growing tilt toward secessionaism were a function of the YSP's obsolescence after 1994 and its association with a partisan opposition unable to curb Northern regime consolidation in the 2000s. Members of the YSP complained that their own party was abandoning its commitments to the South, and to some of its core political principles, in the name of this reform-oriented alliance. Gender equality—and the debate over the women's quota—is a good illustration of this. The socialist party was nominally committed to gender equality, and there was widespread consensus among party leaders that unification had been bad for women overall. But the issue of a possible electoral quota, which critics thought the YSP ought to have supported on principle, was too divisive among the member parties of the JMP for the alliance to adopt a clear position as a unit. Few YSP members, even among the women leaders of the party, risked JMP coherence by publicly supporting it. Instead, they were outpaced by the ruling party's support for the quota, which observers anticipated—correctly—would lead the JMP to agree to delay the 2009 parliamentary elections.

Given how little the YSP could show for itself, then, it is not surprising that a movement for change developed outside of the party. Interviews with YSP members at the time, meanwhile, are rife with grievance. Party leaders spoke of feeling first displaced as a ruling party—'we were the state'—and then almost equally displaced as an opposition by the Hirak.[95] A high-ranking member of the party said in 2009:

> The South is a great problem now…. Under this regime, they believe [the South] has been diminished, because of the divide

between the *sulta* [governing authority] and the people.... The *sulta* didn't behave as a state with a political project. This is why we face such a problem when we talk about democracy. Southerners don't think this will solve their problems.[96]

Despite this clear-eyed assessment of the roots of extrapartisan mobilization in the South, the YSP committed to the dysfunctional partisan politics of the capital and the JMP's reform agenda, giving the Southern movement further momentum.

Ahead of the postponement of the 2009 elections, there was considerable cohesion among the JMP parties, but the cost of this cohesion was a kind of narrow focus on procedural democracy that left the parties sorely out of touch with the priorities of major segments of the country. The same leader who understood that democracy was being discredited by regime practices in the South argued almost in the same breath that institutional reform should continue to be the JMP's top priority:

> There are some differences, of course, but the mainstream in each [member party of the JMP] agrees that there is no choice but democracy....We want to develop democracy by reforming the electoral system. The biggest challenge is the decline of democracy....We are the only opposition in this country.[97]

Of course, the JMP was not the only opposition in the country. It was the only partisan opposition working within the state's institutional structures.

Dr. Muhammed 'Abd al-Malik al-Mutawakkil, one of the architects of the JMP, offered a critical diagnosis months before the delay, arguing that, 'the parties [of the JMP] have opened a dialogue with the ruling party but what they really need is negotiations. Dialogue should take place with constituents. Parties need to focus on how to mobilize popular pressure against the government.'[98] With hindsight, it is possible to see that the agreement between the JMP and the ruling party to postpone the parliamentary elections shifted the balance irretrievably in favor of the extrapartisan mobilization of the Hirak and the Houthis.

Militancy and Repression

While President Saleh had long been credited as governing through a system of managed or 'perpetual crisis,' spiraling developments in the North and the South threatened to become more than he could manage by the end of the decade.[99] The emergence of Al Qaeda in the Arabian Peninsula in 2009 contributed an additional unpredictable element to already volatile conditions. In the short term, however, Saleh was able to make use of this development to secure important (in)security rents that extended the life of his regime.

For decades, Saleh had been able to leverage Islamist militancy—both real and amplified—for political gain. In the 1980s, when still President of North Yemen, Saleh had worked with the Saudis to 'export' Yemeni militants to Afghanistan to fight in the anti-Soviet jihad.[100] These returning 'Afghan Arabs' and others were among the Islamist militias and irregulars that continued to play an important and destabilizing role in the South as vigilantes, before, during, and after the 1994 conflict. Islamist militants were recruited to help prosecute the Sa'ada Wars and were employed against elements of the Hirak. The Saleh regime instrumentalized Islamist militants as a component of governance and as a means of managing political competition.

As other authoritarian regimes were able to do in the 2000s, Saleh also capitalized on the United States' Global War on Terror to secure important material and political guarantees. The proximate risks that Yemen's own Islamist movement might radicalize or that Yemen might prove to be a safe haven for violent radicals from elsewhere were worrisome enough to transform the material relationship between the United States and Yemen over the course of the decade. A series of increasingly deadly attacks against Yemeni forces, tourists, and embassies in the mid-2000s pointed in a troubling direction, and military and counterterrorism assistance ballooned, far outweighing other forms of assistance by the end of the 2000s.[101]

Saleh's ability to instrumentalize risk was hastened by the formal merger of Yemeni and Saudi branches of Al Qaeda into the unified Al Qaeda in the Arabian Peninsula (AQAP) in 2009.[102] This occurred only months after an attack on the US Embassy in which at least 17 people were killed; it was followed by a foiled plot to attack the United States that could be attributed to the organization. I remember well the changing tone around this issue in Sana'a in January 2009. In previous years, my interlocutors would speak with cynicism about the regime's amplification of the threat of militancy. By the time AQAP announced itself that winter, however, there was a real awareness that 'they' were present and a sense that the effect of this would be difficult to anticipate and very hard for the country's various nodes of partisan and extrapartisan opposition to control or direct.[103] On the one hand, members of the opposition were well-aware of the way in which Saleh manipulated the threat of radicals for domestic and international political gain. On the other hand, for many of my interlocutors, there was a genuine concern that there were now too many concurrent crises, too much uncertainty, for Saleh—or anyone—to manage.

Assessing Strategic Engagement with Justice

The two decades of the 'unity regime' were a period in which injustices accumulated and accountability was consistently undermined. While some of the human rights abuses that occurred during this period were committed by non-state actors, state actors themselves were implicated in wrongdoing directly and indirectly, and elites were consistently disengaged from justice demands issued by important segments of society. By 2010, on the eve of Yemen's uprising, there was a secessionist movement in the South and an insurgency in the North, an animated but ineffective political opposition, and a climate of chaos that encouraged the growth and autonomy of Al Qaeda militants.

Alongside the events mapped in this chapter is the history of Yemen's (non)ratification of the Rome Statute and efforts to limit legal accountability for serious crimes committed by state and non-state actors. As signatory of the statute from 2000, Yemen was obliged to bring its national legislation in line with the requirements of the International Criminal Court (ICC) prior to ratification. An agreement between members of parliament from the GPC and opposition parties was nearly reached in 2005 but was scuttled when the government cited 'internal strife in certain areas of Yemen' (i.e. the Houthi insurgency) as a means to delay legislative changes and ratification.[104]

On March 24, 2007, a bill ratifying the Rome Statute was nonetheless moved forward and passed. The day that it passed, Amnesty International provided copies of documents obtained via a Freedom of Information Request that showed a 2003 bilateral agreement between the US and Yemen that would prevent Yemen's full compliance with the obligations of the Rome Statute.[105] Memoranda exchanged between Foreign Minister Abu Bakr al-Qirbi and Secretary of State Colin Powell obliged each state not to surrender to the ICC nationals of either state facing international criminal charges that fall within the court's mandate.[106] Amnesty International produced this document as a part of its campaign for broader ratification of the Rome Statute, but MPs from the GPC used the opportunity of its publication to walk back parliament's action altogether, arguing that there had not been a quorum for the original vote. The bill was returned for a re-vote on April 7; it failed. In its remaining years, the Saleh regime would therefore continue to be unrestrained by international legal mechanisms that might have offered Yemenis some protection.

Domestic legal mechanisms, meanwhile, were both insufficient to produce accountability for abuses and were actively instrumentalized to undermine it. The Specialized Criminal Court (SCC), established in 1999 by presidential fiat, was expanded in 2004 to address crimes of 'state security' and used to surveil and suppress domestic critics of the regime from civil society, the media, and the opposition parties, in addition to those suspected of terrorism. Grounding the SCC in counterterrorism provided the regime with room to maneuver and performed its public commitment to counterterrorism objectives, all while further fueling anti-American grievances in a range of political quarters. By the end of the decade, US officials—even the US Congress—were made aware that counterterrorism support from the United States was abetting authoritarian encroachment and human rights abuses in Yemen, but there were no significant reassessments of policy.[107]

The Saleh regime did show periodic strategic engagement with justice demands, but only in ways aimed at reinforcing its position.

Amnesties were the most common tool, issued after 1994, after various rounds of the Sa'ada wars, and in some other selective instances—such as an amnesty for Houthi and Hiraki detainees charged with sedition in May 2010. Amnesties were employed 'somewhat arbitrarily and for politically motivated reasons, as a kind of release valve at times of particular political tension, rather than in accordance with clear and transparent criteria.'[108] There were also a range of national dialogues during this period, though they did not feature the formality or depth of inclusion as the 2013 National Dialogue Conference, discussed in the next chapter. The regime's selective engagement with such tools in a context that was neither transitional nor 'post-conflict' can be read as a strategic effort to manage crises and navigate the genuine pluralism of Yemeni society without building a polity that could meaningfully satisfy society's demands.

These demands related not only to the deteriorating political climate and increasing violence but to the erosion of Yemenis' most basic needs in an environment of social and economic distress. Already the poorest state in the Middle East and North Africa, inflation was approaching 30 percent by the end of the decade.[109] Food subsidies became a particularly volatile issue, accounting for close to 20 percent of the government's budget. Such subsidies were under constant scrutiny by international financial institutions, but efforts to reduce them were too destabilizing for the regime to consistently sustain.[110] A water crisis 'unprecedented in [Yemen's] history' spurred what one analyst described as a 'race to the bottom—every man for himself,' contributing to conflict in several parts of the country.[111] Non-violent channels through which citizens could pursue grievances were ineffective, while more confrontational strategies were met with punishing force. Human rights work aimed at documenting regime responses to violent and non-violent contention was itself securitized, particularly through the increased reliance on specialized courts.

It would thus be an understatement to say that the Yemeni state did little to address the justice demands of significant groups of Yemeni citizens in the contexts described in this chapter and the previous one. After the 1994 civil war, the justice demands of Southerners directly affected by the war were not even addressable because of the political isolation of the YSP and an overall decline in accountable institutions. New grievances developed as Northern hegemony was extended throughout the South. By the time the Southern movement was formed in earnest, it confronted a more authoritarian state with increased willingness to use force to suppress demands for restitution. But North/South framing does not address powerful intra-Northern grievances, as witnessed by the development of the Houthi movement. The regime's indifference or hostility toward the movement's political demand for cultural rights and protection contributed to the state's suppression of its insurgency—but neither the politics of patronage nor a punishing military campaign were successful in displacing a movement that claimed to speak for a significant proportion of Northern Yemeni society.

Disengagement with justice demands was paired with very minimal strategic engagement in an effort to further protect the regime of 'Ali 'Abdullah Saleh. This succeeded neither in the North nor in the South, as would become clear during the uprising of 2011 and the transitional process that followed. While the scope and dynamics of the uprising that occurred in 2011 may not have been predicted as such, by late 2010 Yemen was clearly facing a 'revolutionary situation'—a period characterized by 'hectic political struggle over ultimate authority that does not depend on revolutionary intentions and need not terminate in a revolutionary outcome.'[112] This concept offers a useful way of conceptualizing the Yemeni uprising as an unplanned coalescence of contention by actors who were making decisions quickly, in relational anticipation of others. The next chapter considers the significance of new practices and institutions that emerged in the context of such a revolutionary situation, as a range of Yemeni actors set justice as their ethical horizon in pursuit of diverse political projects.

THE SHADOW OF TRANSITION

'The Tunisians, then the Egyptians. And now it's our turn.'

Tawakkol Karman
February 2, 2011

As the previous two chapters have shown, the regime of President 'Ali 'Abdullah Saleh spent the better part of two decades disengaged from or strategically engaged with justice claims that echoed throughout different quarters of Yemeni society. Regime repression exacerbated grievances, and by the end of 2010, crises were developing concurrently on several planes. Though Saleh appeared to gamble on the notion that allowing some dissent would continue to enable him to manage these crises, the events that unfolded in 2011–12 would come to 'vindicate the Cassandras who had long warned of the limits of Yemen's political equilibrium.'[1] As dissent turned increasingly toward disorder by the end of the 2000s, Saleh had leveraged the specter of insecurity in order to attract vital insecurity rents in the form of increased military assistance and training, as well as development assistance. This left the regime in control of important instruments of surveillance and coercion but did not address core drivers of conflict—perceived and real inequalities across the social, economic, and political spheres, and rampant corruption.

The 2011 Yemeni uprising and the transitional process that followed are rich with examples of both strategic and substantive justice engagement in Yemen. This chapter highlights the transformative effect of collective action on a rising generation of Yemeni civil actors as they charted a new relationship to state and society during and after the 11-month uprising in 2011. The transitional period that followed the uprising casts a long shadow; it continues to serve as a point of reference for conflict actors and civil actors alike in the context of the current war. This owes to the way that transitional institutions and their international backers approached questions of injustice and to the opportunities that the transitional period offered for Yemenis shaped by the uprising to articulate justice demands inside and outside of those institutions. The legacies of strategic and substantive engagements from this period have been long-lasting, shaping the way in which civil actors imagine more just futures, even—or especially—amid the destruction of the current war.

This chapter also shows how the justice claims of civil actors during the period from 2011 to 2014 were accompanied by growing insecurity and conflict, particularly outside of Sana'a. It is organized more thematically than chronologically, illustrating how substantive engagement with justice claims at the political center of the transition were partially offset by parallel, more strategic engagements elsewhere, as well as by new sources of injustice. Features of the transitional process simultaneously directed Yemen toward war and, paradoxically, shaped important resources for peace that continue to inform civil action today.

Reform or Revolution?

The earliest protests in January 2011 built upon established, even routinized, contention by a familiar cast of characters.[2] They were organized by members of the JMP and urban civil society. In Sana'a, protest organizers erected a dais from which speakers addressed crowds wearing color-coordinated sashes and holding mass-produced posters distributed by the opposition parties.[3] Even as protests began to grow over the course of the month, longtime observers of Yemeni politics—both Yemeni and foreign—remained skeptical of interpretations that linked protests in Yemen to those in Tunisia or Egypt or read the protests as revolutionary. Yemeni analyst 'Abdulghani al-Iryani, for example, offered the following at the time:

> [T]here is no reason for these protests to develop into a movement that could give trouble to the regime... The ruling party can give concessions that will satisfy the demands of JMP without even threatening its dominant position in parliament and political life. I think the positive result [of the protests] will be that the regime will call for national dialogue.[4]

In other words, observers expected to see the regime rely on existing practices, including strategic engagement with justice demands meant to appease the opposition.

There were other considerations, as well, that sowed doubt about the revolutionary potential of growing protests. Grievances in the South and the far North both seemed too locally specific to generate traction as a national movement, whereas the national political opposition seemed too firmly reformist to embrace more revolutionary demands. Protests and sit-ins—even very large ones—were already a well-established part of Yemenis' repertoire of contention and therefore did not signal a major departure from the status quo. My own sense in January 2011 was that Yemen's political opposition was continuing to advance what was a fundamentally reformist agenda, albeit with a more urgent inflection linked to regional enthusiasm for change.[5]

Another factor that appeared to mitigate the early protests' revolutionary potential was Saleh's reinforcement from the outside. The Economist Intelligence Unit reflected a widely shared vision in European and North American policy circles, imagining that 'the toppling of Mr. Saleh would paralyze government, and, in the absence of a single individual able to draw together the country's disparate powerbrokers, a free-for-all ensues as the various tribes and sheikhs battle for control.'[6] There were also significant (and not entirely unfounded) concerns that disorder would enable the continued growth of Al-Qaeda in the Arabian Peninsula, which had been escalating its attacks on Yemeni military targets, including a dramatic attack in early January. Efforts to reinforce President Saleh's position reflected fear of further fragmentation and civil war; the oft-repeated concern that Yemen was 'on the brink' circulated widely even before the uprising.[7] The US launched a multi-front diplomatic effort to ensure that Saleh stay put. The US security establishment, the State Department, and even the US Senate sent representatives to Sana'a in January 2011 to meet with Saleh and his Vice-President, 'Abd Rabuh Mansour Hadi, pledging increased American security and development assistance in support of counterterrorism priorities.

As real as many of Yemen's interlocking challenges may have been, none could be easily separated from Saleh's strategies of governance; the risk of civil war was frequently advanced by President Saleh himself, as he appealed to Saudi and American leaders, in particular.[8] By January 25th, Ben 'Ali had already fled Tunis, and crowds had gathered—and were prepared to stay—in Cairo's Tahrir Square, calling for the fall of the Egyptian regime. Saleh attempted to forestall any similar pressure in Sana'a. On that same day, he announced that he would not run for reelection when his term expired in 2013 and sought to dispel suspicion that he was preparing for his son, Ahmed, to succeed him by explicitly repudiating all forms of hereditary rule.[9] These rhetorical commitments were not enough. By the time Mubarak stepped down a few weeks later in Egypt, protesters in Yemen had unequivocally asserted that it was their turn.[10]

In the weeks and months that followed, members of Yemen's incipient 'Change Revolution' erected protest encampments in provincial cities across the country, launching a sustained critique of the whole of the status quo, from Saleh to tribal shaykhs to partisan opposition. The movement that developed in 2011 is sometimes described as independent, in the sense of having no relationship to any organized party, but it is also in some ways 'postpartisan,' articulated as much in response to the political failures of the parties across the political spectrum as to the regime that they abetted.[11] It was these parties, however, that entered into negotiations with President Saleh to end the uprising, to pacify the justice demands of society, and to reestablish a semblance of order. It was also these parties that captured an overwhelming amount of political power through a brokered transitional agreement and whose practices during the transitional period helped to pave the path to war.

The 'Change Revolution'

Yemen's youth revolution was coequally part of a regional political phenomenon and an extension of political struggles particular to Yemen and the politics that preceded the Arab uprisings. While celebrating successes and adopting some methods of protest witnessed elsewhere, the grievances of Yemen's revolutionaries also bore the clear imprint of previous cycles of contention in the 2000s.[12] Like much of the region, Yemen's population skewed heavily toward its youth, with close to 65% of the population under the age of 25 years in 2011 and a median age of 18.5 years. While the youth revolution did develop its own coherent identity, it did so in a robust and variegated political field, where belonging to the youth movement did not intrinsically foreclose other attachments, including partisan commitments. For some, in fact, the revolution was an important introduction to partisan ideologies. As activist Ala Qasem described it:

> The squares represented a political fair, much like a career fair, where young individuals were exposed to various political ideologies ranging from liberal left to the conservative right simply by walking from one tent in the square to the next.[13]

The effect of exposure to plural interpretations of the country's challenges—and the convergence of those interpretations around the notion that Saleh must go—emerged as a theme in many interviews with and observations of participants in the uprising. In the language of the Capabilities Approach, protest squares offered opportunities for transpositional scrutiny and the development of overlapping consensus regarding the injustices of the regime and those of wider society. It was not uncommon to hear participants praise the unity of the Change Revolution while substantively describing this unity as one composed of difference:

111

One of my fondest memories was a day I had tea at a tea house in the square with four men: an Islahi, an atheist, a secular Socialist, a religious Zaidi, and myself. We laughed a lot, disagreed on politics … there are many unexpected friendships [that started in the square], and they have sustained, even if politically we no longer see eye to eye.[14]

In this recollection, shared at a similarly diverse gathering of Yemeni youth in 2012, an intentional solidarity foregrounds difference in the constitution of a shared revolutionary subjectivity.[15] The refashioning of identity in the revolutionary movement was one that underscores Lisa Wedeen's observation that 'categories are not groups, but they do make groups thinkable and legible, and indeed help constitute groups as objects available for self-identification.'[16]

The uprising helped to constitute the social category of 'independent youth,' which should not be regarded as wholly synonymous with the broader 'youth' though the two were sometimes (and continue to be) used interchangeably.[17] Atiaf al-Wazir has distinguished between the independent youth's 'agenda' (comprised of 'building a civil state with equal citizenship' and commitment to peaceful resistance, women's equality, and social justice) and that of youth more generally. She also argues that:

Politically, independent youth are not affiliated to the traditional political parties, neither JMP nor GPC, neither to ideological groups such as the Southern movement or the Houthis. However, some youth members of these groups state that they too are part of the independent Youth movement, especially when their decisions are taken freely and sometimes against the party/group line. This is mainly because the term 'youth' has become synonymous with demanding a new political reality, rather than reforming the current reality.[18]

This appreciation of youth activists' diverse attachments and relationships to a newly constituted group of independent youth also reflects anxieties expressed by members of the movement who were concerned about the risks of co-optation (by political parties) or militarization (by armed groups). Maintaining non-violence under such conditions was essential to the revolutionary movement's identity and its momentum, provoking powerful symbolic practices, including the theatrical laying down of weapons by tribesmen as they entered protest spaces.[19]

Accounts of the revolutionary movement by activists stress its collaborative and participatory features; they highlight the way in which collective action was transformative on an individual level, affording activists opportunities to interact across social boundaries that few had previously transgressed.[20] It is clear from activist accounts that the experience of collective action in 2011 and even into 2012 transformed them not into undifferentiated Yemeni citizens engaged in a common struggle but into subjects who stood in solidarity even from positions of sometimes deep disagreement.[21] Across this movement of difference, 'injustice—specifically, the state's unwillingness to apply the rule of law equally and its propensity to privilege access to economic resources on a discretionary basis—was the intersecting theme.'[22] This concern with injustice was reflected in dynamic forms of cultural production, from the street art that decorated protest spaces with representations of the unrepresented to the staging of theatrical performances—*masrah haquqi* or 'human rights theater'—that challenged inequitable social norms seen as upholding the country's political system.[23]

The climate of intersectional activism established in the country's protest squares also encouraged a kind of intellectual experimentation and engagement with new ideas. Youth participants described staying up late debating and arguing with others about 'big ideas.'[24] This sometimes took the form of casual collegiality and sometimes it was more formal, as with efforts by youth activists to initiate series of 'Yemen Enlightenment Debates' on core issues of the youth agenda.[25] Some did attempt to form new political parties, but many remained deeply attached to the idea of partisan independence.[26] New media experimentation also sought to widen the scope of engagement through participatory story-telling projects to bridge the gap between disparate Yemeni communities and those who claimed to represent them.[27]

The uprising was a form of collective action that irrevocably altered the political identities of its participants and their forward-looking expectations in ways that are still discernible today in many of the collectives and projects undertaken by civil actors. At the same time, the generational tension between youth activists and members of the partisan opposition, especially, has remained difficult to reconcile. Yemeni youth debating philosophy in Change Square were not the first Yemenis to take ideas seriously, to engage intellectually or practically with ideological others, or to attempt to build broad support for change. Under different circumstances, some in the JMP had done the same over the past decade. Yet many youth activists were engaged in this kind of bridge-building for the first time in their own lives and were doing it with a new level of inclusivity when compared with their partisan elders. The revolutionary movement was unique but also simultaneously indebted in important and rarely acknowledged ways to the politics that preceded it—both the successes and the limitations of building cross-ideological opposition to the Saleh regime.[28]

In this context, the JMP's effort to represent the popular movement was legible—predictable, even—but was also a source of ongoing grievance among both independent and partisan youth. Activists in protest squares organized around the slogan 'no political parties, no partisanship'—yet at the same time, al-Wazir has argued that this 'does not necessarily mean youth were against political parties, but rather condemning the bargaining of the traditional political parties.'[29] Journalist Laura Kasinof recalls in her memoir of reporting on the uprising that JMP leaders were similarly distrustful of the youth:

> [JMP leaders] stood back while the kids were pelted with rocks…. The young generation saw the Egyptian revolution and wanted to take to the streets, beating their chests, sacrificing their lives. The JMP leadership saw the establishment as they knew it changing, but knew they were themselves part of that establishment.[30]

The relationship between independent youth and the JMP was fraught from the first days of the uprising. It was not a relationship that improved with time.

Violence and Non-Violence After March 18

The events of March 18, 2011, are often cited by activists and observers alike as a turning point in the Yemeni uprising. Depicted vividly for a global audience in the Oscar-nominated documentary *Karama Has No Walls* and by longform journalism in the pages of *The New Yorker* or *The Guardian*, this day is cemented in collective memory of the Yemeni uprising with good reason.[31] After more than a month of ongoing protest and intermittent assaults on protesters, met largely with indifference or complicity on the part of security forces, regime agents took direct action against unarmed citizens on a mass scale. Human Rights Watch describes what is remembered as the Friday of Dignity (*Karama*):

> As the protesters finished their midday prayer, dozens of men wearing civilian clothes and armed with military assault rifles converged on the rally from the south and opened fire…. The Friday of Dignity massacre proved to be the deadliest attack on demonstrators of Yemen's yearlong uprising. Over the course of three hours, the gunmen killed at least 45 protesters—most of them university students and three of them children—and wounded 200 while state security forces made no serious effort to stop the carnage.[32]

The immediate aftermath of these events was a regime rupture. Powerful military figures like Brigadier General 'Ali Muhsin al-Ahmar and General Muhammed 'Ali Muhsin and tribal leaders like Shaykh Sadeq al-Ahmar and Shaykh Muhammed Abu Lahoum publicly declared their break with Saleh.[33] 'Ali Muhsin announced his 'support for the peaceful revolution of the youth and their demands,' and cited 'unconstitutional and illegal practices by the authorities, a policy of marginalisation and absence of justice,' as the reasons for his defection.[34] Sadeq al-Ahmar, son of Shaykh 'Abdullah bin Hussein al-Ahmar and his successor as leader of the Hashid tribal confederation, announced that Hashid had 'joined the revolution' and called for a 'safe transfer of power to the people.'[35] Senior figures in the bureaucracy and the General People's Congress (GPC) similarly constructed March 18 as a red line and resigned their posts. Saleh dismissed his entire cabinet before any more had the chance to quit.

The specter of civil war—and of Syria, where an uprising was also fracturing the military—amplified an interest in a quick negotiated solution that would see Saleh out of office. Yemen's regional neighbors initiated negotiations. The earliest draft of what would come to be called the Gulf Cooperation Council Initiative (GCCI) was proposed in early April 2011. Named in reference to the role of Gulf states in brokering the negotiations, it was not a template for a democratic transition, though its institutionalization by the United Nations and its broad endorsement by European donor states would seek to make it so, as discussed below. It was instead an effort by Yemen's elite and neighboring states to reconfigure power in a way that would buy time to stabilize Yemen.[36] As Ginny Hill explained, this 'prolonged the agony in Sana'a by creating a cycle of ambivalence that played directly into the stalemate, affecting the rivals' running calculations of the balance of power that lay between them.'[37]

When Saleh failed to sign the agreement, he faced increasingly overt pressure from external actors. US Defense Secretary John Brennan reportedly issued a veiled threat to Saleh that 'if he doesn't sign, we're going to have to consider other possible steps.'[38] Yet as destructive as the ensuing battles between rival military and tribal factions became, particularly in places like Arhab and Hasaba on the periphery of Sana'a, Yemen's conflict in 2011 did not immediately develop into widespread civil war.[39] Unlike the popular uprisings in Egypt or Tunisia, however, where the military remained intact, Yemen's uprising contributed to fragmentation and disorder over several months, in ways that had lasting consequences.

The Yemeni revolutionary movement continued pressing its aims through non-violent means, surrounded by a protective belt of armed fighters with at least some military equipment and considerable battlefield experience. Some armed actors, especially those surrounding the city of Taiz, described themselves as 'people protectors' there to ensure that the revolution could continue.[40] Others pursued less clear objectives. Some settled scores. Participants in the revolutionary movement recall working hard to maintain the non-violent character of protest spaces. Chants of *silmi, silmi* (peaceful, peaceful) were not enough; they stationed guards at the perimeter of protest encampments to frisk anyone coming in and required that they leave their arms outside.

Even with the fissures after March 18, the regime retained significant military force and diplomatic advantage. In his relationship to Saudi Arabia and the United States, in particular, Saleh instrumentalized insecurity in order to 'regulate both the magnitude and the rhythm of change.'[41] The transitional agreement proposed by the Gulf Cooperation Council in April 2011 was not able to forestall more death and destruction in the months that followed. Saleh repeatedly refused to sign and he rallied loyal factions of the armed forces, several under the command of his relatives, against a coalition of dissident military and tribal leaders as civilian casualties mounted. After a June 3 attempt on Saleh's life and his subsequent departure for medical treatment in Saudi Arabia, the country was engulfed in a summer-long campaign of violence at the direction of Saleh's son, Ahmed, and cousin, Yahya.

A symbiotic but two-track uprising thus unfolded. Protest spaces became more developed and their demands more refined. According to activists, much of the transformational impact of the uprising occurred during this period of sustained encampment, which was also when new initiatives became institutionalized or quasi-institutionalized for the first time in the form of insipient civil society organizations (CSOs) and other kinds of collectives. At the same time, the periphery of these spaces became arenas of armed conflict, with the ever-present risk that violence would encroach on any one of the dispersed nodes of Yemen's Change Revolution. This gave the uprising a fragmentary spatial dynamic that prefigured the development of the decentralized micropolities that would become significant in future conflicts.

By late summer of 2011, loyal factions of the military and security services escalated the use of force against civilians precipitously. In Taiz, which President Saleh was reported to hold in particular disregard because of its longstanding place at the center of Yemen's intellectual life and civil society, protesters' tents were set alight, and civilians, including small children, were indiscriminately killed by loyalist forces.[42] Shortly after Saleh transferred some authority to Vice President Hadi via Presidential Decree, a vicious phase of conflict unfolded between loyalist units of the military—especially the Republican Guards, under the control of Saleh's son, Ahmed— and dissident forces and tribal militias. The latter were not able to effectively hold back violence against unarmed protesters. A days-long battle between defected military units and loyalists ended with a deadly mortar attack on activists in Change Square in Sana'a, at the very moment that the UN Human Rights Council convened to discuss the crisis.[43]

Throughout this escalating violence in the summer and fall of 2011, rather than confirm concerns about Yemen's perilous risk of disunity, revolutionary activists made evident in their ongoing mobilization new forms of solidarity that traversed regional, tribal, sectarian, gender, and ideological boundaries. This occurred through practices of sustained collective action, and effected changes among revolutionary activists that were not registered openly by political elites associated with the opposition parties or those brokering an agreement. By the time Saleh returned to Yemen and ultimately agreed to leave office, 'the opposition' that co-signed on this plan for Yemen's future could not credibly claim to represent the revolutionary movement and became itself a target for activist energies challenging the terms of the transition.

The Gulf Cooperation Council (GCC) Transitional Framework

Finalized on November 23, 2011, the GCCI was conceived by Yemen's neighbors, signed by its political parties, and guaranteed by international institutions. After months of Saleh's prevarication, the Saudis were 'finally persuaded that perpetuating the status quo was doing no one any favors' and applied necessary pressure on the president to commit to a negotiated exit.[44] In October 2011, the UN Security Council issued a resolution that hastened the signing of the GCCI deal and delegated Jamal Benomar to represent the Secretary General by monitoring, reporting on, and generally facilitating its timely implementation.[45]

The GCCI agreement itself is brief, composed of only nine substantive articles, calling for the following steps to be taken in order:

1. Formation by the President of a power-sharing government divided evenly by 'both sides.'
2. Creation by that government of an 'atmosphere of national consensus.'
3. Adoption by parliament of a law granting immunity to the President and 'those who worked with him during his time in office.'
4. Parliamentary acceptance of the President's resignation and the transfer of presidential authority to the Vice-President.
5. Scheduling of Presidential elections within 60 days.
6. Appointment of a committee to prepare a new constitution.
7. Approval of that constitution by national referendum.
8. Establishment of a timeframe for parliamentary elections according to new constitution.
9. Creation of a new government by the leader of the party winning the largest share of seats in parliamentary elections.

Article 10 committed the GCC states, the United States, the European Union, and the Russian Federation to 'be witness to the implementation' of the agreement.[46] In practice, the steps were taken in a different sequence, or not at all. Rather than signing the agreement and following these steps, Saleh issued Presidential Decree No. 24 on September 12, 2011, delegating authority to his Vice President to negotiate on his behalf an implementation mechanism based on the basis of the GCC-brokered agreement.[47] This presidential decree facilitated UN Security Council Resolution (UNSCR) 2014 in October 2011, allowing the finalization of the agreement and adoption of the implementation mechanism on November 23.

The devil, of course, is in the details. Terms in the agreement like 'national consensus' or 'either side' belie the reality of deep (and multiple) divisions in Yemeni society and frayed state-society relations. This is not resolved by the Implementation

Mechanism, despite its greater insight into the way the transition was conceptualized by the drafters of the agreement.[48] Its language persistently describes the signatories as 'the two parties'—a fiction that is evident in the fact that the document was not signed by an entity called the Joint Meeting Parties (JMP) but by a collection of representatives of (some of) its member parties. The extent to which Yemen's opposition political parties did or could meaningfully represent one party to the agreement, let alone the broader field of opposition to the Saleh regime, was unclear.

The issue of developing national consensus is similarly muddy, even in the GCCI's clarifying document. The Implementation Mechanism appears to operationalize consensus differently in two parts of the document. In the first instance, it tasks the unity government with reaching decisions that reflect consensus among the parties, limiting the ability of any one party represented in that government to shape outcomes at the expense of another. In the event that there is no consensus among the parties, the President is given the authority to decide.[49] But it also outlines the plan for a National Dialogue Conference (NDC) designed to build consensus around issues of importance. These include several core justice issues, including political, economic, and social questions central to the JMP, the Southern Movement, the Houthis, independent youth, and women, all of whom were guaranteed representation by the terms of the Implementation Mechanism. It was in the Implementation Mechanism that the issue of transitional justice was mentioned formally for the first time, identifying the National Dialogue as both a reflection of and instrument for substantive engagement with the justice demands of Yemeni society.[50]

Immunity Does Not 'Build a New Yemen'

Despite its reference to transitional justice, at the center of the GCCI were two provisions that bedeviled substantive engagement with justice demands; one included immunity for President Saleh and his closest associates, and another guaranteed a smooth transfer of power by stipulating in advance that the election of the interim President would be uncontested. The first of these was more controversial at the time, but each had long-lasting consequences for the transition and is of continuing relevance from the perspective of accountability and justice.

As discussed in Chapter 1, amnesties are common features of peace agreements and negotiated settlements designed to make it easier for those who have participated in conflict to lay down their arms and/or leave office. Narrow and conditional amnesties are preferable to blanket or unconditional amnesties, since conditions allow negotiators to leverage the promise of amnesty in exchange for some desired outcome. Blanket amnesties, meanwhile, may allow many rights violators to evade accountability.

The amnesty provision of the GCCI was somewhat narrow but imposed few conditions. The GCCI required that President Saleh leave office within 30 days of the agreement entering into force, but stipulated that parliament would first 'adopt laws granting immunity from legal and judicial prosecution to the President and those who worked with him during his time in office.'[51] This provision had been initially resisted by the JMP, but they dropped their objections in a bid to convince Saleh to sign.[52] Not only was the scope of this provision vague, but its terms allowed Saleh to remain in the country and remain politically active through the GPC, where he would continue to play an important and ultimately highly destructive role. Moreover, in extending amnesty to Saleh's family members, several of whom were vitally important to the regime and its security institutions, the provision contributed to impunity for serious human rights abuses. Procedurally, it left the specificities of the law in the hands of a parliament that Saleh himself helped to engineer in 2003.

International condemnation of the immunity provision was widespread. Organizations like Human Rights Watch and Amnesty International launched campaigns against this component of the GCCI, and directed appeals to parliament itself. The International Center for Transitional Justice warned that the draft law was 'manifestly and uncontroversially in breach' of Yemen's obligations under a number of international treaties to which it was bound, adding that 'the idea that you can simply amnesty away the past, provide for official amnesia, and guarantee official impunity, is unacceptable in the current state of international law and international relations.'[53]

While the UN Security Council issued its support for the GCCI through UNSCR 2014 in October 2011, the terms of the parliament's amnesty law were publicly criticized by UN High Commissioner for Human Rights, Navi Pillay. She not only faulted the law for violating Yemen's international legal obligations but expressed concern that it did not 'respect the principle of equality before the law—meaning that there should be no discrimination between individuals who are pro-Government or in opposition and no distinction based on family connections.'[54] Amnesty International called the law 'a smack in the face for justice, made all the more glaring by the fact that protesters have been calling for an end to impunity since mass protests began in 2011.'[55]

Protesters had begun organizing against immunity for Saleh as early as April 2011, even before the most violent months of the uprising, with specific instances of anti-immunity organizing documented in at least fourteen of Yemen's governorates.[56] These grew acutely during the period between the formation of a new power-sharing government on December 7, 2011, and parliament's adoption of the immunity law (Law No. 1 of 2012) six weeks later. After the transfer of power and the formation of the transitional government, however, there was a new obstacle. Members in the new government who might be sympathetic to protesters' positions or who claimed to represent them were required by the terms of the GCCI to govern by consensus with others who doubtless feared that any changes to the immunity law would expose them to risk of prosecution.[57]

Protesters turned to innovative and theatrical forms of non-violent resistance in service of the demand that this provision of the agreement be dropped.[58] Adopting practices recognizably drawn from North Yemen's tribal repertoire of contention, marchers in the 'Life March' (from Taiz), the 'Dignity March' (from Hodeidah), and others staged a form of unarmed *wijah,* a confrontational demonstration designed to concurrently prevent conflict but signal steadfast demands.[59] The adaptation of this form of contention was resonant and succeeded in growing the crowd along the marchers' path, with new recruits joining the cordon of the Life March by the hundreds as it passed through Ibb and Dhamar en route to Sana'a.[60] A contemporaneous account numbers its original members as about 700 men and 18 women:

> It left Taiz on foot on December 20th and passed by many villages and towns. Along the way, the marchers were greeted by fireworks and cheered by chants, welcomed and offered shelter and food and joined in each city by protesters on their way to Sana'a, swelling their numbers....[61]

Images and video from the march from Taiz flooded Twitter but received very limited news coverage.[62] As Murad Alazzany observed at the time, what little media coverage there was also diminished the symbolic power of the marches by describing them as 'peaceful rallies,' difficult to distinguish from other forms of ongoing mobilization on a wide range of issues.[63] The specificity of the marchers' justice demands and the recognizable form of claims-making were inconvenient to a plotline that framed a post-Saleh Yemen as embarking on an orderly transition after nearly a year of tumult.

But it was not precisely a post-Saleh Yemen. When the marchers from Taiz arrived at Hizyaz, a suburb of the capital where members of the former President's tribe, Sanhan, predominate, they were attacked by Saleh loyalists and new protesters were prevented from joining the march. As the marchers pressed into the city, they were then attacked by security forces, now under the command of the new power-sharing government. This resulted in at least seven deaths and hundreds of injuries.[64] Responsibility for the killings was hotly debated; some witnesses claimed that the assailants were from units of the military that remained loyal to former President Saleh, while the Defense Ministry claimed that they were agents of the Interior Ministry, then under the command of a member of the JMP.[65] This highlighted the friability of power-sharing between rival factions of the old elite and foreshadowed the new government's limited ability to advance security from the center.[66]

Opposition to the immunity provision continued into January through protests and marches, but the priorities of the GCCI and its international supporters were elsewhere. According to the terms

123

of the GCCI, the next step in Yemen's transitional process was the formalization of 'Abd Rabbuh Mansour Hadi's position through election. Endorsing Hadi as the sole candidate firmly positioned the former opposition parties as part of the governing coalition. The election sanctified the choice of someone who had been a partisan of 'Ali Nasser, aligned with Saleh in 1994, and built his political career on the ashes of an earlier civil war. It was difficult to understand how he could expect to deliver on his campaign slogan: 'Together, we build a new Yemen.' It was also unclear why he bothered to campaign.

Only about one third of eligible voters ultimately participated in an election process that observers described as a collective rubber stamp.[67] Yet Hadi's election was received at the time with more equanimity among activists than I expected, given his political biography. Many expressed exhaustion from the protracted period of uncertainty and anxiety (if also some excitement) about the challenges and opportunities that other features of the transitional process presented. Having effectively lost on the immunity issue, young activists seemed willing to empower Hadi and the power-sharing government if it could advance movement toward the meatier parts of the transitional process, especially the National Dialogue, and if it meant that the government was able to make progress in restoring basic security.

Some activists did remain mobilized, however, as part of a 'parallel revolution,' shifting focus from Saleh himself to public institutions that protesters had previously deemed 'untouchable.' Through sit-ins, demonstrations, and work stoppages at public utilities and in the military and security apparatus itself, they issued justice claims that struck at the heart of Saleh's continuing ability to exercise political control outside of the Presidency.[68]

The new government's actions against some figures who were targets of this parallel revolution—including members of Saleh's family—created tension between Hadi and the former president. Saleh was out of office, but the amnesty meant that he was free to remain politically active as the head of the GPC, Hadi's political party. Protests demanding the cleanup of the bureaucracy and security sector began even before Hadi was elected; actions described by some as mutinies within the military proliferated across the country at dozens of military bases and in a wide range of units over the course of 2012 and 2013.[69] With Hadi's control over the military only 'partial and tenuous,' Ginny Hill describes his efforts at restructuring—including the formal dissolution of both the Republican Guard and the First Armored Division—as insufficient:

> Far from consolidating the [defense] ministry's authority, Hadi's military restructuring efforts led to further fragmentation in the real and effective chain of command.... At the behest of his international backers, Hadi's ambitious programme of security sector reform amounted to little more than unpicking the fiefdoms of the Saleh era and stoking intense competition among a growing number of veteran and aspiring warlords.[70]

Ongoing contention outside of the security sector may have been more effective in addressing justice demands. Protesters were able to secure the replacement of important Saleh allies in public universities, state-run media outlets, and even the Supreme Commission for Elections and Referenda, which had itself been a bête noir for the JMP. Protesters also halted production at the country's largest oil facility for several days in February. Discursively targeting 'the family,' justice claims were framed against the nepotism that underwrote decades of consolidation of resources and decision-making in the hands of the Saleh family, Sanhan tribe, and other close loyalists.

At a minimum, the parallel revolution made evident a fundamental tension that existed among activists about how—and how quickly—to pursue change. Having seen Saleh removed by street politics, young Yemenis sought to show that the revolution could continue. As Abdulghani al-Iryani described the effort at the time:

> It is a more dramatic and efficient way of effecting change that reflects the grievances of civil servants who have been controlled by corrupt officials for a very long time.... They are not willing to wait for political negotiations to deal with these corrupt officials so they're taking things into their own hands and it's proving remarkably effective.[71]

While demands to replace corrupt officials were partially successful in some parts of the public sector, the parallel revolution as a whole reflects an underlying tension between disruption and governance that was pronounced in the period prior to the National Dialogue.

As the pre-organized parties of the opposition gained formal political power in the new transitional government, they also entered into a new relationship with the revolutionary youth. Whereas party leaders had been willing to leverage youth mobilization to keep pressure on Saleh, they now appeared wary of the power of their younger members. For their part, participation in the uprising had created for youth activists 'a permanent repository of resistance' that posed a challenge to partisan elites.[72] Effectively kicking the ladder out behind them, leaders of the major political parties consolidated power in the early transitional period by closing down their internal mechanisms of deliberation and locking most partisan youth out of internal decision-making.[73]

Yemeni youth therefore had to wrestle with the perceived tradeoffs between the benefits of partisanship—which might guarantee them some limited formal representation but offered little internal space for youth voices or leadership—versus grassroots mobilization. While the youth movement had social credibility, it was 'excluded from the negotiations between members of the politically relevant elite,' which communicated to youth the appeal of partisan belonging as a path to access.[74] At the same time, by the time the GCCI came into force, youth activists had spent nearly a year articulating together their skepticism of the parties. This tension was reflected in surveys of Yemeni youth showing an overwhelming preference for 'decision-making to take place through formal, legal processes rather than informal institutions or unofficial means,' but little faith that the parties themselves could—or would—work to ensure this.[75] Instead, young partisans encountered systemic communication barriers within their parties that led them to seek influence through other channels.

As government and non-government organizations in Washington and London worked to organize events and meetings in advance of the National Dialogue, it was clear that they turned first and foremost to the parties to identify 'relevant' representatives of Yemeni youth.[76]

Indeed, as a study of partisan youth reported, 'one critique that was repeatedly mentioned by international diplomats and political analysts following the protests in Yemen was the lack of an entity that could represent the 'youth'.'[77] Parties might have provided such an avenue, but both youth ambivalence and international organizers' awareness of exclusive party behavior led to parallel investments in other forums—workshops, trainings, capacity-building— oriented toward the development of a cohesive approach to youth representation ahead of the next stage of the transitional process, the cornerstone NDC.

The Inconvenience of Ongoing Dissent

In May 2012, a group of young people on the terrace below my hotel room window kept me awake well into the night, laughing and teasing each other with a comfortable familiarity. I could hear the bubble of a *nargileh* as they played a kind of game that reminded me of a version of 'Truth or Dare.' What marks this evening out in my mind is that a few hours earlier, the same young people had been arguing about varieties of federal institutions, the need for military restructuring, and the role of *shari'a* in a civil (*madani*) state. As a group of about 40 revolutionary activists from across Yemen, they were meeting to consider the possibility of joint 'youth platform' in advance of Yemen's upcoming National Dialogue, but were divided about whether and how they could participate under the demands of the Dialogue's organizational structure.[78]

The group included activists from across the political spectrum— Islahis and Houthis, members of the Hirak, secular liberals, rights activists of different stripes, university students. All had participated in the uprising in 2011 in some way, identified as 'youth activists,' and were involved with exciting new initiatives that flourished during the early months of the transitional period. Many came to this workshop frustrated by what they characterized as a revolution interrupted by the GCCI. The transitional framework signed by 'the opposition' did not represent the full range of their aspirations, and they were struggling to identify the best way to convey their dissent. No participant was satisfied with GCCI, though the reasons for and extent of their critiques varied. My notes reflect extensive disagreement among participants on important particulars as they envisioned Yemen's future, but also note how often they affirmed each other's inclusion in a process of political reimagining even, or especially, in moments of disagreement.

Opposition to elements of the GCC transitional framework voiced by these activists—from the immunity provision to what some described as the reductive approach to representational quotas at the NDC—also fell victim to an international policy environment in which ongoing non-violent dissent went largely unremarked. Justice demands reflected in civil forms of opposition to the substantive terms of transition did not fit with a narrative forwarded by international actors that suggests that the transitional agreement enjoyed the consent of 'the opposition.' Those who sought to criticize or amend the agreement were treated as destabilizing forces to be contained.

Raising the stakes of ongoing dissent, six months into the transitional period, US President Barack Obama signed an executive order authorizing the US Treasury Department to seize the assets of anyone whose actions might:

> …threaten Yemen's peace, security, and stability, including by obstructing the implementation of the agreement of November 23, 2011, between the Government of Yemen and those in opposition to it, which provides for a peaceful transition of power that meets the legitimate demands and aspirations of the Yemeni people for change…[79]

This executive order was issued while I was at the meeting of youth activists described above. As I listened to them deliberate about the pros and cons of working on a common agenda, I received an email from a staffer working for President Barack Obama's National Security Council (NSC) with the text of the President's order attached. I worried that this might have a chilling effect on activists' efforts to issue legitimate grievances through non-violent mechanisms, so I sought immediate clarification. The NSC staffer responded that the intent of the order was 'to ensure the Yemenis meet the transitional benchmarks they agreed to in their transitional agreement.'[80]

In ensuing conversations with activists over the next several days, both the executive order and this clarification were taken to signify the broad failure of the international community to account for civil forms of dissent against an agreement that some revolutionaries said they could not regard as 'theirs.' Elements of the GCCI were viewed instead as reflecting the vested interests of established elites inside and outside of Yemen. Both the George W. Bush and Obama administrations had sustained a relationship with Yemeni President 'Ali 'Abdullah Saleh that rested on security cooperation in the service of counterterrorism. After the failed attack by Al Qaeda in the Arabian Peninsula (AQAP) member 'Umar Farouq Abd al-Muttalib in December 2009, the United States more than doubled its military assistance to Yemen in 2010, with the bulk of the increase earmarked for counterterrorism.[81] Technologies of surveillance central to counterterrorism, however, were easily turned against the civil opposition by Saleh's regime, leading to further encroachments on political freedoms and civil rights. The US Senate Committee on Foreign Relations indicated its knowledge of such misdirection of counterterrorism funds at least a year before the uprising, as such aid was ballooning.[82] In the months immediately preceding the 2011 uprising, journalists were targeted by Saleh's regime, limiting the public's access to information, especially when it related to the developing relationship between the Saleh regime and the United States.[83] This was acutely illustrated by the prominent case of 'Abdulelah Haider Shaea, which spanned the period before, during, and after the uprising.[84]

Concern with the US-Yemeni relationship in domestic Yemeni political debates may help to explain, in part, why it was the GCC that brokered the transitional agreement, though it did so with the United States' support and in ways that promised to minimize the impact of a political transition on US and Saudi security objectives in the country. Saudi Interior Ministry spokesman General Mansour al-Turki was explicit on this point, noting that 'our main concern is al-Qaeda and that is not going to change, whatever happens in Yemen.'[85] Sana'a-based journalist Iona Craig suggested at the time that many viewed Saudi Arabia as 'a proxy for US diplomacy, providing Washington with a back door to prevent civil war and further instability.'[86] A member of Islah living in the UAE suggested that the GCC leadership 'had no real interest in the success of the revolution, nor in its failure,' but voiced the common view that their primary interests were in stability, and containing the reach of revolutionary change.[87] The agreement was positioned to provide quick stabilization, not to enable the kind of durable change to which activists aspired.

That such an agreement might then be framed by the United States government and others as a bilateral pact between Saleh's regime and 'those in opposition to it,' illustrates an elite orientation out of sync with developments on the ground. The GCCI awarded the ruling party half of the seats in a national unity government, left the ruling party's 2003 parliamentary supermajority intact, and called upon that same parliament to immunize the regime through new legislation. It sequenced new parliamentary elections last, to come only after the redrafting of the constitution by a committee appointed by the (new) president, whom the parties to the agreement agreed not to oppose. While the agreement did pledge to 'respond to the aspirations of the Yemeni people for change and reform,' the path to ascertaining those aspirations was opaque.[88] Even on the eve of the transition's centerpiece NDC, activists continued to argue that 'many of the organizational details are still very vague.'[89]

The GCC agreement and its implementation mechanism played a role in obscuring civil actors' dissent and ongoing popular mobilization for justice. Presenting to the international community a portrait of an inclusive agreement that was belied by the transitional government's narrowness, international institutions and important third parties reinforced the notion that Yemen's opposition parties represented 'the' opposition to the Saleh regime. From this vantage point, the decision to sequence the National Dialogue before constitutional revision and parliamentary elections appeared sensible, enabling broader inclusion and social consultation. Yet as the next section shows, the effects of the National Dialogue were mixed, given its failure to account for the transformative power of solidarity among Yemeni youth shaped by the experience of collective action.

The National Dialogue Conference

Core decision-making power under the GCCI was lodged with the president, the ministries, and to a lesser degree, the parliament, distributed on the basis of powersharing among Yemen's formal political parties. Women, youth, and important extrapartisan movements like the Houthis and Hirak—all mentioned specifically as warranting inclusion in the transitional process—had to pin their hopes on the consultative process of the NDC. It was here that they could expect to have the greatest input on the country's future. This difference—between a pact that distributed power and a dialogue that distributed opportunities for voice—highlights different meanings of the concept of inclusion that were concurrently operative during the transitional period and persist in approaches to peacebuilding and post-conflict planning today.

Despite integrating a broader range of Yemeni actors than any other component of the transitional process, analysts nonetheless noted that 'one of the shortcomings of the NDC process is that it failed to recognize and include the demands of major sectors of the population' and was 'driven by old tribal and political parties.'[90] This was reflected in the formal composition of the conference, which allocated the largest share of seats to parties. Half of the delegates were drawn from the South—overrepresenting participation relative to Southerners' demographic share—but here observers correctly noted that 'being of southern origin does not translate into support for the southern cause.' Indeed, many Southerners who participated in the dialogue were not aligned with Hirak, and Hadi himself, elevated to Defense Minister in the middle of the 1994 civil war, was counted among the Southern delegates.[91] Representatives of the Houthi movement, meanwhile, were granted 35 seats, but their share was dwarfed by other groups, most notably Islah, which had 50. Independent youth, women, and civil society—the first two mentioned explicitly in the GCCI implementation mechanism— received shares that collectively amounted to a little more than 21% of the total delegates, recruited by a preparatory committee that received tens of thousands of applications.[92] Other blocs were also required to nominate women and youth among their slate of delegates. The presidium of the NDC included one representative of each of the four named categories indicated by the GCCI—one woman, one representative of youth, one Hiraki, one Houthi—as well as representatives of Islah, the Yemeni Socialist Party (YSP), the Nasserists, and the GPC, in addition to President Hadi.

At the delegate level and in the presidium, therefore, parties continued to dominate at precisely the time when so many had become vocally frustrated by them and as parties themselves were becoming less responsive or internally inclusive. The limited outreach conducted by the parties also left many concerned that it would create recommendations that did not enjoy broad support or buy-in. In an interview shortly before the NDC, Amat al-Alim al-Soswa captured this concern:

> Maybe the national dialogue conference will still take place, even with this [limited] amount of representation. But will it be truly then agreed upon by the vast majority of people who were not there? I doubt it.[93]

Others were critical of the NDC's adoption of a logic of descriptive representation that effectively asked participants to represent single constituencies—or check single boxes—despite the fact that youth activists, in particular, had an increasingly intersectional understanding of their own identities and interests.[94] Asking women, for example, to participate primarily as women blunted the possibility—probability, even—that those women also had partisan, regional, or other important commitments. As one female youth activist explained, 'the way groups are identified [by National Dialogue planners] puts us in closed boxes and reduces our identity to only one.'[95] The NDC's quota-based approach made incipient solidarities less accessible as a resource for civil actors because its representational logic promoted bargaining over consensus building.[96]

This tendency toward bargaining was underscored by practices among delegates to the conference. Southerners associated with the Hirak, for example, boycotted the NDC in August 2013, demanding confidence-building measures directed toward the South specifically.[97] This led to a substantial delay and prompted President

Hadi to establish a new 8+8 committee that further prioritized Hiraki demands and at least partially worked around the NDC structure.[98] It was combined with some limited recognition of and restitution for harms against Southerners after 1994. While this fell short of fully meeting the demands of the boycotting faction, their return to the conference in September showed both sides offering some concessions.[99] Members of Islah also walked out of sessions or threatened to veto them. Those who lacked alternative channels of power, especially women and youth, were more circumspect (if not less frustrated), as participation in the NDC was their primary opportunity to shape outcomes during the transitional period. Practical and institutional asymmetries put such participants at a disadvantage in this bargaining model and undermined the efficacy of the dialogue as a whole.

Moreover, the National Dialogue Conference occurred alongside strategic engagements with transitional justice that occurred outside of NDC channels, casting a shadow over its work. Under pressure from the UN, President Hadi issued a presidential decree in September 2012 calling for the establishment of an investigatory commission to address human rights violations committed during the events of 2011. Beyond this decree, no action was taken to render such a committee operational. Instead, changes were introduced to a draft Transitional Justice and National Reconciliation law that narrowed its temporal scope and put many of the injustices relevant to victims out of reach. Further, any draft law could not contradict Law 1 of 2012, which granted immunity to Saleh and his associates. Despite nominal engagement, then, the prospects of pursuing justice through the legal system were remote due to provisions of the GCCI that protected and empowered existing elites, as well as to the weakness and non-independence of the Yemeni judiciary.[100]

This context makes the work of the NDC's working group dedicated to Transitional Justice and National Reconciliation all the more remarkable. The committee produced recommendations that were capacious in scope and laid out a blueprint for a transitional justice process that could have been genuinely transformative. The concluding document articulated 126 distinct recommendations addressing the purposes, scope, and procedures appropriate to the pursuit of transitional justice in service of national reconciliation and sustainable peace.[101] These reflected both rear-looking and forward-looking guides to understanding the core justice demands of Yemeni society. The document adopted a temporal scope extending well before unification, thus bringing unjust features of governance dating to the People's Democratic Republic of Yemen and Yemen Arab Republic under examination. It addressed the role of *takfir,* or allegations of apostasy, in delimiting public expression and personal freedom, as well as fomenting intercommunal conflict.[102] It adopted a victim-centered approach, identified pathways to reconciliation through individual and collective approaches to reparation, and even accounted for some 'lost life opportunities' of the sort discussed by advocates of reparative development as outlined in Chapter 1.

A substantial proportion of the committee's recommendations focus on material resources and their equitable and transparent handling by government authorities. Several of the provisions call for the cancelation of no-bid contracts, dissolution of monopolies, or return of properties that were allocated or appropriated non-transparently or in punitive ways by the state. These are presented as violating the rights of individuals and those of society as a whole. The working group also addressed the rights of groups, highlighting the need for collective reparations targeting deliberately underdeveloped communities in the Tihama, for example, or places like Sa'ada or Abyan that have faced disproportionate internal displacement and infrastructural destruction from recent periods of conflict.

The work of this committee was certainly not uncontroversial, and it required Hadi's intervention to resolve deadlock on several occasions. In September 2013, the Transitional Justice and National Reconciliation committee was the first NDC committee to signal the need for an extended work period. One member of the working group recalls that part of the struggle within the committee was over the temporal scope of transitional justice. GPC members, for example, wanted to start the clock in 2011, whereas members of the YSP wanted to account at least for events in 1994, if not earlier. Some Nasserists extended their claims back to 1978–9, citing a wave of political disappearances, show trials, and executions that followed an early attempt to overthrow President Saleh.[103] Far from a technical exercise, these temporal decisions were a means of identifying whose harms 'count' in the transitional justice process and were informed by harms suffered directly and indirectly by members of the committee itself, as well as by submissions made to the committee and its own outreach. [104]

The committee was also challenged by the concurrent creation of two investigatory commissions in the South, decreed by President Hadi to address cases of land expropriation and the forced dismissal of Southern military officers and civil servants in the aftermath of the 1994 war.[105] While these commissions and the formal apologies that accompanied them were not considered fundamentally incompatible with the transitional justice committee's work, there were disagreements among NDC delegates about whether it was possible, or desirable, to begin work on a comprehensive approach to justice before these commissions had concluded their own work.[106] In the end, this contributed to the working group's delay, and to some lack of clarity in the scope and jurisdiction of different instruments.

After the NDC's conclusion, international observers of the process expressed concern that the issues addressed by the Transitional Justice and National Reconciliation committee were 'vulnerable to being re-litigated in the subsequent constitution drafting and implementation phases.'[107] This concern is one that continues to haunt members of the committee as they revisit the working group's delays:

> [I]f you're consumed at that moment, you don't realize that you don't have all the time in the world. It's only a matter of time before things get complicated and then things could collapse. And it's hard. I mean, when I think about it. I keep thinking about all the times ... could we have done something different ... could this have been avoided? I'm still not sure.[108]

Indeed, in the short window between the NDC's conclusion in January 2014 and the dissolution of the transitional government the following fall, political elites from a range of partisan backgrounds did take obstructionist moves to undermine the draft transitional justice law.[109]

The committee's report reflects both the product and promise of transitional justice to advance the rights of both individuals and groups.[110] It was a product of transitional justice insofar as the group's recommendations were developed through a sustained and inclusive dialogue process that was more representative than any other institution in Yemen at the time or since then. In its substantive focus, it also represents the promise of transitional justice mechanisms to empower individuals to deliberatively identify and address harms that sustain conflict and to identify appropriate restorative mechanisms for individuals and for groups. It reflects the Capabilities Approach priority on public reasoning in plural contexts, and highlights the possibilities such reasoning offers for the development of overlapping consensus on difficult questions of justice.

The fact that the committee's recommendations remain unrealized, however, is significant. What progress was made at the NDC was undermined by President Hadi's decision to work around the NDC when it became unwieldy and when events outside of the political center did indeed become, as the delegate above put it, 'more complicated.' Much as rescheduled parliamentary elections had earlier been eclipsed by the uprising, the transitional justice component of the GCCI and its intended one-year implementation period were overtaken by events outside of Sana'a, and arguably outside of the formal sphere of Yemen's political transition itself.

Remaking the North

With all eyes on the political transition and the NDC, events in the far North received comparatively less attention, as the Houthis gradually expanded their military control of the region through a combination of coercion and persuasion. They did so in an area of the country laid flat by the six rounds of fighting during the Sa'ada Wars (2004–10), especially during the Operation Scorched Earth campaign in 2009–10, when more than 40,000 Yemeni troops were deployed and Saudi Arabia launched a punishing aerial campaign. The result left more than a quarter of a million internally displaced persons sheltered in the ruins of cities and towns that had already been among the most neglected in the country. The scale of the suffering was difficult to contemplate and fed an established narrative of injustice.

As discussed in Chapter 3, the final and devastating round of fighting in the Sa'ada wars, Operation Scorched Earth, had concluded—inconclusively—through mutual exhaustion in 2010. Internal and external factors had initially appeared to favor a negotiated outcome: a tentative agreement had been floated and modified by mediators and diplomats, Houthi forces had become exhausted by fighting both Yemeni and Saudi forces, and US and European governments were concerned that the government's entanglements were distracting it from counterterrorism objectives.[111] Instead of negotiating, however, the Saudis pulled back on their military campaign and Saleh announced a unilateral ceasefire, putting an end to any effort to engage with the Houthis and changing the calculus for Saleh and the Houthis alike. Even if the Houthis might have had pragmatic reasons to informally abide by elements of the earlier tentative agreement as they pursued Sa'ada's reconstruction, the government's suspension of negotiations made any shared understanding of how to sequence its steps impossible.[112]

When the popular uprising developed in 2011, some of the Houthis' existing and longstanding grievances fit within the broader frame of the revolutionary movement against an unjust and abusive regime. While the participation of Houthi youth in protest activity in 2011 was informed by their own distinct experience with the Saleh regime, they also participated in protest activity against 'the totality of the parties represented in the Yemeni parliament, described as corrupt and self-interested.'[113]

As Luca Nevola's ethnographic research in 2012 and 2013 suggests, the transitional period structured opportunities for recognized groups in a way that propelled a 'rephrasing of traditional lineage identities in political terms' in the far North. *Sada,* many of whom had not previously been active in the Houthi movement during the 2004–10 insurgency, were increasingly drawn to it as a vehicle for political recognition in the transitional period. This had the effect of 'triggering an equal and opposite reaction' that swelled support for Islah among non-*sayyid* tribesmen, contributing simultaneously to political polarization and sectarianization.[114] As

Nevola recounts from the small village of Kuthra, 'at first as a joke, next as a reaction, [non-*sada* residents] reacted blow-by-blow to any Houthi-marked practice.'[115]

Nevola's explanation of the quotidian ways in which descent-based distinctions in predominantly Zaydi communities were increasingly transformed into rival partisan and sectarian affiliations helps to disentangle what many have struggled to understand about the sectarianization of conflict in Yemen. People who were nominally 'born Zaydi' but not *sada* began to adopt 'Sunni' prayer styles not as a form of doctrinal conversion, per se, but as a reaction to the mobilization of descent-based claims among *sada*. This is not precisely the same, but parallels in some important ways the effects of earlier *salafi* evangelism among low-status Zaydis, which scholars in turn characterized as the initial impetus of Zaydi revival. Far from some kind of timeless sectarian conflict that pitted pre-existing groups against one another, North Yemen was a fluid space in which identities were being refashioned and groups made. This was occurring far from the NDC or the politics of Yemen's urban centers, but in ways that became significant for them as well.

Support for the Houthi movement grew during the transitional period through a 'weaponization of nostalgia' directed not toward a restored Zaydi imamate governed by *sada*, but for what 'Ali al-Bukhyati, Houthi delegate to the NDC, called a 'second republic,' in which Zaydis would be afforded equal dignity and protected from forms of discrimination or denigration they associated with the first.[116] Added to this was the Houthis' anti-imperial rhetoric, which found new resonance at a time of external political intervention and escalating US counterterrorism operations in Yemen. The demands of the Change Revolution paired with Houthi rhetoric to articulate a populist version of 'the people' recognizable to revolutionary youth. This created some basis for support for the Houthi movement and its critiques of the transitional government outside of its existing areas of strength, though observers have noted that 'not all sympathizers were staunch defenders of Houthism; many were simply frustrated with the prevailing political stalemate.'[117]

Violence in the North did not develop, however, because the NDC failed. Instead, it was present throughout the transitional process.

From 2011 onward, as transitional institutions provided the Houthis limited voice and no significant decision-making power, the Houthis engaged in a military campaign to consolidate territorial control throughout much of the North. They were also met with counter violence, which shaped Houthi positions at the NDC. The assassination of two of their delegates—notably, two of the movement's 'doves,' 'Abd al-Karim Jadban and Ahmad Sharaf al-Din—strengthened the position of hardliners at the NDC and their movement's commitment to a military strategy outside of the conference.[118]

The issue of Dammaj and the *salafi* institute of Dar al-Hadith, discussed in the previous chapter, also resurfaced during this time as a site of both symbolic and material struggle. While students and supporters of Dar al-Hadith—*ahl al-Dammaj*—had been involved in armed clashes with Houthi fighters in the past, sustained military pressure from Houthi forces during the transitional period led to the eventual expulsion of its students and their families in January 2014. Forces defending *ahl al-Dammaj* were led by Ahmed 'Abu Muslim' al-Zaakari, whose personal biography parallels the familiar pattern; born into a Zaydi tribe, he later studied at Dar al-Hadith and became a leading figure in the *salafi* movement in Dammaj.[119] In January 2014, President Hadi brokered a ceasefire between the two sides, calling for only 'natives' of the area (*ahl al-bilad*) to remain and attempting to refer the conflict to various government committees for more thorough resolution of the competing claims.[120] Instead, government forces were allowed to evacuate *salafi* fighters, students, and their families, but were prevented from redeploying in any of the areas held by Houthi forces.[121] Leaders of the *salafi* contingent were evacuated to the capital in military helicopters, but the majority were relocated to more distant parts of Yemen, filling a convoy of more than 300 buses out of the Sa'ada area.[122] Many of these evacuees went on to join *salafi* militias that were active in the war that developed after 2015 and have consequently been among the most hardline anti-Houthi fighters.[123]

Despite the role of this conflict in further entrenching sectarian polarization, it remained clear that the fighting in Dammaj was more than 'the age-old Sunni-Shiite split.'[124] Those with close knowledge of the area and the antagonists interpreted these events as part of a much broader and complex struggle between Houthi insurgents, the so-called 'republican shaykhs,' and Yemen's partisan elite; tribal shaykhs, many of whom were also by this point partisan elites aligned with Islah, 'capitalized on [*salafi* doctrine] in order to reinforce their own leadership claims against the still-influential *sadah*.'[125]

The conflict in the North had therefore acquired a sectarian dimension, but one not neatly divorced from partisan dynamics or the distribution of and access to resources, nor from a transitional government that empowered Islah at the expense of the Houthis. By the summer of 2014, Houthi militias had defeated rivals throughout the north, including in Islah-aligned 'Amran, and had surrounded the capital. Their military campaign outside of Sana'a had focused not only on the defeat of *salafi* fighters but on forces commanded by 'Ali Muhsin, specifically, and tribal militias aligned with Islah, including the powerful Bayt al-Ahmar.

The Houthis combined their military pressure with a political campaign, erecting an unarmed encampment in the capital and working to build popular support for their demands that fuel subsidies be restored and the transitional government resign.[126] These demands resonated in areas well outside of traditional Houthi influence, including as far south as Taiz. The dynamic relationship between largely unarmed protests in urban areas paired with armed conflict outside of them made it less surprising when, after talks between Hadi and 'Abd al-Malik al-Houthi broke down, armed Houthi forces entered Sana'a on September 21, 2014.

In the capital, eyewitness accounts describe unguarded government buildings taken 'without firing a shot.'[127] It quickly became clear that the Houthis had been working in close cooperation with former President Saleh and elements of the military that were still led or influenced by his allies. Surprising to some observers, a Houthi-Saleh alliance was legible to others as a kind of 'negative coalition, united by what they oppose, not in their prescriptive aims.'[128] The ease with which their forces took over enabled Houthi fighters to move quickly toward symbolic and sometimes even theatrical attacks on the property and homes of prominent Islahis. The targeting of Islahis specifically, rather than generic Sunni or even *salafi* targets, further underscores Houthi claims regarding Islah's privileged access to institutional power and resources during the transitional period.[129]

Disintegration in the South

Preoccupation in Sana'a, first with the uprising and later with formal elements of the transitional process, also contributed to a steep deterioration in security conditions in the South. This was especially acute in Abyan. In partial response, the government strategically engaged South-specific justice demands alongside, but not in coordination with, efforts to pursue accountability at the national level. The effect of a two-track approach deepened regionalism further, and by the time Houthi forces entered Sana'a in 2014, the Hirak was clearly working to advance an independent state in Southern Arabia.

Security conditions in the South were caught in a negatively reinforcing cycle during the transitional period by which militants mobilized a narrative of injustice in undergoverned spaces while moving such spaces even further from the reach of the transitional government. The responses of the transitional government and of local leaders in Abyan to the challenge presented by local AQAP affiliate Ansar al-Shari'a likewise presaged developments that would become more commonplace during the war that developed after 2014. Autochthonous security providers succeeded in displacing militant groups outside of the scope of the transitional government in ways that 'further lowered the expectations for the state' and drove the practical decentralization of security and justice.[130]

Throughout the spring of 2011, AQAP and Ansar al-Shari'a took territorial control of a number of Southern towns and cities throughout Abyan and Shabwa, including the provincial capital of Abyan, Zinjibar. This occurred not through extensive battle, but because 'state control in southern Yemen had essentially evaporated' in the wake of the political and security crisis developing in the North.[131] Aware of and speaking explicitly to the accumulated injustices that animated their local communities, Ansar al-Shari'a declared emirates in territories under their control and quickly worked to establish a system of public provision and local justice.[132]

In testimony before the United States' Senate Committee on Foreign Relations in 2013, Robin Simcox framed Ansar al-Shari'a as a 'rebranding' of AQAP designed for local consumption:

> Aware of al-Qaeda's divisive reputation, AQAP introduced themselves to locals in Yemen as members of Ansar al-Sharia. They empowered local jihadists and rebranded their movement with a positive message that they could restore peace and justice to the area, while also providing key services. They achieved some success with this, providing food, water, and electricity. This only served to highlight the shortcomings of the government in Sana'a, who proved incapable of providing such basics for the population it purports to govern.[133]

While AQAP and Ansar al-Sharia are undoubtedly linked, accounts that seek to understand Ansar al-Shari'a in the context of Yemen's social, economic, and political dynamics at least partially distinguish the organization from AQAP by its origins and its aims.[134] AQAP includes a number of foreign fighters, especially but not exclusively a cohort that migrated from Saudi Arabia following the kingdom's crackdown in 2009. By contrast, Ansar al-Shari'a has been described as a wholly Yemeni 'insurgency' that, while politically sympathetic to AQAP and Al Qaeda's vision of global jihad, was more directly invested in the reordering and governing of Yemeni society in a period of pronounced uncertainty.[135] Its origin in Abyan also connects it to a longer history of Islamist militancy in the area, including the Abyan Islamic Army, responsible for the 2000 attack on the *USS Cole* off the coast of Aden. This attack on US military power by 'Afghan Arabs' returned from the anti-Soviet jihad is another example of the translocalism of Yemeni Islamism, where global flows of ideas, people, and practices take on specific meaning in local contexts. So too, arguably, was the development of Ansar al-Shari'a in dialogue with a global militant Al Qaeda. As Abyan experienced some of the worst of the US counterterrorism campaign against AQAP, this global/local entanglement deepened.

While the non-militant Islamists of the Islah party had done moderately well in elections in Abyan prior to the uprising, the people who would eventually form Ansar al-Shari'a were neither invested in Yemen's republican system nor welcoming of partisan competition. They instead sought an alternative to the *fawda,* or chaos, of the transitional period and the pervasive insecurity. The continuation of US counterterrorism operations, and especially the Obama administration's escalation of drone strikes in 2012 and 2013, contributed to the sense that the transitional government could not (or would not) keep Yemenis safe, feeding Ansar al-Shari'a's narrative. While AQAP was more oriented outward toward global jihad, Ansar al-Shari'a's primary promise was to 'address local grievances, such as corruption and lack of effective justice.'[136] One local politician highlighted the fluid dynamics well, arguing that 'most Ansar followers in Abyan are local....You can strike agreements with them and pull them away from al-Qaeda.'[137] Such a formulation positions AQAP and Ansar al-Shari'a as one, but also as distinct. The distinction offered the government an opportunity to undermine Ansar al-Shari'a by substantively engaging local justice and security demands.

Yet the transitional government was not able to restore security or significantly undercut Ansar al-Shari'a, given the ongoing mutiny of the security sector amid the 'parallel revolution' and the political demands of the transitional process. Sarah Phillips argues that this failure was rooted at least in part by a USAID-backed approach to stabilization during the transitional period that emphasized development over attention to justice.[138] Able to mobilize a 'narrative of injustice' that blended local, especially Southern grievances and broader jihadist aims, Ansar al-Shari'a and AQAP spoke in a resonant language, focusing on forms of injustice seen to 'emanate from the political processes that are entrenched in the regime's core, not in its institutional or administrative failings.'[139] The issue of land expropriation—of particular resonance in the South—was central to militant recruitment appeals, as it signaled a kind of unresolved injustice from which poverty and underdevelopment emerged as a consequence. In this way, militants could dismiss stabilization efforts not only as foreign interference but as efforts to address symptoms without treating the underlying disease.

It was ultimately self-organized Popular Committees, not the Yemeni armed forces, that drove militants out of Abyan in 2012.

These groups have been described by Nadwa al-Dawsari as part of 'an indigenous movement whose mandate and function are rooted in and inspired by the tribal tradition of collective responsibility in which local men volunteer to maintain security in their communities.' At the same time, she is careful to note new features of the Popular Committees, where members included both tribesmen and non-tribesmen, and did not function as representatives of any particular tribe. They were local security providers, organized on the basis of their tie to a specific place, further emphasizing the centrality of land. Al-Dawsari notes that members of the Popular Committees find the term 'militia' to be 'offensive and derogatory, and one that does not fit with the positive things that they have been doing for their communities.'[140]

The Popular Committees were organized spontaneously and, in theory, temporarily. As al-Dawsari argues, 'as the militants withdrew, the PCs stepped in to establish order and protect public interests in those areas, with the hope that this would be a temporary arrangement until the government came back to resume responsibility.'[141] Instead, the government did not develop this capacity, and the Popular Committees instead demonstrated the utility of locally organized protection. The lesson of the Popular Committees acquired additional significance after the war in 2015 fractured any remaining sense of security, demonstrating to autochthonous Southern leaders, in particular, the power that could come from mobilizing sons of the soil.

The transitional government may not have been able to successfully address Southern security needs directly, but it did invest in targeted efforts to strategically engage widely held grievances in the South as a means of undercutting support for the ambitions of Southern secessionists and militant Islamists alike. As the draft transitional justice law failed to advance at the national level, President Hadi issued two presidential decrees in 2013 creating independent commissions to investigate and recommend compensation for victims of unjust land seizures and punitive dismissals of Southern military officers and civil servants in the aftermath of the 1994 war. The need to address these justice claims featured prominently among the recommendations that the Dialogue Preparatory

Committee submitted to President Hadi in August 2012, months before the commencement of the NDC.[142] Given the specter of militant mobilization around these grievances, the President issued decrees in January establishing two independent commissions— the Commission to Consider and Deal with Land-related Issues and the Commission to Address Issues of Employees Dismissed from Their Jobs in the Civil, Security, and Military Sectors. Rather than deferring these issues to the wider NDC deliberation over transitional justice, these two commissions operated independently of the concurrent national-level process. There was redundancy built into this approach, as the same justice demands addressed by the two commissions were also addressed in the draft law and discussed at the NDC, though they were not the sole focus of either.

Though each commission's mandate was set to expire within one year, neither could reasonably complete its work in such a timeframe, and both were at least partially overrun by the wider collapse of the transitional process by the end of 2014. The initial response to the Land Commission was tremendous, to the point of overwhelming its investigative capacity. More than 33,000 cases were opened within the first month after its website was launched, despite there being 'no comprehensive communications strategy prior to the start of the work,' suggesting that even this volume of cases may have underrepresented the number of potential claimants.[143] This contributed to the commissioners unilaterally expanding the scope of their mandate to land violations that occurred prior to 1990, a controversial decision that was retroactively, if only verbally, approved by President Hadi.

The Forcibly Retired Commission similarly began its work in isolation from other transitional justice mechanisms at the national level. It was tasked with identifying three categories of claimants: those who were forcibly retired from the military or civil service after 1994, the spouses of forced retirees who would otherwise have been entitled to their pension benefits, and those who were displaced from state-owned enterprises through privatization following unification in 1990. As with the Land Commission, President Hadi verbally authorized expansion of its mandate, and the commission further ensured that those whom it reinstated would be credited for the years between their dismissal and reinstatement for the purposes of calculating back wages and pensions.[144] From the point when the commission began accepting applications in March 2013 to the point at which its operations were suspended in May 2014, the commission processed over 150,000 applications and judged more than two-thirds of them to be valid claims.[145] While its work has been intermittent in the years since 2014, the Forcibly Retired Commission has remained operative to the present, in part because 'verifying whether forcibly retired employees were eligible for compensation turned out to be relatively easier than examining land-related cases.'[146]

This does not mean, however, that substantial compensation has been paid. In fact, recommended reparations were hampered by the lack of compensation mechanisms in the initial presidential decree establishing the commissions. Instead, both the President and the NDC General Secretary Ahmed Awadh bin Mubarak undertook diplomatic efforts to secure donor support for a compensation fund to address the recommendations of the two Southern commissions, further muddying the waters between different transitional justice channels being pursued at the national level and those related only to the South. While Qatar pledged 350 million dollars to support compensation in 2014, estimates based only on claims received by that point exceed one billion USD.[147] According to one member of the commission, by June 2016, small payments of 100,000YR (then about 336USD) had been issued to all valid claimants among the forcibly retired, constituting an unspecified 'part of their full compensation.'[148]

A 2021 evaluation by the European Institute for Peace (EIP) describes the results of the two commissions as mixed.[149] With a short timetable and deteriorating security and political conditions, it is not surprising that neither commission completed its work as planned. Nonetheless, researchers argue that there was popular enthusiasm for these transitional justice measures in Southern communities and high expectations for their success. This was met with a lack of political will at the center to carry through with the commissions' recommendations for compensation. It was further challenged by staff who received little or inadequate training, leaving investigators to rely on 'learning by doing' or else make use of established but inadequate legal practices and outdated modes of data collection.[150] While the individuals named to the commissions—the overwhelming majority of whom were from governorates in the South—were widely regarded as competent, they were also seen to be resistant to a number of techniques that could have facilitated greater outreach.[151] Legal professionals came out of a system in which regime interference was common and judicial institutions were generally weak,[152] Nonetheless, the Forcibly Retired Commission's use of civil judges to adjudicate claims regarding military dismissals were received as a 'good sign' of the commission's intent to genuinely engage justice claims.[153]

Both the EIP's evaluation and an earlier report from the Center for Applied Research in Partnership with the Orient (CARPO) indicate that the core grievances investigated by the commissions, resolved incompletely, will continue to be a source of justice claims in any future settlement, as I discuss in the next chapter. Land and property restitution was seen by the Yemeni government and external supporters of the GCCI as essential to securing the unity of a disintegrating state.[154] It is clear, however, that both in their failure to deliver on the recommended reparations and in the commissions' development through a parallel process of transitional justice operating outside of the center, that the bodies contributed to Yemen's disintegrative dynamics in the run-up to the current war. Given that the government pushed to 'swiftly complete' the work of the commissions, Yemenis in the South might reasonably have thought they had a greater likelihood of effective response through the Southern-only transitional justice mechanisms.[155] At a minimum, the work of the commissions was understood by some as a 'last chance' before civil war in the South.[156] Divestment from the national transitional justice process, however, furthered the impression that Southern grievances, or the harms experienced by Southerners, were unique to the South—and equally communicated to Northerners that abuses they may have experienced under the prior regime were considered comparatively inconsequential.

The End of the Transition (to War)

Yemen's transitional period arguably ended with the Houthis' takeover of Sana'a in September 2014, or at least with the agreement brokered days later by UN Special Envoy Jamal Benomar that normalized it. Signed at the barrel of a gun, the Peace and National Partnership Agreement negotiated away a significant share of Islah's power in the transitional government, gave the Houthis and the Hirak voice in the appointment of a new but largely incapacitated government, and effectively brought transitional governance to a dangerous standstill. When the UN imposed sanctions on Saleh and two Houthi leaders for their role as transitional spoilers, the GPC's response was to expel President Hadi from the party leadership, underlining the new president's political isolation and cementing the Houthi-Saleh alliance.[157]

Formally, some elements of the transitional process continued, though they acquired new meaning. The draft constitution was completed during this period of paralysis, despite the fact that its work was likely to be opposed by many quarters. Even when the drafting committee had been announced in March 2014, many of Yemen's core political factions (including the YSP and Islah) were unhappy with its composition, which procedurally violated core recommendations of the NDC and was substantially less representative than many expected.[158] The fact that the committee concluded its draft for the federal restructuring of the Yemeni state at a moment when significant portions of the country were outside of the reach of that state meant that the draft was almost guaranteed to provoke greater conflict. And it did.

Framed by the committee members as a fulfillment of recommendations made by the NDC, the draft constitution proposed what appeared to be a federal system but in fact was a system designed to maximize the unity of the Yemeni state, albeit with some notable federal characteristics.[159] It divided the country into six territorial units, none of which were contiguous areas controlled by the Houthis or by separatist Hirakis. Federal borders thus broke up concentrations of power and access to important material resources and infrastructure for both groups.[160] The electoral system prescribed by the draft constitution elected a lower house on the basis of proportional representation in a single national constituency, and overrepresented Sana'a and Aden in an upper house. While the six federal states would have powers greater than those of Yemen's existing governorates, the draft constitution was nonetheless designed to undermine the concentrated power of specific groups seen as threatening the territorial integrity of the state. The draft's divergence from NDC recommendations and the narrow representation of its drafters meant that when it was released in January 2015, it was read as a final provocation by the Houthi-Saleh coalition. Abrogating the Peace and National Partnership Agreement, they soon put Hadi under house arrest and took over the capital in earnest, ultimately prompting the President's escape to Aden, and from there, to Riyadh.

The war in Yemen is sometimes dated to March 26, 2015, when a Saudi-led coalition of forces began a military campaign to restore President Hadi and his government by force. With the benefit of hindsight, however, it is clear that the full decade since 2011 was marked by co-extensive armed conflict and civil action. More Yemenis died from acts of violence during Yemen's 'transitional' period than during the whole of the 2011 uprising. Many, many more have been killed since then. Does this mean that the war itself began in 2011? The Houthis might say that their war began in 2004. Hirakis might reach back to 1994, or even to unification. President Hadi issued an apology in 2013, in which he vaguely acknowledged the effects of both the Sa'ada wars and 'what the previous government did against the Southerners' during and after the 1994 war.[161] But the accumulation of decades of unresolved justice claims—and the development of new claims and new claimants that emerged in response to violations during the transitional period itself—has meant that such an act of recognition was too little, too late.

The fact that earlier and unresolved justice claims have been overshadowed by a catastrophic war makes them no less relevant to Yemen's future. Yet reading the transitional period as simply a prelude to the current war also minimizes this period's mixed record in relation to justice claims. During the transitional period, there were undoubtedly strategic engagements with justice, but there were also some meaningful substantive engagements, particularly through the NDC. This is undoubtedly why the transitional period—and the NDC in particular—remains an important and largely positive referent point for Yemeni civil actors today, despite the flaws that many identify with the process. Even as they acknowledge that it will not be possible to return to the *status quo ante* after years of punishing war and destruction, claims made and tools developed during the sustained mobilization of the uprising and the ensuing transitional period continue to shape the work of Yemeni peacebuilders today as they navigate the current conflict and endeavor to lay the foundations for a more peaceful—and more just—order.

The Transitional Period: A Capabilities Assessment

The period discussed in this chapter, which ranges from the 2011 uprising against the regime of President 'Ali 'Abdullah Saleh through to the internationally brokered transitional process and ending with Houthi militants' takeover of the capital in January 2015, offers a mixed record from a Capabilities standpoint. Participation in the shared experience of collective action allowed for the kind of opportunities for voice and for transpositional scrutiny that helped to refashion the identities of many Yemeni participants in an intersectional revolutionary movement. It laid ground for new solidarities that many civil actors in Yemen continue to exhibit, even after years of conflict. Some elements of the transitional framework built upon these changes, by allowing for greater political participation and representation than ever before—or since.

Other features of the transitional period were less constructive. They relied on flattening, quota-based or 'solitarist' understandings of belonging that asked Yemenis with plural commitments to speak from the standpoint of singular identities. Some were premised on forms of exclusion that hardened divisions or undermined the integrity of participatory institutions. The 8+8 negotiations and the existence of two parallel tracks of official engagement with justice demands stand out among the most visible examples. On the one hand, these institutional approaches recognized the way in which Hirakis were underrepresented in formal decision-making at the ministerial level under the terms of the transitional framework. On the other hand, they undermined the more inclusive national process at the NDC, and therefore perpetuated the idea that some voices matter more than others in determining the future of the Yemeni state.

Individual freedoms also deteriorated during the transitional period as a result of pervasive insecurity, representing a clear setback from a Capabilities standpoint. Theorists emphasize not only the necessity of certain basic capabilities and freedoms that facilitate meaningful life choices, but argue that these capabilities must be secure so that individuals can engage in planning and can work for the futures they imagine.[162] Significant parts of the country witnessed the erosion of physical security, not only during the uprising but throughout the transitional period, whether because of conflict with Houthi militias, the campaign against Ansar al-Shari'a, military infighting, the pervasive risk of drone strikes, or forms of violence with more local or idiosyncratic drivers. Yemenis as a whole also experienced a sharp decline in food security and had irregular access to basic infrastructure during this time.[163]

Institutions—whether organized as a part of the transitional process or emerging from civil society and through activist mobilization—offered plentiful opportunities for (especially urban) Yemenis to express voice and articulate justice demands. From a Capabilities standpoint, however, while voice is essential, it is not itself sufficient to expand human agency. Despite ongoing dissent through Yemen's 'parallel revolution' and other forms of ongoing contention throughout the transitional period, officials remained functionally unaccountable to many citizens, limiting the ability of Yemenis to shape outcomes that mattered to them. The interim President was able to work through old representative institutions—like the parliament, last elected in 2003—to advance impunity for Saleh and his closest associates while circumventing newer representative institutions—like the NDC—to advance priorities around which there was no national consensus. This lack of accountability and uneven inclusion fueled the popularity of transitional spoilers, and impunity allowed former President Saleh and his allies to further aid those who would undermine the transition. Dynamics built into the GCCI ensured its downfall, at immeasurable cost to Yemeni civilians and their well-being.

Using Deneulin's typology, however, it is clear that these liabilities were balanced, in part, by some important expansions of agency. As outlined in Chapter 1, Deneulin grounds agency in social processes that shape an individual's self-trust, self-respect, and self-esteem. Each of these is influenced by a different set of actors and institutions, and each has a connection to developments that occurred during the transitional period. Self-trust involves the ability to form for oneself a conception of the good, informing the nature of one's choices. The opportunities for interaction and development of solidarity among diversely situated activists in the context of popular mobilization shaped many Yemenis' conception of the good in new and richer ways, as evidenced by activist accounts of the expanded worldviews and diverse solidarities shaped through collective action.

Self-respect, by contrast, derives from legal recognition of one's value and rights by the state. Here the transitional period was perhaps more ambiguous. Certainly, the widespread rights violations that occurred at the hand of state actors during the uprising cut against this basis of agency. Yet the recognition in the GCCI of the need for more broadly representative institutions offered some foundation for expanded self-respect by recognizing the rights of specific groups or classes of individuals. Even if existing political elites captured the lion's share of transitional power, the naming of new groups as worthy of official recognition and representation expanded agency.

More than either of these expansions, however, the transitional period was profoundly significant in expanding agency through self-esteem, as Yemenis formed new associations, mobilized in their communities, and advanced justice claims through civil action. Dense forms of associational life that thrived despite (and, in some cases, because of) the insecurity of the transitional period afforded many civil actors and organizations recognition within the communities to which they contributed. As the next chapter will show, civil action—oriented during the transitional period toward tasks of representation and political reimagining—has taken new forms under conditions of war but remains a significant source of agency. Today, civil actors advance justice claims using means often described as or associated with peacebuilding.

5

IMAGINING JUST FUTURES
KNOWLEDGE-PRODUCTION, PEACEBUILDING, AND JUSTICE WORK

As previous chapters have shown, transitional justice mechanisms played a role in both engaging and undermining justice claims advanced by a range of Yemeni actors over the past three decades. The two decades from unification to the uprising featured a combination of regime disengagement and strategic engagement, while the period following the uprising was marked by a sharp disjuncture, with concurrent substantive and strategic engagements and active disengagement from justice demands. Those most empowered by the National Dialogue Conference continued to engage via national institutions and processes, while actors with less access engaged justice questions both through and outside of these channels.

This division has acquired new significance in light of the current war. Unless or until there is greater coordination in the direction of broad, substantive engagement with questions of post-conflict justice, most Yemenis are likely to see their concerns marginalized or ignored at the expense of the priorities of conflict actors. As Tarek Radwan has argued, 'even if the fighting stops tomorrow, the multitude of injustices against different groups by different perpetrators will leave lasting scars that require reconciliation to repair the social fabric and restore trust in state institutions.'[1] Notably, as this chapter shows, it is Yemen's civil actors—not conflict actors, nor international peace brokers—whose work is most explicitly directed toward seriously addressing these injustices through their everyday practices under conflict conditions.

This chapter draws on interviews with, observations of, and knowledge produced by civil actors from different parts of the country to show how civil action relates to the longer arc of justice engagement laid out in previous chapters and how such work addresses new justice demands that have emerged from the current conflict. I consider some of the barriers that currently exist to more fully reflecting the priorities and agency of civil actors in the peace process and focus on the role of Yemeni researchers in forms of knowledge-production that may help to bridge global and local approaches to sustainable peace.

A Brief Synopsis of the War in Yemen

Any overview of the current war is likely to be partial and inadequate, given that the conflict is ongoing. At the point of this writing, more than 150,000 Yemenis have been reported killed in the fighting since 2015, but the scope of destruction caused by the war—to people, to institutions, and to whatever remains of Yemeni society—far exceeds the death toll itself.[2] The aim of this section is to review the main contours of the conflict from 2015 to 2022, outline core features of the UN-led diplomatic process and the three tracks along which peace has been pursued, and identify some of the barriers to progress that have produced a protracted diplomatic stalemate. For several years, there has been broad agreement by Yemeni and non-Yemeni analysts that this is not a conflict that is likely to be settled militarily. Yet that has not stopped the war's most central antagonists from fighting. War is therefore the background against which the ongoing justice work of civil action occurs.

Events moved most quickly at the beginning of the war. After the Houthis and their allies displaced the internationally-recognized Government of Yemen (GoY) in January 2015, President Hadi fled the capital for Aden. On February 15, the United Nations Security Council condemned the Houthis' declaration of a Supreme Political Council to replace the Hadi government. Houthi militias and their allies then pursued their campaign southward, arriving in Aden by late March and prompting President Hadi to leave for Saudi Arabia. On March 26, a Saudi-led coalition of forces from several states (henceforth, the Coalition) launched a campaign to restore the government by force. Seven years later, this campaign is ongoing.

Pushing out of the capital, Houthi forces took control of the Red Sea port of Hodeidah and reached the city of Taiz in March 2015; the city has remained bitterly divided by rival militias ever since. On April 14, 2015, the UN Security Council issued Resolution 2216, imposing an arms embargo and calling on the Houthis to surrender and disarm. In the same month, Al Qaeda in the Arabian Peninsula (AQAP) capitalized on the disorder to take direct territorial control of the governorate of Hadramawt, which it held for the first year of the war before being driven out by a combined aerial and ground campaign under the leadership of the UAE.[3] As Southern forces pushed back the Houthis, the UAE's political priorities introduced an important cleavage in the Coalition. In an effort to limit the influence of Islah (and its ties to the Muslim Brotherhood), the Emiratis patronized *salafi* aligned militias in the South. At least some of the militants displaced from Hadramawt were absorbed by Southern militias who were eager to pursue the Houthis northward for a combination of regional identarian and ideological reasons.[4]

Throughout much of the war, a significant proportion of the government has been located outside of the country, which has had implications for its legitimacy and for the development of rival forms of local governance in different parts of the country. Houthi forces have controlled the city of Sana'a continuously since 2015 and have been able to institutionalize their rule there, absorbing elements of the pre-war bureaucracy and security sector and introducing new instruments of rule that are brutal, discriminatory, and have become progressively more unjust over the course of the conflict.[5] The displaced government was initially reconstituted in Aden, but the formalization of the Southern Transitional Council (STC) in 2017 and its parastatal control over the South's former capital have presented both symbolic and material challenges to GoY authority there, and the city has been effectively ceded to the STC. On Yemen's Red Sea coast, the Emiratis have supported militias under the control of Tareq Saleh, a relative of the former president and a patron of *salafi*-oriented fighters. The hostility of Tareq Saleh's forces and the STC toward Islah, which is a member party in the GoY and has ties to militias in a number of arenas of conflict, has contributed to ongoing conflict fragmentation and to fissures within the Coalition. Government work, to the extent that it can be said to be ongoing, has been based in a small number of areas, including Hadramawt and Marib, though the former is itself divided and the latter became a site of acute military pressure from the Houthis in 2021.[6]

The United Nations established the Office of the Special Envoy to the Secretary General for Yemen (OSESGY) in 2012, but the role and function of this position has changed over the course of the war, as has the person occupying the position. The office was initially created to oversee the implementation of the Gulf Cooperation Council Initiative (GCCI), according to the terms of UN Security Council Resolution (UNSCR) 2014 (2011) and 2051 (2012).[7] Since 2015, however, the office has been reoriented by UN Security Council Resolution 2216, the guiding resolution that authorizes the war in Yemen and which has had an outsized impact on the peace process, as I discuss below.

The OSESGY's work has been organized along three concurrent 'peace tracks.' Track I entails the formal brokering of negotiations between the GoY and representatives of the Houthis. According to UNSCR 2216, these are the war's principals, and negotiations should help to produce an agreement that leads to the full restoration of the internationally recognized Yemeni government and the complete demobilization and disarmament of the Houthis. Track I efforts are supplemented by informal negotiations and dialogue that occurs along Track II, with influential representatives of stakeholder groups identified by OSESGY.[8] For example, the Youth Peace and Security Pact and the Women's Peace and Security Pact (Tawafuk) represent women and youth as Track II actors. Track III is generally where inclusive peacebuilding processes are meant to occur, with a wide range of civil actors engaged in dialogue and representation.[9] As one

OSESGY staff member explained, however, a substantial constraint on Track III is that it must operate according to the logic of UNSCR 2216, which has a particular binary understanding of the war as one between the GoY and the Houthis, meaning that civil action by individuals and organizations that fall outside of this scope may not reach the OSESGY's attention or receive its support.[10]

Track I negotiations have yielded very limited gains since the beginning of the war and have generated substantial frustration among Track III civil actors engaged in peacebuilding work. Despite earlier talks in Geneva and Kuwait, no Track I agreement was successfully negotiated until the Stockholm Agreement was signed at the end of 2018. In the months prior, Emirati and Saudi-backed militias intensified their campaign in Hodeidah, leading to a dramatic uptick in violence. Fighting in Hodeidah constituted close to 40 percent of the casualties reported for 2018.[11] Amid global pressure for negotiations that could prevent the closure of the port and the worsening of humanitarian suffering, the agreement included provisions related to the port of Hodeidah, the stalemate in Taiz, and a plan for a prisoner exchange. While awaiting its implementation, however, tensions within the Coalition became more acute, necessitating the Riyadh Agreement a year later. This agreement was designed to paper over the differences between the STC and the GoY in order to present a common front against the Houthis and enable the implementation of the Stockholm Agreement.

To date, neither agreement has been fully implemented, nor has the comprehensive ceasefire plan known as the Joint Declaration, a draft of which was leaked by the Special Envoy's office in 2020; it attracted considerable criticism from civil actors for reiterating weaknesses of the Stockholm framework.[12] In the words of one Track II negotiator, while those overseeing Track I and II negotiations have been gradually reckoning with conflict fragmentation, formal agreements addressing the war in Yemen have largely been 'belated reactions to stuff that happened 2-3 years ago.'[13] Just before Ramadan in 2022, however, a limited two-month ceasefire was announced— the first in six years—and President Hadi transferred power to an eight-member Presidential Council, raising hope that new options for Track I peacebuilding might emerge.[14]

Whether or not such options materialize, no discussion of the war would be complete without some accounting of the catastrophic humanitarian crisis it has generated. While this deserves (and has received) much attention in its own right, the humanitarian crisis has had a direct impact on the peace process and the work of civil actors engaged in peacebuilding, which I detail below. Before the war, entrenched poverty and declining security had already left many parts of Yemen perilously close to famine but major developments during the war have exacerbated already-bad conditions substantially. These include the impact of internal displacement, the closure of ports and roads, 'taxes' on food and medicine at checkpoints manned by conflict actors, and the collapse of civil service salaries following the relocation of Yemen's Central Bank in 2016.[15] The humanitarian crisis in Yemen is primarily a man-made artifact of war. Regulations on the movement of people and goods and the collapse of Yemeni purchasing power are the core drivers of hunger.[16] The politicization of aid distribution by all conflict actors is well-documented, and revenues generated by black market trade have helped entrench Yemen's war economy.[17] The COVID-19 pandemic has intensified the crisis further, given the damaged health infrastructure, crowded conditions and displacement, and the health effects of years of deprivation.[18] The situation in Yemen is genuinely and abjectly horrible in many ways. An end to the war will not miraculously resolve Yemen's humanitarian crisis, but the continuation of the conflict will surely escalate it further.

Civil Action, Effective Citizenship, and Peacebuilding

Whether despite or because of these conditions, civil actors across the country do the everyday work of holding their communities together. As outlined in earlier chapters, civil action requires both a commitment to pursue objectives through non-violent means but also a minimum recognition of the rights of one's adversaries. The 'mere civility' that civil actors exhibit as they pursue their objectives does not require that they avoid difficult subjects or deep disagreements, but only that they avoid exclusionary rhetoric associated with more confrontational modes of civil resistance. It is 'broader [than civil resistance] because it also includes less conflictual engagement with various stakeholders—legally and illegally, institutionally or extra-institutionally.'[19] Non-violence is definitionally central to civil action, but it is this non-exclusionary aspect that is most important for the character of the change that civil action seeks to produce and to its ability to contribute to sustainable peace and reconciliation.

'Mere civility' is not an intrinsic property of all non-violent collective action. Some civil society organizations (CSOs) and less formal, even ad hoc, providers of community services may not exhibit this essential characteristic of civil action; exclusionary rhetoric or practice—including the politicization of access to aid, access to programming, sectarian or identarian programing that is oriented toward an in-group, even incendiary tweets—means that some organizations' non-violent work may not meet the threshold of mere civility and should not be considered a form of civil action. However, much of the work being done by local activists, CSO staff, and other Yemeni non-combatants does display both definitional characteristics of civil action. Such work is often considered a component of peacebuilding insofar as it is aimed at goals articulated in the United Nations' peacebuilding architecture, including not only 'preventing the outbreak, escalation, continuation, and recurrence of conflict,' but also promoting reconciliation and 'moving toward recovery, reconstruction, and development.'[20]

Some civil action in Yemen occurs as a component of what scholars have critically described as 'Peace, Inc.,' or the 'global project' of liberal peacebuilding.[21] To the extent that Yemeni civil actors work on projects funded by international peacebuilding organizations, they have become proficient in the language of the international peacebuilding industry. While many acknowledge the impact of donor agendas on their organization's work, such partnerships do not entirely efface Yemeni agency; as one practitioner explained, experienced actors and organizations working with peacebuilding donors, 'have learned how to negotiate with donors and resist top-down donor dictates.'[22] Other civil actors do work that they may not describe as peacebuilding, though it advances the objectives of positive peace. In some cases, as I discuss below, this is because civil actors encounter explicit and implicit constraints on peacebuilding work and choose different labels to describe their work. But it is also because civil action often reflects quotidian forms of problem-solving drawing on different terms of reference in sometimes hyperlocal contexts.

Amid the country's fragmentation, civil action—like forms of public provision, security, and more—has taken on an increasingly local character. This has allowed for the development of what international peacebuilding organization Search for Common Ground calls 'pockets of stability' and resembles what Séverine Autesserre describes as the 'pieces of peace' that can develop from below.[23] Such local successes can help to build effective citizenship and, if integrated into a 'peace learning' approach, can support sustainable peacebuilding and justice work concurrently. As Susan Campbell's work on international peacebuilding shows, national-level or international actors who learn from, integrate, and build upon positive experiences of effective citizenship in local communities will be better positioned to support post-conflict institutions with the kind of legitimacy they need to function effectively and secure peace.[24] This is not the same thing as international peacebuilding organizations promoting local ownership, which still reflects a top-down logic, but begins with practices of effective citizenship and justice work advanced locally.

Effective citizenship itself has a powerful conceptual connection to justice. As described in Chapter 1, effective citizenship is best understood as 'the actual capacity of citizens to make use of formal and civic political rights,' and has been both unevenly distributed and far from secure in Yemen.[25] The expansion of effective citizenship would entail eroding entrenched social inequalities that uphold informal and formal systems of subordination. Local justice work has the capacity to do this in some places and for some people, though this relationship is not automatic.

The gap between the rights of citizens of Yemen's republic on paper and their practical experience of rights-bearing has been a significant focus of justice claims across the period described in this book. By the onset of the war, fragmentation had already produced a terrain in which there were 'de facto different rights for different groups across the country, as well as possibilities for different strength and ability to legally contest violations of these rights.'[26] The war has only intensified and entrenched this fragmentation. As the previous chapters have shown, many of the core justice claims of Yemeni actors—whether met with disengagement, strategic engagement, or substantive engagement—have explicitly or implicitly focused on calls for greater effective citizenship. The desire to be recognized by state and society as deserving of equal dignity cuts across justice claims. The continuing centrality of the National Dialogue Conference in the political imagination of many civil actors today affirms the notion that effective citizenship is viewed as a central and necessary remedy to a wide range of abuses faced by individuals and by groups. Local peacebuilding work is often directed at such de facto expansions of effective citizenship and agency, even in the absence of a national political settlement.

In 2020, I worked with two Yemeni colleagues on a project commissioned by an international peacebuilding organization which included mapping hundreds of CSOs engaged in peacebuilding work across the country.[27] These were formally registered organizations, but responses from our interviews and survey suggest that a far larger number of projects likely exist. In a series of focus group discussions conducted in areas facing different conflict conditions, we were repeatedly told of formal and informal limits on peacebuilding work carried out by civil actors that drive such an undercounting. Respondents in areas under the control of both the Houthi authorities and forces commanded by Tareq Saleh, for example, reported explicit prohibitions on peacebuilding as 'political work,' prompting them to register their work under different rubrics and/or carry out small projects without registering with any authority. One respondent described the Houthis as treating peacebuilders like 'they work for intelligence agencies,' while another argued that the STC is 'discriminatory' in the limits it imposes in its areas and considers peacebuilding CSOs to be fronts for Islah, recalling animosities from the Saleh era that have extended to the present.[28] The substantive politics of concern may differ by conflict actor and area, but the clear lesson is that civil action framed as peacebuilding is viewed by at least some conflict actors as threatening.

In addition to the direct risks of violence or material retaliation from conflict actors, Yemen's civil actors must contend with the consequences of a humanitarian crisis of unfathomable proportions— one that affects the needs and capacities of their communities, but also of themselves and their families. Moreover, the humanitarian crisis has shaped the relationship of donors to Yemeni peacebuilders; despite donors' rhetoric of inclusion and local ownership, Yemeni civil actors repeatedly describe donor pressure to adopt roles as distributors of aid for donor projects and programs designed by outsiders, and lament that while they are sometimes consulted, they are rarely invited to participate in shared decision-making.[29]

This is a part of why, despite its flaws, the NDC remains a powerful symbolic touchstone for many civil actors in Yemen. International observers and those involved in facilitating Track II and III dialogue sometimes express frustration with what they see as the NDC's outsized role in civil actors' imagined futures. As one put it, the NDC may be a rhetorically useful starting point, but reflects 'a Yemen that, for all intents and purposes, no longer exists.' Instead, he continued, the NDC contributed to 'Sana'a-centric processes that characterized pre-war diplomacy … and effectively paved the way for the Houthis to gradually take over northern Yemen while everyone was focused on the proceedings of a bunch of meetings taking place in the conference rooms of a five star hotel.'[30] This critique makes some sense to me, which is why I found it so puzzling that the NDC outcomes continue to be cited as a 'starting point' by so many civil actors, even those who have been deeply critical of the NDC and other features of the transitional process. If it was flawed, what makes it so important to the way people imagine pursuing justice?

It is important to distinguish civil actors' focus on the NDC from the wider context of the transitional period. According to staff at Mwatana for Human Rights, one of Yemen's most widely recognized rights organizations, 'all of the warring parties are very aware of what happened in the GCC deal and they expect that as a bare minimum, they will get the same if not more protection.'[31] The impunity institutionalized by the GCCI has set expectations that current conflict actors will be afforded immunity for crimes that have occurred during the war and those that precede it; civil actors, by contrast, cite the need to return to the recommendations for transitional justice and accountability issued by the NDC, many of which would implicate these same actors. In the eyes of one mediator, while there is a 'general reluctance to reckon with how fundamentally the country has changed,' international peace-brokers do not take adequate account of Yemen's historical context in efforts to understand the current conflict.[32] That context includes the history of engagement with justice demands.

The central place of the NDC as an example of substantive and historically grounded engagement with justice in the future imaginings of civil actors might be read as unrealistic or nostalgic, but an alternative interpretation is also possible. The NDC was premised on forms of mere civility that afforded civil actors with deep disagreements greater opportunities to shape outcomes than any form of participatory decision-making at the national level—before or since. As one independent youth delegate to the NDC reflected:

> [L]ike any other process, you know, you can always make the argument that it could have been better. There's always room for improvement. However, in the whole period of the Yemen's recent history, and at least if I go from the period from 1990 onwards when the multiparty system was announced, there hasn't been any process that has been more inclusive than the National Dialogue.[33]

In describing a 'return to the NDC outcomes,' civil actors like this one are gesturing toward a period of unprecedented agency. Whereas critics have tended to view the NDC as a flawed exercise in voice over decision-making, its repeated resurfacing among civil actors today suggest that it means something more. Understanding this recurrence is important for considering future pathways for the pursuit of justice through civil action.

How Conflict Shapes Civil Action

As Yemen's civil actors seek to engage with others on the basis of mere civility and employ practices that expand effective citizenship at different scales, they do so under the profoundly uncivil conditions of war. The primary effects of the war on civil action can be broken into four categories, each of which has had bearing—in uneven ways in different parts of the country—on the focus and reach of civil action in the context of the war in Yemen. These include:

- Fragmentation
- Securitization
- Polarization
- Humanitarianization.

In the context of these four interlocking processes, peacebuilding aims have been advanced through myriad local-level projects and practices of civil actors; their successes have concurrently advanced peacebuilding but have also sometimes contributed to the centrifugal pull of the Yemen's unplanned, de facto decentralization. This has been one of the most consistent features of the current war and poses a challenge to any kind of post-war political settlement, whether or not the war ultimately marks 'the end of Yemen.'[34]

Fragmentation

While the process of fragmentation began before the 2015, the current war has divided Yemen's territory and its sense of shared peoplehood in ways that are quite profound. At a material level, the country has been divided into areas with often dramatically different local conflict conditions. Three years into the war, a former member of the UN's Panel of Experts described it as three distinct wars; by 2021, he had upgraded his estimate to seven.[35] Regardless of specific enumeration, there is a clear consensus among analysts of the war in Yemen that the operative issues, central actors, and forms of combat differ substantially across the country—and that these differences are only multiplying as the war extends.

Cross-national research shows that conflict fragmentation makes it much more difficult to negotiate successful agreements and can extend the duration of armed conflict.[36] Relatively few civil conflicts are characterized by dyadic regime-opposition dynamics, and opposition groups (and regimes) often function as composite actors whose constituent parts may adopt divergent tactics concurrently.[37] Fragmented oppositions can sometimes leverage regime fears of disintegration to secure concessions, but these concessions themselves often contribute to peace frameworks that are unsustainable or lead to relapsing conflict.[38] All of these dynamics are evident in Yemen.

What unites analyses of conflict fragmentation in Yemen is often a frustration with the UN-led peace process underwritten by Security Council Resolution (2216). International organizations and actors guided by this framework approach the question of peace through the lens of the war between the Houthis and the internationally recognized GoY despite clear evidence that the conflict is far more variegated. The framework established by UNSCR 2216 predates some of the most significant fragmentation, most notably the 2017 declaration by members of the Hirak of the STC as a shadow Southern government. Having secured the support of the United Arab Emirates, the entrenchment of the STC, especially in Aden, has significantly altered the course of the war and introduced a major division within a coalition that is at least theoretically aligned together against the Houthis. Additional fragmentary dynamics exist along the Red Sea coast, where forces loyal to Tareq Saleh—also supported by the UAE, but mobilized more through *salafi* ideology than regionalism—exhibit loyalty to neither the GoY nor the STC in their own battle against the Houthis and their allies. The far eastern province of al-Mahra, which has remained largely 'untouched by the conflict between the Houthis and their opponents, and far from the Northern Zaydi insurgents' radars' has nonetheless become another arena of 'collateral militarization' by rival members of the Coalition itself.[39] Hadramawt, meanwhile, with its history of regional distinctiveness, has experienced dramatic shifts, falling under the territorial control of AQAP for the first year of the war and since 2016 experiencing a period of protracted calm that has enabled something like regular political life to resume.[40] But even here, fractures were emerging by late 2021 between the Saudi-supported GoY and local Hadrami Elite forces backed by the UAE.[41]

Track I negotiations have struggled to adapt to a fragmenting conflict in which a significant and growing number of actors 'have repeatedly declared that they will reject any settlement in which the UN has given them no say.'[42] Over the course of seven years, the UN-led process has produced only three agreements—the 2018 Stockholm Agreement and the 2019 Riyadh Agreement, neither of which has been fully implemented by the time of this writing, and a temporary ceasefire in April 2022. The very need for the Riyadh Agreement, which was designed to 'mend the fractures within the anti-Houthi alliance' by directly engaging the STC, shows instead how easily conflict fragmentation can outpace or otherwise derail diplomacy.[43] A unilateral Coalition ceasefire in April 2020 was followed by the UN Special Envoy's plan for a comprehensive and negotiated ceasefire known as the Joint Declaration, which proved difficult to fully realize and has faced considerable criticism both for failing to reckon realistically with conflict fragmentation and for failing to address core justice demands from civil actors.[44] Amid a highly fragmented multi-actor conflict, peacebuilding has remained anchored to an international diplomatic framework that has been described as 'increasingly anachronistic' or even 'fanciful,' by mediators themselves.[45]

The reality of conflict fragmentation shapes what civil actors identify as the core issues in their communities, the resources that are available to them, and their capacities for action. For example, across all areas, women report the devastating impact of economic crisis as a driver of conflict and a source of militant recruitment. What this means in different localities differs, however, as do the ways women engage in peacebuilding. In 2019, women in a rural community outside of Sana'a, for example, devoted resources to the construction of a gender-segmented space in which they could market home-produced goods, offset economic pressures on their families, and address drivers of child recruitment by the Houthis. They negotiated with tribal authorities to secure permission for the project and avoided addressing Houthi authorities directly. In an equally rural part of Lahj, by contrast, women sought to change social attitudes toward women's economic participation by filling vacancies in male-dominated fields and sought the support of STC authorities in doing so.[46] In Sana'a in 2020, professional class women organized and arranged construction of a multifunction space for women, with a conference room, computing center, library, on-site childcare, an indoor children's recreation space, and a gym. It is, in effect, a kind of co-working space that can function within the framework of increased gender segregation enforced by Houthi authorities while enabling women to build community, maintain professional networks, and contribute to both income-generation and knowledge-production, as I discuss below. The broad range of such projects underscore the fact that there is no single portrait of civil action because there is no single set of conflict conditions or community needs.

On the positive side, fragmentation constitutes a kind of 'unplanned decentralization' that has the capacity to enhance the effective citizenship of at least some Yemenis under some conditions.[47] Gains of this sort appear most possible in areas that are neither frontlines in armed conflict nor, interestingly, areas where governing authorities have restored or developed existing institutions.[48] But fragmentation also raises considerable coordination challenges for peacebuilders who would like to scale their work up to the national (or even governate) level. Staff at CSOs report difficulty coordinating programming or organizational work across territorial divisions. Technology enables some coordination but can be unreliable, and differences in both formal rules and informal limits on CSO activity across conflict areas constrain the kind of work that is possible. When Coalition airstrikes hit critical infrastructure in January 2022, the entire country was knocked offline for four days.[49] This kind of large-scale disruption made international headlines in a way that pervasive but more localized disruptions rarely do. Under sometimes wildly different local circumstances, CSOs with branches in different parts of the country unsurprisingly find it difficult to carry out 'national' projects. CSOs that operate in a single area, meanwhile, find it difficult to access national-level dialogue processes and express frustration that Track III actors are offered, at best, a consultative role. All of this limits the extent to which Yemen's civil actors can ensure that their priorities are reflected in any negotiated settlement and curtails their effective citizenship.

Civil actors' relations to various local authorities differ as well. In Hadramawt, for example, where the GoY is quite firmly entrenched, there are robust public–private partnerships capable of fueling reconstruction and underwriting civil actors' projects.

Some semblance of normal political life has been facilitated by the relative stability of the area since 2016.[50] In Aden, where the GoY is nominally in control but the STC functionally governs, civil actors report jurisdictional confusion, redundancy, and physical insecurity. This is nonetheless where many international organizations now base their operations. Relocating operations from Sana'a to Aden after 2015 has created opportunities for Yemeni civil actors to engage with international organizations. On the other hand, some Adenis complain that it remains difficult to access these organizations, which prefer to work with relocated elites who moved to Aden from Sana'a and have sought to reconstitute their social networks there.[51] Civil actors in areas under the control of Ansar Allah, or the Houthis, are increasingly limited in what they can do, must navigate a labyrinthine and politicized permit system, and even report fear that their colleagues will report them to the authorities if their work crosses red lines.[52] The imposition of new limits on women's mobility in Houthi-controlled areas, in particular, significantly shape options for civil action. In al-Mokha, staff at local peacebuilding organizations report explicit limits on their work imposed by Tareq Saleh's forces, who disallow work carried out by people they associate with Islah. The specific dynamics in each area differ and remain fluid but the fact of material and political limits on civil action is shared, as are the challenges civil actors face in connecting projects across Yemen's diverse conflict landscape.

One additional consequence of the disconnect between the UN-led process and the kinds of work done by civil actors under a wide range of local conditions is that it makes it more difficult to constructively connect or vertically integrate the various peace tracks. This is a persistent theme in discussions with civil actors—perhaps the most persistent theme of all. Whereas civil society organizations are considered possible Track III partners who can help to make the peace process more 'inclusive,' in reality, civil actors complain that it has been very difficult to establish meaningful linkages. Staff at the OSESGY acknowledge that Track I functions largely autonomously of the other two, and while they 'welcome' linkages with Track III civil actors, the work of local peacebuilders and civil actors is 'not always relevant to Track I,' where the most consequential decisions are made. The Special Envoy's office, moreover, can only support or engage with initiatives that operate within the narrow scope of UNSCR 2216.[53] These constraints are well-recognized by civil actors, who express frustration at their limited opportunities to communicate the priorities of non-combatants or shape the outcome of negotiations.

Securitization

The war has also deepened the preexisting tendency by non-Yemeni actors—in the Gulf region, certainly, but also in Europe and North America—to approach Yemen through the lens of regional (in) security. Research on the war itself contributes to this. As I discuss in greater detail below, knowledge-production related to Yemen has ballooned during the conflict but is narrowly oriented toward mapping core conflict dynamics and rendering groups and territories legible to an audience with little prior interest in or knowledge of Yemen's internal dynamics. 'Proxy war' narratives abound in the security community, exacerbating the core weakness of the formal diplomatic approach to the conflict in Yemen. If UNSCR 2216 is defined by a binarism that defines the war as GoY-Houthi, substituting an equally binary competition between Saudi Arabia and Iran is not an improvement. Such an approach renders longstanding justice demands identified in the previous chapters and current efforts to hold conflict actors accountable to civilians reasonably irrelevant to a significant component of the policy community in Europe and North America. This is particularly true in those states that have supported the Coalition's military campaign through arms sales and logistical support.[54]

There is absolutely no question that Saudi Arabia and Iran—and several other regional states—have played and continue to play a significant role in shaping the war in Yemen.[55] Indeed, they have contributed to the conflict fragmentation described above through direct and indirect military engagement and both material and diplomatic support for different factions on the ground. Their involvement in the conflict—but absence from the authorizing resolution that frames diplomacy—sets back efforts to broker peace. That said, the proxy war framing of Yemen as a contest between Iran and Saudi Arabia neither accounts for the conflict's emergence from Yemen's own political ecosystem, nor reckons with the consequences of important internal fissures within the coalition.

It also fails to account for some apples-and-oranges differences in the nature of external involvement. For example, Iranian support has taken material form—including the transfer of ballistic missiles—as well as forms of ideological and organizational influence and diplomatic recognition of the Houthi government. Saudi Arabia's approach has included a combination of airstrikes, patronage to diversely aligned local militias, and sponsorship of some intra-Yemeni diplomacy. The Emiratis, meanwhile, first committed (and later partially withdrew) ground forces and intelligence services.[56] Each of these interventions is significant; international support for rival Yemeni factions has not only slowed UN-led diplomacy designed to broker a Yemeni agreement but has even necessitated intra-Coalition diplomacy (and contributed to its breakdown). Qatar was in the original coalition in 2015, expelled in 2017 as part of the Gulf Crisis, and in 2021 received Yemen's foreign minister in Doha as part of a broader Gulf normalization. Oman's neutrality—criticized sometimes virulently by its Gulf Cooperation Council (GCC) neighbors—has provided an essential back channel for substantive negotiations.[57] Collectively, this shows that a binary 'Saudi Arabia vs. Iran' framing fails to capture the complexity of the international dimensions of the war in Yemen, as well.

More insidiously, however, securitization and proxy war framing direct attention away from important forms of Yemeni agency and push justice demands to the side. While many of the war's injustices have been the result of direct or indirect military action taken by outside actors, Yemeni conflict actors have and are continuing to carry out gross violations for reasons of their own, abuses that Yemeni rights organizations endeavor to document and for which civil actors hope to hold them to account. Moreover, regional and international actors work against accountability-oriented justice work by Yemeni civil actors, undermining documentation efforts and campaigns for legal accountability and taking action to advance impunity.

This became particularly clear and unapologetic in 2021. In December 2020, the UN Human Rights Council's Group of

Eminent Experts (GEE) for Yemen, building upon documentation provided by Yemeni civil actors, briefed the UN Security Council on its ongoing investigations. In his remarks before the council, GEE chair Kamel Jendoubi argued that the group had 'confirmed rampant levels of serious violations of international human rights law and international humanitarian law, many of which may amount to war crimes.'[58] The GEE therefore recommended that the Security Council refer parties to the war, including states that supply weapons to the Coalition and to Yemeni groups, to the International Criminal Court (ICC).

As a staff member at a prominent Yemeni human rights organization explained, the GEE focused on state actors not because the Houthis carried out fewer violations, but because members of the Coalition and those who equip them are more legally accessible.

> If you're talking about who you want to be in front of a court or to be in front of a justice mechanism, it's probably not, you know, whatever bureaucrat exports arms. It's probably people within the Ansar Allah armed group or the Saudi Air Force.[59]

At the same time, she continued, the GEE's recommendation reflected the realities of access, and the difficulty of pursuing legal channels against a non-state actor whose properties and personnel are almost exclusively housed in Yemen. Instead, she and other rights workers viewed the GEE's call to refer members of the Coalition and their suppliers to the ICC as means of pressuring North American and European actors to support renewed efforts to bring about a negotiated settlement.

After the European parliament called on member states to use universal jurisdiction to hold parties accountable outside of the ICC context in February 2021, the GEE and its investigatory work itself became targets of securitization by external parties to the conflict and their allies.[60] Using a combination of threats and inducements to shape the outcome of the United Nations Human Rights Council's vote to renew the GEE's mandate, members of the Saudi-led coalition successfully brought the body's fact-finding mission to an end.[61] As Dutch Ambassador to the UN, Peter Bekker, said on the day of the vote, 'with this vote, the council has effectively ended its reporting mandate; it has cut this lifeline of the Yemeni people to the international community.'[62] In early December, more than 90 representatives of over 60 Yemeni rights organizations and international allies addressed the General Assembly, calling for the creation of an alternative body housed at that level.[63] The fate of this initiative is still to be determined.[64] What is clear is that the period following the dissolution of the GEE saw a sharp increase in civilian casualties from Coalition airstrikes, a reality that the Yemen Data Project attributes to a climate of international impunity.[65]

Polarization

In addition to the fragmentation of the conflict and the securitization of justice demands, the polarizing effects of the war in Yemen on the country's social fabric cannot be overstated. While earlier chapters have sought to complicate characterizations of the conflict in Yemen as sectarian in origin, conflict dynamics have unquestionably furthered the process of sectarianization. Yemeni civil actors often express concerns about this as one of several ways in which social cohesion is eroding—at the national level, certainly, but even in local communities. Internal displacement, which is one of the durable features of the conflict, has exacerbated this erosion and may have a lasting legacy on the geographies of difference that come to characterize post-conflict Yemen.

Polarization—whether sectarian, regional, or otherwise—has been fueled by an utterly fragmented and highly partisan media.[66] Houthi and Islahi media are particularly virulent sources of misinformation, disinformation, and inflammatory rhetoric, amplified by social media.[67] Such media also play a role in campaigns of targeted harassment that deter (or at least seek to deter) civil actors who engage in peacebuilding work. Women engaged in civil action complain of smear campaigns that target their reputations and impugn their character in ways that are very personally damaging and that amplify the physical risks they face.[68] For example, women engaged in mediating prisoner releases—both for prisoners randomly abducted and for political detainees held by different conflict actors—report direct threats of physical and sexual violence, as well as smear campaigns to discredit their reputations and jeopardize their positions in their communities.[69] To the extent that community recognition has an impact on individual agency, the costs of such campaigns for the agency of civil actors can be significant. While feminist social networks have mobilized in clandestine ways to help some women in jeopardy, their reach has thus far been limited.[70]

Polarization, however, is not only sectarian or gendered, but also regional and ideological. The UAE's emergence as a regional patron of the STC and Security Belt forces has contributed to protracted conflict in the South. So have other intra-South divisions, such as those between Abyan and Shabwa, where UAE-backed forces aligned with the STC clashed with those loyal to the government.[71] Since the drawdown of Emirati forces in 2019, the UAE has adopted an indirect strategy that the UN Panel of Experts identified as driven by three concurrent aims—combatting the Houthis, limiting the reach of Islah, and suppressing terrorist violence. Forces that it supports have clashed with rivals aligned with Islah well outside of the South, in Taiz and along Yemen's Red Sea coast.[72] Emirati support for *salafi*-oriented militias, in particular, reflects the UAE's own discomfort with the role of Muslim Brotherhood influence among Islahis and has had the effect of polarizing Sunni Islamists, now divided between those who are more closely aligned with the GoY (Islahis, primarily) versus Southern *salafi* factions.[73] While both oppose the Houthis in different theaters of the war, they also remain in conflict with one another in Aden and, increasingly, in other parts of the South, including Hadramawt.

The sharp end of polarization includes assassination, forced disappearance, and other acts of targeted violence against civilians. Such violence both reflects the kind of fragmentation described above but also entrenches the polarization of society around existing cleavages. As the UN Panel of Experts explained in its 2021 report to the Security Council, 'all parties continue to commit egregious violations of international humanitarian law and international human rights law, including indiscriminate attacks against civilians, enforced disappearances and torture.'[74] In areas under their control, Houthi militias use ordinance and land mines that disproportionately harm civilians, while they tighten repression of journalists and rights activists who might document or report on such crimes. In Aden, the putative home of the internationally recognized government, car bomb explosions have targeted journalists, missiles have been fired at government officials, and individuals have disappeared off the streets. Southern Security Belt forces have carried out 'retaliatory' attacks against civilians who are known to be or simply suspected of being from the North.[75] The object of such retaliation can be read in both its immediate and historical contexts concurrently. These and other examples of Yemen's polarization are why one former member of the UN Panel of Experts concluded that 'as painful as this is to say,' he no longer believes that Yemen will emerge from the current conflict as a single country.[76]

Humanitarianization

Alongside these risks, those who want to engage in reconciliation work face additional barriers stemming from the overwhelming scope of the humanitarian crisis. Across the country, civil actors engaged in peacebuilding work describe being driven explicitly or implicitly toward humanitarian service provision by donor organizations whom they believe place little value on the work of reconciliation.[77] The scope of the humanitarian crisis in Yemen—already acute in some areas during the transitional period—is difficult to convey. It is something that weighs on every Yemeni interlocutor I have spoken with over the course of the war and there is little question that need far overwhelms available resources and institutions. While crisis-level conditions existed in parts of the country during the transitional period and there were major protection needs even before the 2011 uprising, the war adds to these factors extensive internal displacement, the collapse of civil service salaries, and the development of a war economy that benefits core conflict actors.[78]

The humanitarian crisis has shaped the possibilities for civil actors engaged in peacebuilding, pushing them in the direction of direct aid provision and/or needs assessment for aid agencies. Research conducted by the Sana'a Center for Strategic Studies indicated that 'the UN security framework as it is applied in Yemen and managed by the UN Department of Safety and Security (UNDSS) has played a significant role in limiting international aid workers' ability to tend to needs where they exist.'[79] One of the consequences of this has been pressure from international donors on Yemeni civil actors to realign their own work to assist aid agencies in providing services that international agencies cannot otherwise easily provide. Given the disproportionate impact of humanitarian suffering on Yemeni women, it is something that women are particularly engaged in addressing through various channels.[80] This reallocation of work and expertise has consequences for civil actors, insofar as it saps the Yemeni peacebuilding sector of staff and resources and works to transform the nature of Yemeni agency, as I explore in the next section.

The humanitarianization of peacebuilding is both reflected in and driven by the humanitarian-development-peace nexus articulated by the UN's 2030 Agenda for Sustainable Development. My own conversations with civil actors over the past several years exhibit Yemenis' explicit awareness of 'the nexus' and a need to align their work with its priorities, though activist assessments of humanitarianization have varied somewhat based on the conflict conditions they face and their own positionality. The starkest critique of humanitarianization has come from civil actors working in organizations or on projects devoted to documentation, accountability, and reconciliation. These are people who have developed specific skills and capacities related to one kind of work and describe being pressed by donor agendas to do something they see as quite different. While not indifferent to human suffering, some see this shift as a loss for peacebuilding and justice, arguing that 'peace cannot be achieved through food baskets.'[81]

To some extent, this is about the specific skills of different civil actors, but it is also about attributions of cause and effect. Yemenis in the peacebuilding field tend to view the humanitarian crisis as an effect of the war itself and therefore want to direct their work at the drivers of conflict.[82] In interviews and focus groups, women are sometimes less critical of humanitarianization, pointing to gendered effects of the humanitarian crisis that make addressing needs justice work in its own right. But even among such women, there is a keen awareness that directing civil action toward humanitarian relief does not straightforwardly address the country's need for accountability, reconciliation, social cohesion, or other peacebuilding objectives.

Moreover, some civil actors criticize projects that are funded under peacebuilding rubrics but involve programming with little or no clear connection to these concepts. One offered an example of a major donor-funded peacebuilding project that included lessons for school children in rural Lahj about the importance of hand hygiene in containing the spread of communicable disease. While undoubtedly related to the imperative to help contain the spread of COVID-19, she saw this as cutting against the need to 'start teaching children about peace, security, and stability.'[83]

The humanitarianization of peacebuilding is seen as stripping the capacity of civil actors in the peacebuilding sector, but it may also be doing something more. In November 2021, the Sana'a Center for Strategic Studies published a six-part series on the impact of humanitarian aid operations in substantively sustaining the war. The organization summarized its concerns as follows:

> To date, humanitarian operations in Yemen have received more than US\$17 billion, making Yemen the most expensive international relief effort in the past decade, other than Syria. The UN's consistent narrative that famine is imminent, however, misrepresents the situation. Famine is not the key issue facing Yemen. Rather, the key issues are food security, malnutrition, access to water and problems related to purchasing power. There is food available, but people struggle to afford to buy it. Endlessly delivering food baskets does not help people develop the means (or the money) to feed themselves. In fact, this form of rapid response helps to reproduce the kinds of food insecurity that Yemenis experience because it diverts attention from the deeper structural issues at play—and the emergency food supplies are readily diverted to fund the war.[84]

The Sana'a Center staff rightfully 'wrestled with the question of whether going ahead [with criticism of humanitarianization and the aid sector] could ultimately do more harm than good to vulnerable Yemenis' or would be seen as minimizing the genuinely dire conditions they face.[85] This same worry is evident in conversations with many civil actors and peacebuilders across the country who criticize humanitarianization. Yet for those who view the material suffering of

Yemenis as a consequence of war, first and foremost, the need to build peace and pursue justice remain not only justifiable but essential.

The Sana'a Center is not alone in its critical research on the way humanitarian aid is affecting peacebuilding. Attention to structural features of Yemen's economy—its war economy and the features of the economic system that were built by the previous regime and sustained during the transition—has become an explicit focus of the 'Rethinking Yemen's Economy' project, leveraging the work of Yemeni economists and development experts to think about how the war economy builds upon and entrenches existing dynamics of Yemen's political economy while it introduces new challenges. Such projects—led largely by Yemeni researchers—are a key illustration of where civil action, peacebuilding, and Yemeni knowledge-production most powerfully intersect.

Knowledge-Production as Civil Action

To the extent that the four processes outlined above are well recognized, it is because of the proliferation of research and documentation that has accompanied the current war. This growth represents both a quantitative and a qualitative shift in knowledge-production on Yemen. As Laurent Bonnefoy argued in a 2021 review of these changes, understanding the terrain of conflict has become an imperative that has displaced other forms of knowledge, particularly those that relied on the kind of ethnographic work done by an earlier generation of scholars.[86] Most research on Yemen is today conducted through think-tanks or international donor-funded projects shaped by the imperatives of the war or its humanitarian consequences. Notably, a significant proportion of this work is done directly by or in collaboration with Yemenis themselves, which marks a consequential change in the dynamics of knowledge production.

It does mean, however, that the substantive focus of research on Yemen has been thoroughly permeated by the war, shaping the vocabulary of analysis and truncating the range of questions that researchers are able to address. Non-Yemeni researchers are constrained by one set of realities: limitations on research access and grant funding, especially for areas under Houthi control, university restrictions on travel to conflict settings, and—most recently—the global COVID-19 pandemic and the range of restrictions this has generated. Yemeni researchers face some of these limitations but also encounter different constraints: the fragmentation and polarization of the country, the collapse of the economy, the politicization of universities, and difficulty accessing some kinds of research materials. When the entire country was knocked offline in January 2022, this brought temporary attention to the fragility of communication infrastructure, but more localized interruptions shape daily life for Yemeni civil actors across the country, limiting who they can work with and how.

A number of new hybrid research-and-advocacy organizations have emerged over the course of the war to support field-based social science research on Yemen and communicate findings to a global policy-oriented readership. A founding member of one such organization explained the connection between research and peacebuilding:

> Peacebuilding requires debate, which is ideally not only informed by values but also knowledge that is produced in academically sound ways. So research can contribute to this debate, simply by producing knowledge that can be discussed and that can serve as the basis for political or social visions. But research and the entire process of collaborating on research projects also pushes individuals to question things they haven't questioned before. They are pushed to think beyond the ideas they have taken for granted, and hopefully the knowledge produced allows others to also challenge old ideas. Part of peacebuilding is changing attitudes.[87]

It is unsurprising that many Yemeni researchers working in such environments participated as activists during the uprising and transitional period. The notion that learning about or encountering new information and perspectives has transformative potential reflects the legacy of transformations that occurred through forms of collective action.

Seen this way, research can be a form of substantive engagement with Yemeni justice demands in its own right. The push for a more inclusive peace process, for example, has emerged not (or not only) as part the liberal peacebuilding discourse from the outside but has been grounded in and validated by research on an by Yemenis who have been or feel themselves to have been unrepresented in the peace-brokering process and, to a lesser degree, the transitional process that preceded the war. For some Yemeni researchers, knowledge production has been a means of self-representation, as when communitarian organizations issue research reports detailing conditions in communities to which they belong. One civil actor from a marginalized community in Yemen said that at a fundamental level, he writes about conflict dynamics affecting his community 'because I belong.' He explains that because 'no one from the region has made it to research circles, I feel a personal obligation to put [my region] on the research agenda.'[88]

Research produced by differently situated actors has played a role in showcasing the need for greater inclusion, but also highlights the perceived insufficiency of the 'inclusion' frame underwriting the peace process by documenting the work of Yemenis who operate outside of the formal peace tracks. Interviews and focus group discussions suggest that many civil actors are frustrated with a consultative model that engages few Yemenis, prioritizes Track I and II actors (who are often living outside of the country), and offers little by way of substantive decision-making, whether in the diplomatic process or in donor initiatives linked to it. Knowledge-production, by contrast, empowers Yemenis to feel that they are doing something, as they observe not just the data that they generate but also the arguments and interpretations that they offer influencing donors and international organizations.

Knowledge-production has emerged as an opportunity for Yemeni civil actors not only to describe and interpret challenges facing the country but also a space in which to imagine and partially enact more inclusive alternatives through which they may be able to shape outcomes. A founding member of one research organization devoted to Yemen explained why she views knowledge-production as form of civil action that contributes directly and indirectly to peacebuilding:

> [W]e have empowered new and young researchers to engage directly with OSESGY, for example. Our work also empowers Yemenis to participate in international media discourses, which

allows them to speak for themselves as experts on their own country. Finally, it empowers Yemenis to engage with donors, design their own projects and learn project management, which is still often dominated by non-Yemenis because of the technical knowledge it requires. And this is really a goal that we are trying to work towards as an organization, acknowledging that we are really fighting against structural inequalities that are very real. But peacebuilding requires independent, empowered individuals, that are able to maneuver these different contexts, and research and academic practice, from my perspective, is a vehicle to achieve this goal.[89]

Knowledge-production by Yemeni researchers may thus both describe and constitute civil action and contribute directly to peacebuilding. This occurs, first, through the documentation of harm, and second, through the documentation and concurrent enactment of Yemeni agency. In the words of one researcher reflecting on her own role as a peacebuilder:

> The peace process does not consist only of a ceasefire and the meeting of warriors around the dialogue table ... but also writing of all kinds: preserving the memory of society before it is penetrated by the victors, documenting what has happened and what is happening and how it changes, sharing with the world what is really happening, clarifying ambiguity or [addressing] the marginalization that the media may intentionally or unintentionally practice, writing people's stories, continuing to write about the atrocities of war so that they do not become something 'regular' or 'normal.'[90]

Where the investigatory capacity and political neutrality of the state has itself been fractured by the war, civil actors engage in documentation work that creates a record essential to post-conflict accountability, reconciliation, and reparative policies. Creating a record of the kinds of abuses perpetrated by different conflict actors requires research. Such research and documentation can contribute to a form of preservative justice.

Documentation may also involve an invitation to narrate one's experience, making it a political act that expands the scope of individual agency. As Wendy Pearlman has argued in relation to Syria, narration by those who have experienced violence involves 'deciphering the pressures and constraints that structure their environments, tracing the events that delineate their lives, and determining their paths as political agents.'[91] Noha Aboueldahab has similarly described the role that narration can play in 'wider social change processes,' even when carried out by those whom international experts tend to approach as 'so-called "non-professionals."'[92] Analysis of the role of the arts further elaborates this argument, with a 2022 report showing how creative writing, in particular, has become a vehicle by which Yemenis identify conflict-related and socio-political injustices and make forward-looking justice claims.[93] This research builds upon other work on Yemeni visual and performing arts as justice work.[94]

One noteworthy dimension of Yemeni knowledge production is its multidimensionality. People can and often do wear more than one hat. For example, in March 2022, the Yemen Policy Center (YPC) published an animated work of short fiction by Rim Mugahed called 'Bus of Hope,' which details the challenges many women face in navigating public space under conditions of pervasive physical insecurity and outlines some possibilities for practical solidarity.[95] It was part of the YPC's 'Kaleidescope' project, which advances justice work and peacebuilding through the arts. Yet Mugahed is trained in sociology, produces research-based reports for the Sana'a Center for Strategic Studies, and has participated in training sessions for Track II women.[96] Her short fiction was informed by her research work—indeed, it integrates some data visualization and statistics on conditions depicted by the narrative arc of the story's characters. It is only one of several ways in which Mugahed is helping to expand the scope of Yemeni women's agency, including her own. This movement across platforms and across modes of narration has grown over the course of the conflict, particularly as organizations recognize the potential representational and reconciliatory work that can be done through narration. Staff at the YPC report that within a month of its publication, the Arabic-language version of 'Bus of Hope' had become the most accessed content on the YPC website.[97]

The claims-making implicit in documentation and narration of harm is no doubt part of why human rights organizations and those who work in the field of documentation have faced extensive threat and violence throughout the war.[98] Researchers themselves may not always be regarded as professionals among Yemenis. As one notes, the job title of 'researcher' is 'barely recognized or valued by the majority of people in Yemen. They look at such a field as invented to give local jobless people positions through which they do the job of local informants to international agencies.'[99] This heightens the sense of insecurity that many researchers face, if or when their work is seen as akin to espionage.

The security environment shapes knowledge-production in other ways as well. For example, one social scientist who works at a Yemeni research and advocacy organization describes the terrain in this way:

> Conflict dynamics have created blind spots in research mainly due to challenges in the feasibility of doing research openly in certain areas in the county.... [D]ata has always been limited in Yemen but during the war getting hold of accurate and up to date data is a serious challenge. We also see a change on who's leading research, from academic to policy centers which means weaker theoretical development and possibly a lax approach to research ethics. But with no monitoring of research practices in Yemen it's difficult to know what's really going on.[100]

Security risks influence research decisions beyond questions of access; for example, one-on-one interviews are more common in areas under Houthi control, whereas many researchers use focus groups in STC or GoY areas, and there is not often much discussion in published work about how such methodological differences might shape analysis. Despite such concerns, however, researchers tend to describe their work as a valuable counter to the war's 'erasure of facts, and the writing of history by the victor.'[101] This desire for representation, or to capture perspectives and priorities that researchers view as marginalized by the formal peace process, is an extension of activists' substantive engagements with justice that date to the transitional period.

Documentation both relies on and records the agency of civil actors. Research may be oriented toward accounts of the conflict, maps of battle lines, descriptions of negotiations, and so on, but much of it includes extensive documentation of everyday peacebuilding, local conflict mediation, and other forms of civil action. When Yemeni researchers narrate these forms of agency—and especially when they use the kind of qualitative techniques that highlight the sense-making and claims-making of Yemenis themselves—they both describe and enact the kind of inclusion and dignity that has long been the focus of justice demands.

Enacting Justice Projects in Real Time

The fragmentary nature of the conflict in Yemen since 2015 has meant diverse possibilities for differently located actors. One consequence of this is that it has been possible for Yemenis to enact a range of justice projects even in the absence of a negotiated settlement. In areas under the control of the internationally recognized government, these may involve working with governing authorities and/or with civil society organizations or institutions that predate the war. In areas under control of conflict actors like the Houthis, this work is unlikely to be framed or organized in the same way. And in many parts of the country with contested jurisdiction or where no national authority is recognized, the work may draw on local or hyperlocal sources of authority.

What this means is that in many parts of Yemen, substantive engagement with justice demands is ongoing in the absence of any national transitional justice program or even the near prospect of a negotiated settlement. This cuts against a 'trickle-down peace' model that, in the words of Dustin Sharp, assume that 'institutions induce liberalism and peace rather than the other way around, or some other way.'[102] This is particularly true in light of the humanitarian-development-peace 'nexus' that now underwrites UN programming. In my own experience of observing and working on donor-funded peacebuilding projects and speaking with staff of both Yemeni and international peacebuilding CSOs, while nexus-informed language is often adopted by Yemeni participants when speaking to international donors, participants still carve out ways in which to pursue specific, locally resonant peacebuilding priorities. These include programs to build social cohesion in divided communities, the use of arts to support forms of self-representation and build the basis for intersectional solidarities, and more.[103] Projects to train local mediators begin at an often hyper-local level, drawing in participants with preexisting sources of social trust, including midwives and other local health professionals, lawyers, and others. One such project uses a Yemeni-designed curriculum to train mediators recruited from the communities in which they work; 'insider mediators' help deescalate conflicts in their communities and eventually develop community resolution committees to facilitate communication with local authorities. This can even include mediation between armed conflict actors, as with a woman in Abyan who negotiated a ceasefire between STC forces and those of GoY. The facilitator who helped recruit and train this mediator stressed that she was not a Track II actor or working for a CSO but was simply an unremarkable local woman who did remarkable work.[104]

Civil action of this sort can help to bridge peace tracks and address the expressed desire of many local-level civil actors for opportunities to shape outcomes on a broader scale. For example, one organization has hosted workshops in Lahj, Abyan, and Taiz that bring their own local mediators together with Track II actors recommended by the OSESGY or UN Women, local CSOs, and media professionals to engage in a process of jointly establishing policy priorities. According to the facilitator of this program,

> the key priority that they all agreed on was that they wanted a woman on the local council. And the first success that we had was that one of the local mediators that we trained was elected, or hired, in the local council…and now across the three governorates, there are now 10 women in the local councils, whereas previously it was all men.[105]

This is an example of the way transpositional scrutiny allowed differently situated actors to identify overlapping consensus on a shared policy priority and remediate a lack of representation that they could agree, for different reasons, was unjust.

Other examples of everyday peacebuilding by civil actors underscore the centrality of 'mere civility,' where important gains can be made by offering recognition even without broad consensus. In a village on the Red Sea coast, for example, where authorities disallow peacebuilding as 'political,' the director of a local CSO explained his approach to mediating a conflict related to educational access. In his community, families who wanted to send their daughters to school were unable to do so because the school building itself, damaged by a fire, lacked separate spaces for male and female students. The convictions of conservatives in the community—and of the militia with functional control over the area—prioritized gender separation, whereas others in the community asserted their daughters' equal right to an education. Conflict between partisans of each position escalated to the point where the school's operations were entirely suspended for all students. His organization was able to broker an agreement between both parties to the conflict, arrange for the construction of a separation barrier, and enable children—male and female— to return to school.[106] The underlying difference in priorities did not need to be resolved for both groups to be recognized. This seemingly small victory must be considered in the context of the catastrophic impact of the war on Yemen's education sector, where close to 8 million students have seen at least some interruption in their schooling, and two million—disproportionately girls—are unable to attend school at all.[107] Local-level conflict mediation outcomes like this one are critical and showcase the diffusing potential of mere civility to expand effective citizenship even in the face of deep polarization.

Such local-level successes are reflected routinely in research on Yemen generated by Yemeni researchers and through Yemeni research organizations. This helps to explain the frustrations that civil actors express about international peacebuilding initiatives that do not appear to engage constructively with civil actors. As one researcher explained:

> [Th]e discourse on Yemeni peacebuilding is stuck within a box. I mean it is literally a path dependency of the UN approach that has ruined a lot in terms of peacemaking in Yemen. So we are trying to ignore all factors that are causing this discourse to

be stuck in this box, namely regional actors, UN resolutions, international interests, power dynamics and territorial control. And we look at factors that allow communities to generate some stability/dignity or some sort of peace for themselves.[108]

This brings to mind the popular Twitter hashtag #YemenCantWait. While it is often used to describe the county's pressing humanitarian needs and mobilize aid, it can also be read in light of the volume of civil action ongoing throughout the country. Yemeni civil actors are not waiting for Track I to deliver an agreement before they begin to address the injustices that exist in their communities.

There is an important difference, however, between not waiting and rushing. Rushing to forestall crisis in 2011 was a part of why transitional institutions were unable to successfully grapple with existing Yemeni justice demands and, indeed, why the transitional period perpetuated what some have viewed as new injustices. For this reason, Tarek Radwan encourages intentionally planning for post-conflict justice now:

> With the benefit of hindsight, it is possible to get a head start on finding the appropriate mechanism to address different grievances without hurrying the process. In fact, one of the main drivers that led to the current crisis includes the pressure placed on Yemeni officials to rush to peace.[109]

The civil action of Yemeni peacebuilders is doing some of this work already, albeit largely outside of the formal process led by the United Nations. Documentation of this work, often done by Yemeni researchers, can provide an essential guide for the conscious scaling of justice work in planning for a post-conflict future.

CONCLUSION
PEACE LEARNING AND JUSTICE

In Chapter 1, I argued that a Capabilities Approach framework could be useful in addressing injustice insofar as it would encourage institutions and practices that could register both liberal and communitarian claims. This is borne out by the way justice work has been enacted by civil actors in several communities, including shifting expectations about representation. It includes copious (but not uncomplicated) work referencing the rights and roles of women, regional identity groups, tribal groups, and marginalized minorities. Examination of justice work by Yemeni civil actors addressing such rights shows that there is a tricky balance to strike between the recognition of communitarian claims on the one hand and practices or institutions that avoid solitarist or essentializing approaches to identification and representation.

My participation in two recent collaborative research projects brought this tension into particular relief. In the first project, my co-authors and I explored the diverse experiences of women as everyday peacebuilders in different parts of the country. The second project was based on observations and interviews conducted in conjunction with a training workshop for partisan women. Both projects were 'about women,' but each highlighted elements of women's identities that were not defined solely by gender and that shaped their work as civil actors.

In the fall of 2021, the Sana'a Center for Strategic Studies facilitated a project for partisan women designed to expand their role in the formal (Track I and II) peace process.[1] I had the opportunity to observe women participants in the training sessions and arrange interviews with several participants from different political parties and different areas of the country. Women who belong to political parties are eager to help their party leadership be more aware of and mobilized around gendered impacts of the current conflict. Some are critical, however, of being asked to serve as 'representatives of women' in generic terms and are wary of being deployed by their parties only on issues related to gender. Partisan women with distinct political-ideological commitments and preferences thus face a dual struggle—against male party members who view them primarily as women, and against independents who view them largely as partisans.

Such women expressed some concerns that echoed the sentiments of women in independent civil society organizations (CSOs) and some that were distinct. Women interviewed for both projects expressed a clear awareness that gender mediates the experience of conflict, and many voiced some version of the argument that 'women are the greatest victims of the war'—to illustrate this claim, they cited vulnerabilities produced by displacement, hunger, economic collapse, violence, pressure for early marriage, and shifting household dynamics, all of which are documented features of the conflict. Women working in peacebuilding, however, also expressed concern about the reputational risks they faced from a hostile media, whereas partisan women did not. Instead, partisan women saw the biggest barrier to their inclusion coming from their marginalization within their own parties. They noted that they are often appreciated by partisan men for their points of view, but most have experienced difficulty translating this voice into decision-making within party institutions.[2]

In comparing interviews between partisan women and women in CSOs, however, the most striking distinction to me was their understandings of the representational expectations of others. Women in CSOs often expressed the view that they were interpreted by others primarily as women, whereas partisan women clearly understood their representational roles as more intersectional—they were oriented toward shifting their parties toward greater gender sensitivity but also aimed to advance the interests of their parties in negotiations and other inter-party forums. Partisan women have had sustained opportunities to interact with men on the basis of a shared commonality—political ideology—in a way that was far less evident in interviews with women civil actors. Those who were most satisfied with their parties suggested that their satisfaction stemmed from experiences representing the party as a whole, not just women in the party, or where their input was sought on issues not strictly related to gender and their perspectives (including those informed by their gender) were viewed as valuable by male and female party members alike.

One legacy of the transitional period's focus on inclusive institutions—especially via the National Dialogue Conference (NDC)—is that members of marginalized groups now expect a measure of representation (even if there may be differences among them about what that should look like). Activism by *muhamasheen*, for example, emerged quite strikingly during the uprising and in its transitional aftermath. It has continued in the context of the current conflict and led to new research and advocacy on the war's disproportionate impact on marginalized and racialized minorities and their treatment by different conflict actors.[3] Research on the experiences of *muhamasheen* during and before the war highlights their 'caste-like status and structural discrimination' and argues that 'the social isolation and stigmatization of Muhammasheen magnify vulnerabilities and deny them the support of their fellow Yemenis.'[4] Yet the period since 2011 has also seen an expansion in *muhamasheen*-led CSOs and, following participation in the NDC by representatives of the community, the draft constitution offered them specific recognition. Today, such organizations host events and publish work in which they articulate claims for the full legal equality and integration of *muhamasheen* in a human rights framework.[5] This reflects both a communitarian call for recognition and a liberal assertion of individual rights on the basis of equal dignity.

Similarly, attention to the distinctive regional plight of the Tihama region and Tihamis as a distinct community has developed in the context of domestic and international support for a more inclusive approach to peacebuilding. As Ibrahim Jalal has documented, a regional movement developed in the Tihama during the uprising but remained largely unrecognized by transitional institutions. He notes that

> unlike the southern Hirak, al-Hirak al-Tihami does not seek secession. Instead, it demands the reversal and correction of deep-rooted political, economic, military, security, and social grievances. The movement also demands self-governance (autonomy) for the region and the allocation of a fair share of its wealth to fund local development and economic growth, consistent with the federal aspirations in Yemen or the outcomes of the NDC.[6]

When Tihamis hold sit-ins blocking the road to Sana'a, they do so in order to 'highlight injustice and demand their rights,' in the absence of any institutional recognition of the distinctive harms that have affected their region and its long history of marginalization.[7]

In Hadramawt, by contrast, civil actors have made considerable gains in advancing communitarian justice claims in part because they have been able to build consensus through inclusive and self-organized dialogue. The 2017 Hadramawt Inclusive Conference (HIC) empowered Hadrami leaders to negotiate considerable autonomy for the region, including a greater share of its natural resource wealth. But there is a reciprocal relationship here between conflict dynamics and the capacities of civil actors. The HIC was possible because of the region's relative stability and has simultaneously helped to secure that stability. Cooperation depended on 'the intersection of a long-standing, unique Hadhrami identity—both within Yemen and in the centuries-old Hadhrami diaspora—and a de facto decentralization.'[8] Few other places in Yemen have the confluence of those two factors concurrently, perhaps limiting the extent to which Hadramawt might serve as a replicable 'blueprint' for other areas of Yemen. It has nonetheless inspired some similar efforts in Tihama, as with the launch of the National Council in 2019 and more recent efforts at a multidimensional dialogue akin to the HIC.[9]

Claims-making by and attention to claims by distinctive communities outside of the context of those already recognized by formal institutions is an important feature of current justice work in

Yemen. In some cases, it is generating the kind of formal recognition that claims-makers seek. In others, it is perhaps at least laying ground for the recognition of collective claims in a future reparative approach to post-conflict justice. Communitarian claims-making both informs and, in many cases, emerges from the kind of Yemeni-led knowledge production discussed in Chapter 5.

Justice Work and Global-Local Dynamics

In *Rethinking Transitional Justice for the Twenty-First Century,* Dustin Sharp warned that 'there is danger that as transitional justice is 'mainstreamed' into the postconflict policyscape by UN policy organs, it will come to be seen as yet one more box to tick on the 'postconflict checklist,' a routine part of the template deployed in the context of postconflict peace operations.'[10] This was already evident, to some extent, in the way in which the Gulf Cooperation Council Initiative approached the inclusion of transitional justice in its mandate over a decade ago. Yet it was the flawed and perhaps even insincere inclusion of questions of justice on the transitional agenda in 2011 that opened space for Yemen's civil actors to engage justice demands substantively on the basis of the transformations that many experienced during and after the uprising.

The forms of engagement that occurred then and continue now during the war highlight the importance of what Sharp calls 'liberal localism' in advancing forms of popular peace that address 'everyday problems faced by ordinary individuals and communities as part of the peacebuilding process: social services delivery, economic and social rights; basic needs such as shelter, clean water, sanitation, electricity, jobs; and human security.'[11] So much of the civil action detailed by Yemeni researchers, as well as their documentation work itself, is of this character already. Whether and to what extent such work can 'trickle up' depends less on attributes of the work than it does on whether international institutions and donors are prepared to adopt a peace learning approach that recognizes this work as beginning to substantively address justice demands even as the war is ongoing.[12] A bottom-up approach to justice is one that could be framed in a way that is recognizable as liberal to transitional justice practitioners but is also able to integrate lessons from local justice work—understandings of what went wrong and why, and approaches to repairing harm—when that work includes communal claims that fall outside of a liberal frame.

Building up from local justice work offers a way to 'make transitional justice into more of a truly global project' in the sense that it can accommodate more.[13] Liberal localism is not illiberal or anti-liberal, nor does it excessively valorize versions of the local that are indifferent to dynamics of power, privilege, or hierarchy in local practices. Doing so, as Sen warned, risks giving 'commanding voice to the "establishment figures"' in local communities in ways that impose solitarist identity claims or marginalize the plural identities of individuals.[14] But liberal localisms can shape the content and practice of global approaches to justice as institutions and practitioners learn from, amplify, and help to scale up successes of local civil actors that allow individuals—including groups of individuals who constitute communities—to do justice work together.

It is clear that such practices are not simple and those advancing them may encounter significant resistance. Susanna Campbell shows how the UN's own internal auditing reflects an institutional awareness that 'neither peace agreements nor the implementation processes that follow them will likely prosper unless they look beyond the narrow interests of belligerents.'[15] And yet Track III civil actors struggle to see their priorities reflected in the UN-led process in Yemen. The remedies that the UN identified in its 2015 self-assessment focus on identifying local 'needs' in order to promote local ownership, but do little to recognize the agency, or learn from the existing successes, of local civil actors. Consistent across the peacebuilding research projects I have been involved with over the past three years has been civil actors' frustration with precisely the resistance to such recognition.

It is clear that diversely situated civil actors who are engaged in both peacebuilding and peacebuilding research must navigate not just time zones and languages but also complex dynamics of representation as they seek to link their work to international peacebuilding and justice frameworks. Like the work that it describes, peacebuilding research and knowledge-production is shaped by international donor agendas and priorities that, among other things, tend to blunt the language of justice in descriptions of projects and programs. At the same time, Yemeni civil actors do more than implement projects designed at a distance. They frame (and reframe) projects that are resonant in their communities, even when these do not conform (only) to liberal prescriptions.

This does not always happen. Some collaborative projects are poorly conceived or poorly executed from the perspective of expanding Yemeni agency. I have seen this directly, as when international staff at donor organizations direct questions to me, speak over, ignore, or otherwise minimize the contributions of Yemeni researchers with whom I am collaborating. In other cases, however, my Yemeni partners' understanding of local conditions, needs, and possibilities have led to important reassessments by donor organizations, and Yemeni expertise has driven project redesign. Transnational collaborations in peacebuilding can work to create capacities for action in ways that reflect the ethical impulse of the Capabilities Approach and help to answer Abduallahi an-Naim's call for a decolonial approach to justice.

An-Naim identifies the prevailing global approach to transitional justice as neocolonial insofar as it compromises on core justice claims in society in order to facilitate political transition and/or peacebuilding while sidelining indigenous conceptions of justice or questions of justice that are not seen as central to the requirements for transition.[16] In Chapter 1, I argued that the Capabilities Approach could accommodate the desire to decolonize transitional justice and reorient international practice so that '*global* is not a simple byword for *Northern* or *Western*.'[17] An-Naim's call for decolonization is not simply (or even primarily) a defense of the local but rather asserts that the universality of conceptions of justice, and of human rights specifically, can only be accessed through the development of 'an overlapping cross-cultural consensus, and not by universalizing relativist liberal values.'[18]

A peace learning approach in which the agency of Yemeni civil actors and their (sometimes incongruent) understandings of justice is recognized and valued can aid in the development of such cross-cultural consensus and help to wrest the notion of 'the global' from its association with the Western/Northern. The growing role of Yemeni researchers in knowledge-production for a global readership, as well as the growth of intentional transnational partnerships in peacebuilding research, work in this direction.[19] I have chosen to write about my own experience with such collaborations not only because they inform my understanding of conflict dynamics and peacebuilding in Yemen but because I believe that if such partnerships are undertaken reflexively, collaborative research can play a part in building greater cross-cultural consensus in relation to injustice.

Peace Learning and Justice in the Shadows

As I write this in 2022, a tenuous ceasefire holds. Houthi forces have only narrowly been prevented from taking over Marib City and further consolidating political and military control over Yemen's North. The Southern Transitional Council continues to govern de facto in significant parts of the South, and the internationally recognized Government of Yemen has little real capacity outside of a small number of cities. Taiz is a wrenching site where the worst of the war comes together and is far too easily forgotten. This means that the work being done by civil actors will remain central to whatever potential for justice exists, as Yemenis endeavor to build futures that they imagine without waiting for the international community to give them permission.

Meanwhile international peacebuilding too often continues to sidestep opportunities for peace learning of the sort that could matter for the justice projects of civil actors. In late November 2021, a group of Yemeni civil actors walked out of a training workshop organized by a prominent UN agency involved in brokering Track II participation. As activists later recounted, close to one third of participants walked out in opposition to what they interpreted as the workshop's 'shaykhly' model of inclusion: Zoom participants were not allowed to use the chat functionality, questions were not permitted, and invitees who believed they would be participants were rendered into an audience. Women and youth activists said they were 'treated as though they were minors' and expected to passively receive a lesson on advocacy from experts who did not account for existing peacebuilding practices in which participants are already engaged. Members of this same group reported retaliation for raising critiques in a closed WhatsApp group created by the sponsoring organization. Activists described this matter-of-factly as part of a wider practice imposing limits on how civil actors engage in peacebuilding at an international scale.[20]

This version of peacebuilding from above is accomplishing little. At the same time, local civil actors work in vibrant ways to make claims on local authorities and on each other as they advance versions of justice. These are not all congruent conceptions of justice; some of them may even be incompatible. This is why so many civil actors stress the need for a transitional justice process that offers real opportunities for transpositional scrutiny and the development of overlapping consensus.

The Track I process is at a standstill. Track II efforts to broker greater inclusion are widely criticized among civil society actors, and Track III engagement suffers from top-down, tutelary models that continually emphasize the need for training. What I have endeavored to show in this book is the need for a peace learning approach in which the capacities and successes of Yemeni civil actors are recognized as the kind of justice work that can help to reorient the peacebuilding process. I am encouraged to see some small movements in this direction, such as a June 2022 conference in Stockholm that convened Yemeni civil actors with the express aim of outlining an approach to 'reconciliation and approaches to addressing postwar grievances and injustices.' This conference was sponsored by the Swedish Ministry of Foreign Affairs but was planned and administered by one of the new hybrid research and advocacy organizations discussed in Chapter 5, largely through the work of Yemeni civil actors.[21]

International peacebuilders frequently speak of the need to address the core drivers of conflict. In Yemen, the repeated denial of or strategic engagement with justice demands over 30 years has been and remains a core driver of conflict. Deferring these demands until some indeterminate time 'after' conflict is unrealistic, not only because a history of limited engagement with justice demands already brutally informs Yemen's present but because Yemeni civil actors are simply not waiting. They have set about the work of enacting more just futures where and when they can. They do so in the shadow of decades of unresolved injustice, in the shadow of a failed transitional process, and now, in the shadow of war. A Capabilities-informed approach requires that those who support peace in Yemen ask how they can better work to expand the agency of those who are already pursuing justice amid these shadows.

ACKNOWLEDGEMENTS

This book draws on fieldwork I began in Yemen in 2004 and extends through interviews and correspondence with Yemeni interlocutors through April 2022. The workshops, conferences, drafts, emails, WhatsApp messages, and casual conversations that contributed to the thinking and rethinking reflected here cannot possibly be catalogued adequately. Restrictions on travel during the pandemic ultimately opened up new forms of remote communication that facilitated the completion of the book, as did the fact that I had the time to write it because of a much-needed sabbatical from teaching.

Michael Dwyer and Lara Weisweiller-Wu at Hurst were exceptionally helpful throughout the process. I am grateful to Lara for securing reviewers who engaged the normative and empirical elements of the manuscript thoughtfully and quickly. From the beginning, she 'got' the project and was committed to bringing it into being.

Yemeni colleagues and co-authors are acknowledged more fully in the book's introduction, but on a personal level, I also want to thank them here: without Iman, Bilkis, Maged, Yazeed, and Rim this book simply would not have been possible. Likewise, Marie-Christine Heinze at the Center for Applied Research in Partnership with the Orient and Mareike Transfeld at the Yemen Policy Center substantially facilitated this work. I feel fortunate that they have become friends in the process and look forward to our continuing collaborations. Laurent Bonnefoy and Kate Nevens, with whom I have worked on some joint projects and whose research is cited throughout the book, have given me new ways of thinking about the relationship between knowledge-production and activism that have shaped the concluding two chapters especially.

I have also had the good fortune to work with some tremendous colleagues who have helped me understand Yemen in its broader regional and global context. Mariam Salehi and Jillian Schwedler each graciously read drafts of the book in different stages of completion, and I am grateful for their many insights, as well as to Sarah Parkinson for important discussions of ethics. The Project on Middle East Political Science has been a central and meaningful intellectual network, and Marc Lynch has been an unflagging ally for nearly two decades. At Hobart and William Smith Colleges, I cannot thank Kevin Dunn enough—for everything. I am grateful to Jenny, Feisal, Kristen, and Whitney for support and friendship as I finished the book and to students in my 'Transitional Justice' seminar who were an early sounding board for this project. Special thanks to Julia, my research assistant, and to Charlotte, Shannon, and Nuzhat for brining so much of themselves to our work together.

Amid the dual isolation of the pandemic and book-writing, four text threads on my phone have functioned as vital lifelines. For conversations that seem to have no beginning or end, all I can say to Ian, Ricky, Sarah, and Jillian is...

People often assume that being married to another political scientist means that we read each other's work. Vikash and I do not and never really have. But as I drafted the bulk of the book between May and December 2021, we took a walk after lunch every day with our dog, Snickers, and we talked. When I was deep in my head, he pushed me to explain myself clearly and I have no doubt that these discussions improved the book. Writing books—not together, but alongside each other—was about as close as we have ever come to the life we imagined for ourselves as grad students. But it was only a small part of a life together that has been and remains much richer than I imagined possible.

Our daughters responded differently—and wonderfully—to it all. Kieran reminded me often that 'book writing looks boring' and pushed me to take frequent *Gilmore Girls* breaks with her. Lila wrote endless books of her own, most notably ghost-writing the dog's autobiography, 'Snickers: My Life in Black and Brown.' Some days it was hard to pivot from reading and writing about genuinely dark things to suburban American parenting. The transition was not always graceful but a hug or a snuggle or a ride in the car listening to music together never failed to help me reset. Thank you to both of my beloved girls for every little bit.

NOTES

INTRODUCTION

1. Nadwa al-Dawsari, 'Twitter Post,' November 17, 2021, https://twitter.com/Ndawsari/status/1461048814761041936.
2. The concept of peace learning, explored more fully later chapters, comes from Susanna P. Campbell, *Global Governance and Local Peace: Accountability and Performance in International Peacebuilding* (Cambridge University Press, 2018).
3. For a review of ways in which knowledge production has been affected by the war, see Laurent Bonnefoy, 'Revolution, War and Transformations in Yemeni Studies,' *Middle East Report* 301 (2021), https://merip.org/2021/12/revolution-war-and-transformations-in-yemeni-studies/.
4. For a general discussion of civil action in conflict settings, see: Deborah Avant et al., *Civil Action and the Dynamics of Violence* (Oxford University Press, 2019).
5. Stacey Philbrick Yadav, 'Civil Action Under Uncivil Conditions in Yemen,' Institute for Social Justice and Conflict Resolution, May 2021.
6. Teresa M. Bejan, *Mere Civility* (Harvard University Press, 2017), 165.
7. Avant et al., *Civil Action and the Dynamics of Violence*, 4.
8. Avant et al., *Civil Action and the Dynamics of Violence*, 5.
9. Amartya Kumar Sen, *The Idea of Justice* (Cambridge: The Belknap Press of Harvard University Press, 2011); Martha C Nussbaum, *Creating Capabilities: The Human Development Approach* (Cambridge, Mass.: Belknap Press of Harvard University Press, 2013).
10. Séverine Deneulin, *Wellbeing, Justice and Development Ethics* (Routledge, 2014). She takes the vocabulary of the Capabilities Approach as a set

of concepts and the grammar as the way these are used as tools for sense-making.

11. Kevin Dunn, *IR If People Matter*, video recording, April 7, 2021; https://youtu.be/dqOi7zpz-MQ. The film was shown at the 2021 annual meeting of the International Studies Association as part of a roundtable discussion by the same name.

12. Wendy Pearlman, 'Narratives of Fear in Syria,' *Perspectives on Politics* 14, no. 1 (2016): 21–37.

13. I was—and remain—excited by the invitation implicit in Dunn's question and am encouraged to see that the ensuing discussion that followed the film was formalized in a collection of essays published by the *Journal of Narrative Politics* in late 2021 that addresses the meaning-making and world-remaking potential of narrative quite vibrantly.

14. I thank Mariam Salehi for pushing me to make this directionality explicit.

15. For a discussion of the ethic of world disclosure, see Anne Norton, 'Political Science as a Vocation,' in *Problems and Methods in the Study of Politics*, ed. Ian Shapiro, Rogers Smith, and Tarek E. Masoud (Cambridge University Press, 2004), 67–82. Dvora Yanow and Peregrine Schwartz-Shea describe a hermeneutic circle by which puzzles are rendered less puzzling by the sustained reconsiderations of interpretive work but, in turn, open up new puzzles. Peregrine Schwartz-Shea and Dvora Yanow, *Interpretive Research Design: Concepts and Processes* (Routledge, 2012).

16. Charli Carpenter, '"You Talk of Terrible Things So Matter-of-Factly in This Language of Science": Constructing Human Rights in the Academy,' *Perspectives on Politics* 10, no. 2 (2012): 363–83.

17. Ibid., 369.

18. Iman al-Gawfi, Bilkis Zabara, and Stacey Philbrick Yadav, 'The Role of Women in Peacebuilding in Yemen,' CARPO Brief 14, February 27, 2020, https://carpo-bonn.org/wp-content/uploads/2020/02/carpo_brief_14.pdf.

19. Maged al-Kholidy, Yazeed al-Jeddawy, and Stacey Philbrick Yadav, 'Civil Society in Yemen: Identifying Opportunities for Peacebuilding,' Internal report (Interpeace, February 2021).

20. Stacey Philbrick Yadav and Rim Mugahed, '"One Hand Does Not Clap": The Dual Challenge of Partisan Women's Inclusion in Yemen' (Sana'a Center for Strategic Studies, December 2, 2021), https://sanaacenter.org/publications/analysis/15809.

21. Stacey Philbrick Yadav, 'Ethnography Is an Option: Learning to Learn in/through Practice,' in *Political Science Research in the Middle East and*

North Africa: Methodological and Ethnical Challenges, ed. Janine A. Clark and Francesco Cavatorta (Oxford University Press, 2018), 165–74.

22. Yolande Bouka, 'Collaborative Research as Structural Violence,' *Political Violence at a Glance* (blog), July 12, 2018, https://politicalviolenceataglance.org/2018/07/12/collaborative-research-as-structural-violence/.

23. Ibrahim Fraihat, *Unfinished Revolutions:Yemen, Libya, and Tunisia After the Arab Spring* (Yale University Press, 2016), 75. Fraihat attributes this language to the United States Institute for Peace, one of the leading organizations promoting the adoption of national dialogues globally. The language appears here: 'Dialogue Versus Debate,' United States Institute for Peace, accessed July 23, 2021, https://www.usip.org/public-education/educators/dialogue-versus-debate.

24. Jillian Schwedler, 'Against Methodological Nationalism: Seeing Comparisons as Encompasing Through the Arab Uprisings,' in *Rethinking Comparison: Innovative Methods for Qualitative Political Inquiry* (Cambridge University Press, 2021), 172–89.

25. For an excellent collection of essays mapping experiences with transitional justice in the MENA region—but not in Yemen—see Chandra Lekha Sriram, ed., *Transitional Justice in the Middle East and North Africa* (Hurst, 2017).

26. For a discussion of the post-war 'tweaks,' see Bassel Salloukh, 'The Architecture of Sectarianization in Lebanon,' in *Sectarianization: Mapping the New Politics of the Middle East*, ed. Nader Hashemi and Danny Postel (Hurst, 2017), 215–34. Ussama Makdisi traces continuities in the confessional regime—and in efforts to resist it—to the Ottoman and French colonial periods. Ussama Makdisi, *Age of Coexistence:The Ecumenical Frame and the Making of the Modern Arab World* (University of California Press, 2019).

27. Hiba Bou Akar, *For the War Yet to Come: Planning Beirut's Frontiers* (Stanford University Press, 2018).

28. Chandra Lekha Sriram, 'Unfinished Business: Peacebuilding, Accountability, and Rule of Law in Lebanon,' in *Transitional Justice and Peacebuilding on the Ground: Victims and Ex-Combatants*, ed. Chandra Lekha Sriram et al. (Routledge, 2012), 121–38.

29. From the 'You Stink' movement in 2015 to the October 2019 movement in which Lebanese protesters directed their criticism at the sectarian elite as a whole with the slogan 'All of you means all of you,' desectarianization has emerged as a persistent justice demand. Victories in the Bar Association elections in 2019 and Engineering Syndicate elections in 2021 suggest some limited opening for anti-

sectarian candidates (as opposed to cross-sectarian alliances, which are a longstanding feature but do not disrupt the basic regime logic). Partnerships between grassroots organizations like Umam-DR and international organizations like the International Center for Transitional Justice put some pressure on parliament to establish a commission to investigate disappearances from the 1975–1990 civil war. Fares Halabi, 'From "Overthrowing the Regime" to "All Means All": An Analysis of the Lebanonisation of Arab Spring Rhetoric,' *Arab Reform Initiative*, December 18, 2019, https://www.arab-reform. net/publication/from-overthrowing-the-regime-to-all-means-all-an-analysis-of-the-lebanonisation-of-arab-spring-rhetoric/; Kareem Chehayeb, 'Anti-Gov't Engineers Hopeful after Lebanon Syndicate Victory,' *Al Jazeera*, July 1, 2021, https://www.aljazeera. com/news/2021/7/1/anti-government-lebanese-engineers-win-syndicate-elections; 'Umam D&R,' accessed July 2, 2021, https:// umam-dr.org//about/; International Center for Transitional Justice, 'The Missing in Lebanon Inputs on the Establishment of the Independent National Commission for the Missing and Forcibly Disappeared in Lebanon,' January 2016, https://www.ictj.org/sites/ default/files/ICTJ-Report-Lebanon-CommissionMissing-2016_0. pdf; International Center for Missing Persons, 'ICMP Welcomes Appointment of Members of the Lebanon National Commission for the Missing and Forcibly Disappeared,' July 17, 2020, https://www. icmp.int/press-releases/icmp-welcomes-appointment-of-members-of-the-lebanon-national-commission-for-the-missing-and-forcibly-disappeared/.

30. Features of the reparations program that recognized gender-based harms for women as both direct and indirect victims of repression and collective reparations were paid to specific geographic areas of the country that the Equity and Reconciliation Commission identified as collective victims of state policy. Bettina Dennerlein, 'Remembering Violence, Negotiating Change: The Moroccan Equity and Reconciliation Commission and the Politics of Gender,' *Journal of Middle East Women's Studies* 8, no. 1 (2012): 10–36; International Center for Transitional Justice, 'The Rabat Report: The Concept and Challenges of Collective Reparations' (International Center for Transitional Justice, 2009), https://www.ictj.org/sites/default/ files/ICTJ-Morocco-Reparations-Report-2009-English.pdf; International Center for Transitional Justice, 'Truth and Reconciliation in Morocco,' 2009, https://www.ictj.org/sites/default/files/ICTJ-Morocco-TRC-2009-English.pdf.

31. Susan Slyomovic, 'Morocco's Justice and Reconciliation Commission,' MERIP, April 4, 2005, https://merip.org/2005/04/moroccos-justice-and-reconciliation-commission/; Fakhro, 'Truth and Fact-Finding in the Arab Monarchies.'

32. Mariam Salehi, *Transitional Justice in Process: Plans and Politics in Tunisia* (Manchester University Press, 2021).

33. Nadia Marzouki, 'Whatever Happened to Dignity? The Politics of Citizenship in Post-Revolution Tunisia,' *Middle East Report* 301 (December 15, 2021), https://merip.org/2021/12/whatever-happened-to-dignity-the politics of citizenship-in-post-revolution-tunisia-2/.

34. Séverine Autesserre, *The Frontlines of Peace: An Insider's Guide to Changing the World* (Oxford University Press, 2021).

CHAPTER 1. AN UNCOMPROMISING COMPROMISE

1. For earlier critiques outlining the relationship between transitional institutions, especially the NDC, and conflict, see: Stacey Philbrick Yadav and Sheila Carapico, 'The Breakdown of the GCC Initiative,' *Middle East Report* 273 (2014): 2–6; Stacey Philbrick Yadav and Jillian Schwedler, 'Toward a Just Peace in Yemen,' *MERIP* 289 (2018), https://merip.org/2019/03/toward-a-just-peace-in-yemen/.

2. Empirically, rights can be said to exist—or to be violated—only when they have been created by states, or by international frameworks to which a given state is a party. That said, the literature on transitional justice emerges from a human rights tradition that asserts rights-claims as a normative stance. When I say 'restored or recognized,' I therefore mean the restoration of rights that were previously created and then violated, the extension of those rights to previously excluded categories of persons, or the creation of rights that did not previously exist in a given context.

3. Lia Kent, 'Transitional Justice and Peacebuilding,' in *An Introduction to Transitional Justice*, ed. Olivera Simic (Routledge, 2017), 201–22.

4. Nussbaum, *Creating Capabilities*.

5. Ruti G. Teitel, *Globalizing Transitional Justice.* (Oxford University Press, 2015), 3.

6. Anja Mihr, 'An Introduction to Transitional Justice,' in *An Introduction to Transitional Justice*, ed. Olivera Simic (Routledge, 2017), 11.

7. Lavinia Stan, 'Lustration and Vetting,' in *An Introduction to Transitional Justice*, ed. Olivera Simic (Routledge, 2017), 137–55.

8. Lavinia Stan, 'Lustration and Vetting,' 144.

9. H. Zeynep Bulutgil, 'War, Collaboration, and Endogenous Ethnic Polarization: The Path to Ethnic Cleansing,' in *Rethinking Violence: States and Non-State Actors in Conflict*, ed. Erica Chenoweth and Adria Lawrence (Cambridge, MA (MIT Press, 2010), 57–81.

10. Susan E Waltz, 'Linking Transitional Justice and Human Rights,' in *Transitional Justice in the Middle East and North Africa*, ed. Chandra Lekha Sriram (Routledge, 2017), 40.

11. Lars Waldorf, 'Anticipating the Past: Transitional Justice and Socio-Economic Wrongs,' *Social and Legal Studies* 21, no. 2 (2012): 178.

12. Waltz, 'Linking Transitional Justice and Human Rights,' 44.

13. Doris H Gray, Terry C Coonan, and Chandra Lekha Sriram, 'Reframing Gender Narratives through Transitional Justice in the Maghreb,' in *Transitional Justice in the Middle East and North Africa* (Routledge, 2017), 120.

14. Nevin T Aiken, *Identity, Reconciliation and Transitional Justice: Overcoming Intractability* (Abingdon: Routledge, 2013), 18.

15. Mahmood Mamdani, *Neither Settler nor Native: The Making and Unmaking of Permanent Minorities* (Harvard University Press, 2020), 17.

16. Priscilla B Hayner, *Unspeakable Truths: Transitional Justice and the Challenge of Truth Commissions*, second ed. (New York: Routledge, 2011), 22–3.

17. Agata Fijalkowski, 'Amnesty,' in *An Introduction to Transitional Justice*, ed. Olivera Simic (Routledge, 2017), 116.

18. Sriram C.L, 'Beyond Transitional Justice: Peace, Governance, and Rule of Law,' *Int. Stud. Rev. International Studies Review* 19, no. 1 (2017): 54.

19. Kent, 'Transitional Justice and Peacebuilding,' 205–6.

20. I use the language of peace-brokering to refer to formal Track I diplomatic efforts to achieve negotiated settlements.

21. Kent, 'Transitional Justice and Peacebuilding.'

22. Kent, 204–5.

23. Noha Aboueldahab, 'Writing Atrocities: Syrian Civil Society and Transitional Justice,' *Brookings Doha Center Analysis Paper*, no. 21 (May 2018): 42.

24. Par Engstrom, 'Transitional Justice and Ongoing Conflict,' in *Transitional Justice and Peacebuilding on the Ground: Victims and Ex-Combatants*, ed. Chandra Lekha Sriram *et al.* (Routledge, 2012), 42.

25. Teitel, *Globalizing Transitional Justice,* 57.

26. Kate Nevens, Maged al-Kholidy, and Yazeed al-Jeddawy, '"Broken People Can't Heal a Nation": The Role of Arts in Peacebuilding in

Yemen' (Center for Applied Research in Partnership with the Orient, March 25, 2021), https://carpo-bonn.org/en/category/author/kate-nevens/.

27. Avant et al., *Civil Action and the Dynamics of Violence*, 6.
28. Yadav, 'Civil Action Under Uncivil Conditions in Yemen,' 1.
29. Dustin N Sharp, *Rethinking Transitional Justice for the Twenty-First Century Beyond the End of History* (Cambridge University Press, 2019), 105–6.
30. Duncan McCargo, 'Transitional Justice and Its Discontents,' *Journal of Democracy Journal of Democracy* 26, no. 2 (2015): 5–20.
31. Teitel, *Globalizing Transitional Justice*, 125–6.
32. Waldorf, 'Anticipating the Past,' 173.
33. Juan Carlos Ochoa-Sánchez, 'Economic and Social Rights and Transitional Justice: A Framework of Analysis,' *Journal of Human Rights* 18, no. 5 (December 11, 2019): 528–9.
34. Waldorf, 'Anticipating the Past,' 175.
35. Robbie Shilliam, *Decolonizing Politics: An Introduction* (Polity Press, 2021), 119–20.
36. Robbie Shilliam, *Decolonizing Politics: An Introduction*, 121.
37. Abdullahi Ahmed An-Naim, 'From the Neocolonial "Transitional" to Indigenous Formations of Justice,' *International Journal of Transitional Justice* 7, no. 2 (2013): 197.
38. Mamdani, *Neither Settler nor Native*, 17.
39. Gabriela Lucuta, 'Peacemaking, Peacekeeping, Peacebuilding and Peace Enforcement in the 21st Century,' Peace Insight, April 25, 2014, https://www.peaceinsight.org/en/articles/peacemaking-peacekeeping-peacebuilding-peace-enforcement-21st-century/.
40. Sharp, *Rethinking Transitional Justice for the Twenty-First Century beyond the End of History*, 109.
41. Teitel, *Globalizing Transitional Justice*, 63–6.
42. Teitel, *Globalizing Transitional Justice*, 63.
43. Lucuta, 'Peacemaking, Peacekeeping, Peacebuilding and Peace Enforcement in the 21st Century.'
44. Thomas Carothers, 'The End of the Transition Paradigm,' *Journal of Democracy* 13, no. 1 (2002): 5–21.
45. For example, Interpeace cites the Stockholm Declaration as the basis of its own Frameworks for Assessing Resilience, which guides its own programming and donor priorities, https://www.interpeace.org/programme/far-1/. The ICTJ, for its part, has convened a Working Group composed of NGOs, governments, and international organizations designed to integrate transitional justice priorities into the sustainable development goals, consistent with the Stockholm

Declaration, https://www.ictj.org/news/fits-and-starts-making-transitional-justice-part-sustainable-development-agenda. The working group published its first report in 2019: International Center for Transitional Justice, 'On Solid Ground: Sustainable Development After Massive Human Rights Violations,' Report of the Working Group on Transitional Justice and SDG+16, May 2019.

46. Sharp, *Rethinking Transitional Justice for the Twenty-First Century Beyond the End of History,* 107–8.

47. It is for this reason that I have opted throughout the rest of the book to drop the language of transition altogether in favor of a less teleological 'post-conflict' framing. I retain 'transitional justice' when authors or practitioners use this language themselves, but otherwise avoid it.

48. Séverine Deneulin, *Wellbeing, Justice and Development Ethics* (Routledge, 2014), 22. For an elaboration on the critique of GDP as the central measurement used by development economists and practitioners, see the report by Joseph Stiglitz, Amartya Sen, and Jean-Paul Fitousi for the Commission on the Measurement of Economic Performance and Social Progress: Commission on the Measurement of Economic Performance and Social Progress (France), *Mismeasuring Our Lives: Why GDP Doesn't Add up: The Report by the Commission on the Measurement of Economic Performance and Social Progress* (New York; London: New Press, 2010).

49. Nussbaum, *Creating Capabilities,* 18.

50. Nussbaum, *Creating Capabilities,* 18.

51. Sen, *The Idea of Justice,* 231.

52. Sen, *The Idea of Justice,* 321–37.

53. The language of 'achievements' is Sen's, while Nussbaum uses the term 'functionings' to refer to the same concept. In both cases, one might think of these as the specific outcomes of choices. If individuals are freely enabled to choose their paths – and indeed, both theorists set a high bar for what constitutes informed and enabled choice – then the substantive content of those choices and the consequent outcomes in terms of distributional inequalities should not be a source of concern. This, too, is profoundly liberal, though it is partially offset by consideration of the effect of entrenched inequalities on the ability to reason through one's choices and to act upon them. See Amartya Kumar Sen, *The Idea of Justice* (Cambridge: The Belknap Press of Harvard University Press, 2011), 238.

54. Sen, *The Idea of Justice,* 233.

55. Nussbaum, *Creating Capabilities,* 19.

56. Nussbaum, *Creating Capabilities,* 20.

57. Nussbaum, *Creating Capabilities,* 35.

58. Sen, *The Idea of Justice,* 246.

59. Amartya Kumar Sen, *Identity and Violence: The Illusion of Destiny* (New York: W.W. Norton, 2007), xiii.

60. Evan S Lieberman and Prerna Singh, 'The Institutional Origins of Ethnic Violence,' *Comppoli Comparative Politics* 45, no. 1 (2012): 1–24.

61. Nussbaum, *Creating Capabilities,* 39.

62. Deneulin, *Wellbeing, Justice and Development Ethics,* 95.

63. Nussbaum, *Creating Capabilities,* 18.

64. Sen, *The Idea of Justice,* 344.

65. Martha C Nussbaum, *Creating Capabilities: The Human Development Approach*, 19.

66. Sen, *The Idea of Justice*, 15–18. Sen discusses this point throughout the book, but this is a short introduction to his juxtaposition of a transcendent approach to justice, which he associates most directly with John Rawls and his own comparative approach to evaluating states of injustice.

67. Deneulin, *Wellbeing, Justice and Development Ethics*, 58.

68. An-Naim, 'From the Neocolonial "Transitional" to Indigenous Formations of Justice.'

69. Nussbaum, *Creating Capabilities,* 39.

70. Nussbaum, 34.

71. Waldorf, 'Anticipating the Past,' 180.

72. Balasco L.M, 'Reparative Development: Re-Conceptualising Reparations in Transitional Justice Processes,' *Conf. Secur. Dev. Conflict, Security and Development* 17, no. 1 (2017): 2.

73. Balasco, 'Reparative Development: Re-Conceptualising Reparations in Transitional Justice Processes.'

CHAPTER 2. THE SHADOW OF UNIFICATION

1. Lisa Wedeen, *Peripheral Visions: Publics, Power, and Performance in Yemen* (Chicago: University of Chicago Press, 2009), 23.

2. John M Willis, *Unmaking North and South Cartographies of the Yemeni Past* (Oxford University Press, 2014), 198.

3. Sharif Ismail, 'Unification in Yemen: Dynamics of Political Integration, 1978-2000' (M.Phil thesis, Faculty of Oriental Studies, University of Oxford, 2007), 23.

4. For example, Stephen Day interprets union as a strategic move, where 'the southern YSP leadership was in a risky position because northern President Salih held most of the political cards at a time when Marxist

socialism was in retreat around the world.' By contrast, Dresch sees the situation as last-ditch effort, concluding that 'the rulers of the South faced otherwise the prospect of losing power entirely.' Stephen W. Day, *Regionalism and Rebellion in Yemen: A Troubled National Union* (Cambridge University Press, 2012), 85. Paul Dresch, *A History of Modern Yemen* (Cambridge University Press, 2000), 182. These are subtle distinctions, but relevant to the eventual revival of Southern political aspirations.

5. Fred Halliday, 'Catastrophe in South Yemen: A Preliminary Assessment,' in *Arabia Incognita*, ed. Sheila Carapico (Just World Books, 2016). This essay was originally published in Middle East Report 139 (March/April 1986) and republished in Carapico's Arabia Incognita collection.

6. Nada Choueiri et al., *Yemen in the 1990s: From Unification to Economic Reform,Yemen in the 1990s* (International Monetary Fund, 2002), 3.

7. Dawud Ansari, 'Resource Curse Contagion in the Case of Yemen,' *Resources Policy* 49 (September 2016): 444–54, https://doi.org/10.1016/j.resourpol.2016.08.001.

8. Dresch, *A History of Modern Yemen*.

9. Asher Orkaby, 'Benefiting from the Misery of Others,' *Middle East Report Online*, May 26, 2021, https://merip.org/2021/05/benefiting-from-the-misery-of-others/.

10. Dawud Ansari, 'Resource Curse Contagion in the Case of Yemen,' 447.

11. Sheila Carapico, 'The Economic Dimensions of Yemeni Unity,' in *Arabia Incognita: Dispatches from Yemen and the Gulf*, ed. Sheila Carapico (Just World Books, 2016), 72. This essay was originally published in Middle East Report 184 (September/October 1993) and republished in Carapico's Arabia Incognita collection.

12. Paul Dresch, *A History of Modern Yemen*, 156–7. Dresch notes, for example, that 'as Sana'a imposed restrictions, Aden's government was loosening others. State farms were allowed to move towards less stringent forms of cooperative agriculture and planners in the South placed more emphasis on the private sector, whose share of the economy rose from 66 to 72 percent between 1980 and 1985.' He echoes Carapico's analysis that the convergence of the two economies was primarily 'due to the priorities of foreign donors.'

13. Day, *Regionalism and Rebellion in Yemen: A Troubled National Union*, 80. Both Day's directional analysis and Carapico's argument regarding convergence capture features of the conditions preceding unification. See also: Carapico, 'The Economic Dimensions of Yemeni Unity.'

14. Dresch, *A History of Modern Yemen*, 157.
15. Halliday, 'Catastrophe in South Yemen: A Preliminary Assessment,' 61.
16. Noel Brehony, *Yemen Divided: The Story of a Failed State in South Arabia* (London: I.B. Tauris, 2011), 145–6.
17. Halliday, 'Catastrophe in South Yemen: A Preliminary Assessment,' 63.
18. Brehony, *Yemen Divided: The Story of a Failed State in South Arabia*, 146.
19. Noel Brehony, *Yemen Divided: The Story of a Failed State in South Arabia*, 141.
20. Brehony, *Yemen Divided: The Story of a Failed State in South Arabia*, 124.
21. Dresch, *A History of Modern Yemen*, 169. Estimates for the number of supporters range generally from Brehony's 'tens of thousands' to Dresch's 'perhaps 30,000.'
22. Dresch, *A History of Modern Yemen*, 170.
23. Brehony, *Yemen Divided: The Story of a Failed State in South Arabia*, 142. Dresch also discusses the significance of the NDF defeat on both sides of the 'irregular' border. Paul Dresch, 152–4.
24. Sheila Carapico, *Civil Society in Yemen: The Political Economy of Activism in Modern Arabia* (Cambridge University Press, 1998), 38.
25. Dresch, *A History of Modern Yemen*, 160.
26. Day, *Regionalism and Rebellion in Yemen: A Troubled National Union*, 79. See Table 2.6. Note that the term 'native' is used by Day and has more autochthonous connotations than may be warranted.
27. Fred Halliday, 'North Yemen Today,' in *Arabia Incognita*, ed. Sheila Carapico (Just World Books, 2016), 51–3. This essay was originally published in Middle East Report 130 (January/February 1985) and republished in Carapico's Arabia Incognita collection.
28. Halliday, 'North Yemen Today,' 57.
29. Thomas Stevenson, 'Yemeni Workers Come Home: Reabsorbing One Million Migrants,' in *Arabia Incognita: Dispatches from Yemen and the Gulf*, ed. Sheila Carapico (Just World Books, 2016), 87–92. This essay was originally published in Middle East Report 181 (March/April 1993) and republished in Carapico's Arabia Incognita collection.
30. Dresch, *A History of Modern Yemen*, 181.
31. Robert D. Burrowes, 'Oil Strike and Leadership Struggle in South Yemen: 1986 and Beyond,' *Middle East Journal* 43, no. 3 (1989): 451.
32. Brehony, *Yemen Divided: The Story of a Failed State in South Arabia*, 175.
33. Dresch, *A History of Modern Yemen*, 181.
34. Noel Brehony recalls that 'the deadlock was broken when, during a car journey the two presidents took together without advisers, al-Bidh

suggested that they should disregard the earlier proposals and instead agree to unite on the basis of the constitution agreed in Kuwait in 1980—that is, through union, rather than confederation. A surprised Salih immediately agreed. At the end of the journey, the presidents instructed their ministers of unity affairs to draw up an agreement on this basis.' Brehony, *Yemen Divided: The Story of a Failed State in South Arabia*, 178.

35. The 128-member Consultative Council was elected in July 1988; all candidates ran as independents because political parties were not allowed, but roughly 40% of those elected were aligned with the Islamic Front and another 31% had ties to important Northern tribes. 'Yemen Parliamentary Chamber: Majlis al-Chura' (Interparliamentary Union, July 5, 1988), Parline-E, http://archive.ipu.org/parline-e/reports/arc/2353_88.htm. The 111-member Supreme People's Council was last elected in October 1986 after a postponement in 1985 that immediately foreshadowed the violent conflict that erupted within the party in January 1986. Burrowes, 'Oil Strike and Leadership Struggle in South Yemen,' 449–50.

36. Michaelle Browers, *Political Ideology in the Arab World: Accommodation and Transformation* (Cambridge University Press, 2009), 145.

37. 'Agreement Establishing a Union between the State of the Yemen Arab Republic and the State of the People's Democratic Republic of Yemen,' April 22, 1990, 1–2 https://peacemaker.un.org/sites/peacemaker.un.org/files/YE_900422_AgreementEstablishingUnionYemen.pdf.

38. Brehony, *Yemen Divided: The Story of a Failed State in South Arabia*, 173, 181.

39. 'Yemen After the Sixth War,' *Al-Sharq al-Awsat*, March 5, 2010, BBC Monitoring Middle East-Political.

40. Maysaa Shuja al-Deen, 'Presidential Councils in Yemen: Exploring Past Attempts at Power Sharing and Possibilities for the Future' (Sana'a Center for Strategic Studies, April 2021), 12. https://sanaacenter.org/files/Presidential_Councils_in_Yemen_en.pdf.

41. Shuja al-Deen, 'Presidential Councils in Yemen: Exploring Past Attempts at Power Sharing and Possibilities for the Future,' 13.

42. Interview #24 with author, Aden, September 17, 2005.

43. Interview #42 with author, Sana'a, January 7, 2009.

44. Stacey Philbrick Yadav, *Islamists and the State: Legitimacy and Institutions in Yemen and Lebanon* (I.B. Tauris, 2013). Chapter 3.

45. Interview #7 with author, Sana'a, October 7, 2005.

46. Interview #17 with author, Sana'a, January 3, 2005.

47. Brehony, *Yemen Divided: The Story of a Failed State in South Arabia*, 191.

48. Election results originally reported by the National Election Commission. Brian Whitaker, 'Yemen: 1993 Parliamentary Election,' *Al-Bab*, accessed August 2, 2021, https://al-bab.com/albab-orig/albab/yemen/pol/election1993.htm.

49. Dresch, *A History of Modern Yemen*, 194.

50. Renaud Detalle and Joost Hiltermann, 'The Yemeni Elections Up Close,' *Middle East Report*, no. 185 (1993): 8. In 1991, the interim parliament approved and President Saleh signed Law No. 66, which established these rules. Republic of Yemen, 'Law No. 66 of 1991 Governing Parties and Political Organizations,' October 16, 1991, Tab 58, IFES_21, https://www.ifes.org/sites/default/files/el00256.pdf.

51. 'Promoting Participation in Yemen's 1993 Parliamentary Elections' (National Democratic Institute for International Affairs, 1994), https://www.ndi.org/sites/default/files/331_ye_promoting.pdf.

52. Brehony, *Yemen Divided: The Story of a Failed State in South Arabia*, 190.

53. Carapico, 'From Ballot Box to Battlefield,' 103. For example, members of the Bakil were frustrated by the overrepresentation of those from Sanhan, members of the Hashid confederation, and took part in disruptive actions.

54. Dresch, *A History of Modern Yemen*, 195.

55. Brian Whitaker, 'Fragile Union at Mercy of Outside Forces,' *The Guardian*, April 7, 1994.

56. Carapico, 'From Ballot Box to Battlefield,' 104.

57. 'Yemen's New Ruling Presidential Council Elected,' *Xinhua General Overseas News Service*, October 11, 1993.

58. Brehony, *Yemen Divided: The Story of a Failed State in South Arabia*, 193.

59. 'Presidential Council Sworn in; Bid Message of Apology Read,' *BBC Summary of World Broadcasts*, October 19, 1993.

60. Interview #16 with author, Aden, September 17, 2005.

61. 'King Husayn Addresses the Signing Ceremony for the Document of Pledge and Accord,' *BBC Summary of World Broadcasts*, February 22, 1994.

62. Sheila Carapico, 'From Ballot Box to Battlefield: The War of the Two 'Alis,' in *Arabia Incognita: Dispatches from Yemen and the Gulf*, ed. Sheila Carapico (Just World Books, 2016), 105. This essay was originally published in Middle East Report 190, September/October 1994.

63. Carapico, 'From Ballot Box to Battlefield,' 105.

64. 'Sit-Ins Call for Implementation of Document of Pledge and Accord,' *BBC Summary of World Broadcasts*, March 12, 1994.

65. Brehony, *Yemen Divided: The Story of a Failed State in South Arabia*, 196.

66. The full list of ministers, including their regional origin, can be found in Table 5.1 in Day, *Regionalism and Rebellion in Yemen: A Troubled National Union*, 136.

67. Peter Salisbury, 'Yemen's Southern Powder Keg,' *Middle East and North Africa Programme* (Chatham House, March 2018), 10.

68. Brehony, Noel Brehony, *Yemen Divided: The Story of a Failed State in South Arabia*, 197.

69. Day, *Regionalism and Rebellion in Yemen: A Troubled National Union*, 138.

70. Leslie Campbell, 'Party-Building in the Middle East,' *International Journal* 65, no. 3 (2010): 564.

71. Dresch, *A History of Modern Yemen*, 194–7; Brehony, *Yemen Divided: The Story of a Failed State in South Arabia*, 193. The 'internal colonialism' phrasing is also mentioned by Day, who attributes it to Abu Bakr al-Saqqaf. Day, *Regionalism and Rebellion in Yemen: A Troubled National Union*, 138.

72. This was done in a rather superficial way that ignored almost entirely the context of racial oppression in the United States, or the way in which Reconstruction was rolled back and replaced by the Jim Crow system. I mention the US civil war analogy because of the frequency with which it was invoked in interviews; it is an analogy with significant limits.

73. Interview #6 with author, Aden, September 16, 2005.

74. Interview #1 with author, Taiz, August 11, 2005.

75. Interview #1 with author, Taiz, August 11, 2005.

76. Jillian Schwedler, *Faith in Moderation: Islamist Parties in Jordan and Yemen* (Cambridge University Press, 2006), 105–6.

77. Schwedler, *Faith in Moderation: Islamist Parties in Jordan and Yemen*, 107.

78. '1997 Human Rights Report: Yemen' (United States Department of State, January 30, 1998), https://1997-2001.state.gov/www/global/human_rights/1997_hrp_report/yemen.html.

79. 'Yemeni Socialist Party to Boycott April Elections,' *Associated Press*, March 6, 1997.

80. This was recounted to me by a Yemeni politician with one of the smaller opposition parties and was attributed to an interview President Saleh gave to *Al Jazeera*. Interview #36 with author, Sana'a, January 11, 2009.

81. 'The April 27, 2003 Parliamentary Elections in the Republic of Yemen' (National Democratic Institute for International Affairs, 2013), 24. https://www.ndi.org/sites/default/files/1701_yem_elect-rep.pdf.

82. Sarah Phillips, 'Evaluating Political Reform in Yemen,' *Democracy and Rule of Law Program* (Carnegie Endowment for International Peace,

February 2007), 10. https://carnegieendowment.org/files/cp_80_phillips_yemen_final.pdf.

83. 'Yemen's Constitutional Referendum and Local Elections' (Human Rights Watch, February 2001), accessed August 10, 2021, https://www.hrw.org/legacy/backgrounder/mena/yemen-bck-0201.htm. As Phillips observed, 'the idea that Yemen is a transitional democracy remained an important part of the Yemeni government's credibility with Western donors, despite the fact that the liberalism outlined in the first constitution was substantially eroded in subsequent constitutional amendments in 1994 and 2001.' Phillips, *Yemen and the Politics of Permanent Crisis*, 39.

84. 'Human Rights Watch World Report 2001: Yemen: Human Rights Developments,' 2001, https://www.hrw.org/legacy/wr2k1/mideast/yemen.html.

85. 'Yemen's Constitutional Referendum and Local Elections (Human Rights Watch, February 2001).'

86. Interview #36 with author, Sana'a, January 11, 2009.

87. Note that Browers identifies the 1997 election period as the beginning of these conversations, when Islah worked with the Higher Coordination Council for the Opposition to address flaws in the voter registration process. Browers, *Political Ideology in the Arab World*, 146.

88. Campbell, 'Party-Building in the Middle East,' 565.

89. Sarah Phillips, *Yemen and the Politics of Permanent Crisis* (Routledge, 2011), 109.

90. Browers, *Political Ideology in the Arab World*, 150–60.

91. Stacey Philbrick Yadav, 'Antecedents of the Revolution: Intersectoral Networks and Post-Partisanship in Yemen,' *Studies in Ethnicity and Nationalism* 11, no. 3 (2011): 550–63. Clark mapped similar effects in the Islah Charitable Society; while the charity overlaps with but is distinct from the party, it is nonetheless still embedded in its class and professional networks. Janine A Clark, Islam, *Charity, and Activism: Middle-Class Networks and Social Welfare in Egypt, Jordan, and Yemen* (Bloomington: Indiana University Press, 2010).

92. I spent a lot of time in such shared taxi settings, and my field notes describe them as spaces of shared sociability that appeared largely generational and reflected shared cultural references, such as taste in music and film. One particularly vivid memory includes two members—an Islahi and a Nasserist, each in their 30s—sharing one ear bud each from a set of headphones, listening to a favored artist's new release. While transportation time could sometimes include substantive discussion of politics, my experiences indicated that it

helped reinforce social bonds among alliance members, which could in turn become a resource in moments of internal tension within the alliance or among its member parties.

93. Wedeen, *Peripheral Visions*, 114.

94. Staff at NDI and IFES explained to me that any programming offered to Yemeni political parties had to include representatives of the GPC in order to conform to regulations issued by the Ministry of Social Affairs. This means that any 'capacity building' or electoral systems trainings offered to members of the opposition were also made available to the ruling party. It was little wonder that senior members of the GPC were fluent in the relevant buzzwords and concepts.

95. Browers, *Political Ideology in the Arab World*, 149.

96. 'Corruption Perception Index,' Transparency International, accessed August 11, 2021, https://www.transparency.org/en/cpi/2020/index/nzl.

97. 'Freedom in the World Methodology,' Freedom House, accessed August 11, 2021, https://freedomhouse.org/reports/freedom-world/freedom-world-research-methodology.

98. In 2012, in an effort to better understand this process, I participated in the Freedom House coding process and wrote a corresponding section of the Freedom in the World report. In that context, I learned who was responsible for the 2010 coding change. I was not surprised to learn this person was the coder responsible for the shift in score, since we had been in Yemen at the same time and observed many of the same deteriorating developments.

99. 'Courageous Yemeni Editor Undaunted by Harassment' (Committee to Protect Journalists), accessed August 6, 2021, https://cpj.org/awards/amer/.

100. Interview #29 with author, Sana'a, March 13, 2005. It is relevant that none of the three—the person who showed me the paper, the person who called me, and the editor with whom I discussed this—were from the same political party.

101. Yadav, 'Antecedents of the Revolution: Intersectoral Networks and Post-Partisanship in Yemen.'

102. Sarah Phillips, 'Evaluating Political Reform in Yemen,' *Democracy and Rule of Law Program* (Carnegie Endowment for International Peace, February 2007), 9. https://carnegieendowment.org/files/cp_80_phillips_yemen_final.pdf.

103. Interview #1 with author, Taiz, August 11, 2005.

104. Browers, *Political Ideology in the Arab World*, 162.

105. This was a consistent message across interviews with JMP members, and even with some activists who were critical of the JMP. No one genuinely expected Saleh to lose in 2006. They were paying attention to the margin, how many of the opposition's claims he had to answer, and how much money he had to spend.

106. Yadav, *Islamists and the State*, 57; Phillips, *Yemen and the Politics of Permanent Crisis*, 111.

107. Interview #36 with author, Sana'a, January 11, 2009.

108. Browers, *Political Ideology in the Arab World*.

109. Participant in focus group #4 with author, Sana'a, January 1, 2009.

110. 'World Report 2009: Rights Trends in Yemen,' Human Rights Watch, January 13, 2009, https://www.hrw.org/world-report/2009/country-chapters/yemen.

111. Anna Würth, 'Mobilizing Islam and custom against statutory reform: bayt al-tâ'a in Yemen,' *Égypte/Monde arabe*, no. 1 (June 30, 2005): 277–98.

112. Participant in focus group #4 with author, Sana'a, January 1, 2009. He clarified that this meant that the opposition would be fucked by Saleh.

113. Interview #35 with author, Sana'a, January 3, 2009.

114. Interview #35 with author, Sana'a, January 3, 2009.

115. Interview #46 with author, Sana'a, January 12, 2009.

116. 'Yemen's Parliament Rejects Election Law Amendments,' *Associated Press*, August 18, 2008.

117. Participant in focus group #4 with author, Sana'a, January 1, 2009.

118. Participant in focus group #5 with author, January 3, 2009.

119. Interview #38 with author, Sana'a, January 4, 2009.

120. Participant in focus group #4 with author, Sana'a, January 1, 2009.

121. Interview #46 with author, Sana'a, January 12, 2009.

122. Interview #38 with author, Sana'a, January 4, 2009.

123. Interview #38 with author, Sana'a, January 4, 2009.

124. Participant in focus group #4 with author, Sana'a, January 1, 2009.

125. Participant in focus group #5 with author, January 3, 2009.

126. 'Yemen Delays Polls to Redesign Political System: MP,' *Agence France Presse*, February 25, 2009.

127. In addition to the ample documentation in human rights reports, several of which I cite in the next chapter, I was personally subjected to surveillance while conducting research in Yemen. This occurred in more or less obvious ways throughout the time that I conducted fieldwork, but it was especially evident in 2009. Sometimes, however, it was difficult to determine who was the object of scrutiny, such as

when an interviewee received a phone call in the middle of an interview from a security agent who observed me entering the building. Each of us was convinced that we were the one being monitored, and it is likely that we were right.

128. Participant in focus group #5 with author, January 3, 2009.

129. Interview #46 with author, Sana'a, January 12, 2009.

CHAPTER 3. THE SHADOW OF PAST SOVEREIGNTIES

1. Paul Dresch, *A History of Modern Yemen* (Cambridge University Press, 2000), 27.

2. Dresch, *A History of Modern Yemen*, 24.

3. Paul Dresch, *A History of Modern Yemen* (Cambridge University Press, 2000), 25.

4. Shelagh Weir, *A Tribal Order: Politics and Law in the Mountains of Yemen* (University of Texas Press, 2007).

5. Readers interested in an elaboration on this topic or a discussion of the gradual evolution of Zaydism in the broader context of Shi'ism should see Najam Haider, *Shi'i Islam: An Introduction* (Cambridge University Press, 2014).

6. Marieke Brandt, *Tribes and Politics in Yemen: A History of the Houthi Conflict* (Hurst, 2017). This was a constant source of discussion among my interlocutors in Sana'a, as well, who would point out the lavish homes or businesses owned by shaykhs from more distant parts of the North.

7. Gabriele vom Bruck, *Islam, Memory, and Morality in Yemen: Ruling Families in Transition* (Palgrave Macmillan, 2005). Vom Bruck identifies ways in which educated *sada* refashioned themselves as constitutionalists and technocrats in the decades that followed. Brandt also mentions that some became career civil servants, but 'their new salaries were in no way comparable to their previous *waqf* income.' Brandt, *Tribes and Politics in Yemen*, 64.

8. Brandt, *Tribes and Politics in Yemen*, 64.

9. vom Bruck, *Islam, Memory, and Morality in Yemen*, 146–51.

10. Shelagh Weir, *A Tribal Order: Politics and Law in the Mountains of Yemen* (University of Texas Press, 2007), 64–5.

11. Gokh Amin Al-Shaif, 'On Origin Myths and Geneaological Imagination: The Marginalization of Yemen's Black Community' (Crown Center for Middle East Studies, Brandeis University, March 24, 2021). Al-Shaif describes five social tiers, whereas Brandt locates al-Shaif's third, fourth, and fifth stata in the broad grouping of *Ahl al-*

Thulth, the people of the (bottom) third. Brandt, *Tribes and Politics in Yemen,* 23.

12. Shelagh Weir, *A Tribal Order: Politics and Law in the Mountains of Yemen* (University of Texas Press, 2007), 64–5.

13. Stevenson, 'Yemeni Workers Come Home: Reabsorbing One Million Migrants.'

14. Bernard Haykel, 'Dissembling Descent, or How the Barber Lost His Turban: Identity and Evidence in Eighteenth-Century Zaydī Yemen," *Islamic Law and Society* 9, no. 2 (2002): 194–230.

15. Shelagh Weir, *A Tribal Order: Politics and Law in the Mountains of Yemen* (University of Texas Press, 2007), 63.

16. vom Bruck, *Islam, Memory, and Morality in Yemen,* 145.

17. Weir, *A Tribal Order,* 48.

18. Vom Bruck, *Islam, Memory, and Morality in Yemen,* 146.

19. Brandt, *Tribes and Politics in Yemen,* 146.

20. Brandt, *Tribes and Politics in Yemen,* 114.

21. Brandt, *Tribes and Politics in Yemen,* 121. Brandt cites Hamidi (2009, 169) on this.

22. Najam Haider, *Shi'i Islam: An Introduction* (Cambridge University Press, 2014), 178. See also Gabrielle vom Bruck, 'Regimes of Piety Revisited: Zaydi Political Moralities in Republican Yemen,' *Die Welt des Islam* 50 (2010), 202, fn. 50.

23. It is worth noting that al-Mansur himself was a teacher and mentor to Husayn al-Houthi, the *sayyid* from Sa'ada who would eventually lead the movement bearing his name. Before he initiated an insurgent campaign, however, al-Houthi was an elected member of parliament following al-Mansur's prescription.

24. Boucek, 'War in Sa'ada: From Local Insurrection to National Challenge.' In *Yemen on the Brink,* Carnegie Endowment for International Peace, 2010, 46.

25. Lisa Wedeen, *Peripheral Visions: Publics, Power, and Performance in Yemen* (Chicago: University of Chicago Press, 2009), 165.

26. Shelagh Weir, *A Tribal Order: Politics and Law in the Mountains of Yemen* (University of Texas Press, 2007), 297.

27. vom Bruck, *Islam, Memory, and Morality in Yemen,* 150.

28. Shelagh Weir, *A Tribal Order: Politics and Law in the Mountains of Yemen* (University of Texas Press, 2007), 297.

29. In scholarly accounts, Weir uses this terminology in several published works. Given how differently this term circulated when I was conducting fieldwork, I am inclined to think that there is both a temporal dimension and also, perhaps, a spatial difference. Her

primary research was in Razih in the 1990s, whereas mine was in Sana'a in the 2000s. Brandt bridges this gap, and also uses both terms, sometimes hyphenated as Salafi-Wahhabi.

30. This is also consistent with what Bonnefoy describes, though we were working in different parts of the country. Laurent Bonnefoy, *Salafism in Yemen: Transnationalism and Religious Identity* (Hurst, 2011).

31. Interestingly, both *salafi* and *anti-salafi* members of Islah used the expression 'we are all Muslims' with regularity, to different ends. In *salafi* usage, it appeared to be a call to other Muslims to adhere to correct belief and practice, whereas Muslim Brothers or others in the center of the Islah party tended to use it to mean that *salafis* ought to respect different views.

32. Interview #27 with author, Sana'a, October 3, 2005. Interview #26 with author, Sana'a, October 3, 2005.

33. Bonnefoy, *Salafism in Yemen,* 227.

34. Laurent Bonnefoy, *Salafism in Yemen,* 226.

35. Laurent Bonnefoy, *Salafism in Yemen,* 27; Marieke Brandt, *Tribes and Politics in Yemen: A History of the Houthi Conflict,* 106.

36. This is not to deny that there is a relationship between the expansion of Yemeni *Salafism* and Yemeni ties to Saudi Arabia. This is tied not only to Saudi financial support for religious institutions, but to decades of labor migration and cultural exchange across a border that was only settled in 2000. Particularly prior to unification, large numbers of workers from the North traveled predominantly to Saudi Arabia, where some Yemenis were largely exempted from the exploitative restrictions of the Kingdom's *kafala* system and were more able to experience the (male) egalitarianism that was being preached by evangelists at home. Stevenson, 'Yemeni Workers Come Home: Reabsorbing One Million Migrants.'

37. Bonnefoy, *Salafism in Yemen,* 228. As Bonnefoy explains elsewhere, 'the *sada* are allegedly Arabs of the north, supposed descendants of 'Adnan. They are thus from a different line than the local tribes who descend from Qahtan, the legendary ancestor of the Arabs of the South. Qahtani tribes therefore claim a territorial presence that well predates the arrival of the first Zaydi imam in Yemen, Yahya bin al-Husayn, in the ninth century.' Laurent Bonnefoy, *Yemen and the World: Beyond Insecurity* (Oxford University Press, 2018), 21. The Qahtan-'Adnan distinction is thus used as a convenient gloss for those 'from here' and those 'from away.'

38. Bernard Haykel, 'A Zaydi Revival?' *Yemen Update* 36, no. Winter/Spring (1995): 20–1.

39. Sheila Carapico, ed., *Arabia Incognita: Dispatches from Yemen and the Gulf* (Just World Books, 2016), 48.

40. Lisa Wedeen, *Peripheral Visions: Publics, Power, and Performance in Yemen.* (Chicago: University of Chicago Press, 2009), 167.

41. Nader Hashemi and Danny Postel, 'Introduction: The Sectarianization Thesis,' in *Sectarianization: Mapping the New Politics of the Middle East*, ed. Nader Hashemi and Danny Postel (Hurst, 2017), 4.

42. Lisa Wedeen, *Peripheral Visions: Publics, Power, and Performance in Yemen*, 161–2.

43. For a discussion of early republican reforms to religious education under President Ibrahim Hamdi (1974–7) and later shifts to move religious education outside of the Ministry of Education, see Franck Mermier, 'L'islam Politique Au Yémen Ou La "Tradition" Contre Les Traditions?' *Monde Arabe Maghreb Machrek*, 6–19, 155 (1997). On the role of private funding, see Maysaa Shuja Al-Deen, 'Yemen's War-Torn Rivalries for Religious Education – Islamic Institutions in Arab States: Mapping the Dynamics of Control, Co-Option, and Contention,' accessed September 13, 2021, https://carnegieendowment.org/2021/06/07/yemen-s-war-torn-rivalries-for-religious-education-pub-84651.

44. Al-Deen, 'Yemen's War-Torn Rivalries for Religious Education.'

45. Haykel, 'A Zaydi Revival?' 21.

46. Bonnefoy, *Salafism in Yemen*, 55.

47. Bonnefoy, *Salafism in Yemen*, 55.

48. Al-Deen, 'Yemen's War-Torn Rivalries for Religious Education.'

49. Stacey Philbrick Yadav, 'Yemen's Muslim Brotherhood and the Perils of Powersharing,' Rethinking Political Islam (The Brookings Institution, August 2015), 3.

50. Haykel, 'A Zaydi Revival?' 20.

51. Barak A. Salmoni, Bryce Loidolt, and Madeleine Wells, *Regime and Periphery in Northern Yemen: The Huthi Phenomenon* (RAND National Defense Research Institute, 2010).

52. Haykel, 'A Zaydi Revival?' 20.

53. Brandt, *Tribes and Politics in Yemen,* 128.

54. Marieke Brandt, 'The Irregulars of the Sa'ada War: "Colonel Sheikhs" and "Tribal Militias" in Yemen's Huthi Conflict,' in *Why Yemen Matters: A Society in Transition*, ed. Helen Lackner (Saqi Books, 2014), 117.

55. Boucek, 'War in Sa'ada: From Local Insurrection to National Challenge,' 54.

56. Brandt, 'The Irregulars of the Sa'ada War.'

57. On the broad changes in civil-military relations in the 2000s, see Adam C. Seitz, 'Ties That Bind and Divide: The "Arab Spring" and Yemeni Civil-Military Relations,' in *Why Yemen Matters: A Society in Transition*, ed. Helen Lackner (Saqi Books, 2014), 50–67. For the implications of posting colonel shaykhs far from home, see Brandt, 'The Irregulars of the Sa'ada War,' 113–16.

58. Shelagh Weir offers a compelling account of the relationship between violence and restraint in Razih, whereby violence 'has a legitimate place in human relations, but should be curbed and regulated. Every effort should be made to prevent conflicts escalating, and to channel them into peaceful negotiations.' Weir, *A Tribal Order,* 190.

59. Brandt, 'The Irregulars of the Sa'ada War,' 116.

60. Maysaa Shuja Al-Deen, 'Media Absent from Yemen's Forgotten War,' *Arab Media and Society*, May 6, 2009, https://www.arabmediasociety. com/media-absent-from-yemens-forgotten-war/.

61. 'World Report 2009: Taking Back the Initiative from Human Rights Spoilers' (Human Rights Watch), accessed August 23, 2021, https:// www.hrw.org/world-report/2009/country-chapters/yemen.

62. Interview #11 with author, Sana'a, October 10, 2004.

63. Ginny Hill, *Yemen Endures: Civil War, Saudi Adventurism, and the Future of Arabia* (Oxford University Press, 2017), 77.

64. One personal experience illustrated to me the power and reach of 'Ali Mushin's mythology. After some trial and error in the first weeks of fieldwork, when I was in Sana'a I generally wore a black 'abaya covering my clothes and a scarf around my neck, but not my hair. One of only two occasions on which this created an obvious problem involved the specter of 'Ali Muhsin. Riding to a *qat* chew with some members of the JMP in 2009, I asked to exit a taxi about one block from my host's home, in an area close to where 'Ali Muhsin lived. The driver nervously advised me to pull up my scarf and cover my hair. When I explained that my scarf was too short, he turned the car around and drove several blocks out of the way so that I could reach my destination without needing to walk in proximity to 'Ali Muhsin's home. He was concerned, he said, that I would have an encounter with 'Ali Muhsin's 'associates.' There existed by then a kind of common knowledge of 'Ali Muhsin's relationship not only to *salafis*, but to those among them who would use extrajudicial violence. When I reached the home of my host, I asked them about this—in large part because I had never had an interaction like this in Sana'a. Across the board, attendees at the chew applauded the driver's rerouting.

65. JMP members were aware of this internal tension within Islah, as they worked to generate a common JMP critique of the human rights violations and collective punishment in Sa'ada. Stacey Philbrick Yadav, *Islamists and the State: Legitimacy and Institutions in Yemen and Lebanon* (I.B. Tauris, 2013), 52–4.

66. Yadav, *Islamists and the State,* 208–10.

67. Interview #35 with author, Sana'a, January 3, 2009.

68. Interview #35 with author, January 3, 2009.

69. Interview #40 with author, Sana'a, January 4, 2009.

70. Interview #38 with author, Sana'a, January 4, 2009.

71. Boucek, 'War in Sa'ada: From Local Insurrection to National Challenge,' 52–3.

72. Boucek, 'War in Sa'ada: From Local Insurrection to National Challenge,' 55.

73. Stephen Day, 'The Political Challenge of Yemen's Southern Movement,' in *Yemen on the Brink*, ed. Christopher Boucek and Marina Ottaway (Carnegie Endowment for International Peace, 2010), 66.

74. Day, 'The Political Challenge of Yemen's Southern Movement,' 66.

75. It is worth noting, however, as Carapico does, that the economic systems of North and South were not as different as they are often rhetorically positioned, given the role of development projects financed or sanctioned by international financial institutions in the North and the fact that the PDRY never fully eradicated the private sector. Carapico, 'The Economic Dimensions of Yemeni Unity.'

76. Day, 'The Political Challenge of Yemen's Southern Movement,' 65–6.

77. Susanne Dahlgren, 'The Snake with a Thousand Heads: The Southern Cause in Yemen,' in *Arabia Incognita: Dispatches from Yemen and the Gulf*, ed. Sheila Carapico (Just World Books, 2016), 170–1. This essay was originally published in *Middle East Report* 256 in 2010.

78. Stevenson, 'Yemeni Workers Come Home: Reabsorbing One Million Migrants,' 91.

79. Susanne Dahlgren, *Contesting Realities: The Public Sphere and Morality in Southern Yemen* (Syracuse University Press, 2014), 83.

80. Dahlgren, 'The Snake with a Thousand Heads,' 171.

81. Stephen Day, 'The Political Challenge of Yemen's Southern Movement,' in *Yemen on the Brink*, ed. Christopher Boucek and Marina Ottaway (Carnegie Endowment for International Peace, 2010), 66.

82. Dahlgren, *'Contesting Realities,'* 83.

83. Dahlgren, *'Contesting Realities,'* 84.

84. Dahlgren, *'Contesting Realities,'* 84.

85. Interview #6 with author, Aden, September 16, 2005.

86. Day, 'The Political Challenge of Yemen's Southern Movement,' 68.
87. Boucek, 'War in Sa'ada: From Local Insurrection to National Challenge,' 58.
88. Dahlgren, 'The Snake with a Thousand Heads.'
89. As cited in Dahlgren, 'The Snake with a Thousand Heads,' 169.
90. Sheila Carapico, 'Kill the Messengers: Yemen's 2009 Clampdown on the Press,' Middle East Institute, June 2, 2009, https://www.mei.edu/publications/kill-messengers-yemens-2009-clampdown-press.
91. 'CPJ Protests Conviction of "Al-Ayyam" Journalists,' IFEX, August 5, 1999, https://ifex.org/cpj-protests-conviction-of-al-ayyam-journalists/.
92. 'Government Seizes Newspaper Offices in Yemen,' Committee to Protect Journalists, May 4, 2009, https://cpj.org/2009/05/government-seizes-newspaper-offices-in-yemen/.
93. 'CPJ Calls on Yemen to End Siege of Independent Newspaper,' Committee to Protect Journalists, January 5, 2010, https://cpj.org/2010/01/cpj-calls-on-yemen-to-end-siege-of-independent-new/.
94. Notably, this occurred during the transitional period after the 2011 uprising, highlighting the continuing threat that the Hirak was seen as posing to the Yemeni state even under its new transitional regime. 'Witnesses in Al-Ayyam Case Turn against Prosecution,' *Committee to Protect Journalists* (blog), January 10, 2012, https://cpj.org/2012/01/witnesses-in-al-ayyam-case-turn-against-yemeni-pro/. Yemen's Specialized Criminal Court (SCC) was established in 1999 by presidential decree, with expanded jurisdiction in 2004 to address vaguely framed 'state security' crimes. In 2009, branches of the SCC were established in Aden and Hodeidah, in addition to Sana'a, and a second specialized court specifically for press crimes was introduced. See Amnesty International, 'Yemen: Cracking Down Under Pressure,' August 25, 2010, https://www.amnesty.org/en/documents/MDE31/010/2010/en/.
95. Shelagh Weir, *A Tribal Order: Politics and Law in the Mountains of Yemen* (University of Texas Press, 2007).
96. Interview #46 with author, Sana'a, January 12, 2009.
97. Interview #46 with author, Sana'a, January 12, 2009.
98. Rafiah al-Talei, 'Interview with Dr. Muhammad Abd al-Malik al-Mutawakkil, Assistant Secretary-General of the Federation for Popular Forces,' Arab Reform Bulletin (Carnegie Endowment for International Peace, August 19, 2008).

99. This expression can be attributed to Phillips, *Yemen and the Politics of Permanent Crisis*.

100. Dresch, *A History of Modern Yemen*, 172.

101. Stacey Philbrick Yadav, 'No Pink Slip for Salih: What Yemen's Protests Do (and Do Not) Mean,' in *Arabia Incognita: Dispatches from Yemen and the Gulf*, ed. Sheila Carapico (Just World Books, 2016), 176.

102. Alistair Harris, 'Exploiting Grievances: Al-Qaeda in the Arabian Peninsula,' in *Yemen on the Brink*, ed. Christopher Boucek and Marina Ottaway (Carnegie Endowment for International Peace, 2010), 31–44.

103. The winter of 2009 was the first time that Yemeni friends began to express concern about my safety, offering to drive or pick me up from meetings so that I could avoid taking taxis or being on the streets. After years of being able to move reasonably freely in the capital, I had to begin planning much more carefully.

104. 'Yemen and the Rome Statute,' Parliamentarians for Global Action, accessed August 3, 2021, https://www.pgaction.org/ilhr/rome-statute/yemen.html.

105. Amnesty International, 'Yemen: Amnesty International Urges Yemen to Complete the Ratification of the Rome Statute,' March 24, 2007, https://www.amnesty.org/download/Documents/68000/mde310042007en.pdf.

106. United States Department of State, 'Diplomatic Note,' December 10, 2003, https://foia.state.gov/documents/IntAgreements/0000BA1E.pdf.

107. Stacey Philbrick Yadav, 'No Pink Slip for Salih: What Yemen's Protests Do (and Do Not) Mean,' in *Arabia Incognita: Dispatches from Yemen and the Gulf*, ed. Sheila Carapico (Just World Books, 2016), 176. This essay was originally published by *Middle East Report* on February 9, 2011.

108. Amnesty International, 'Yemen: Cracking Down Under Pressure,' 23.

109. International Monetary Fund, 'Republic of Yemen: 2008 Article IV Consultation: Staff Report; Staff Statement and Supplement; Public Information Notice on the Executive Board Discussion; and Statement by the Executive Director for the Republic of Yemen,' *IMF Staff Country Reports* 2009, no. 100 (March 24, 2009), https://doi.org/10.5089/9781451840834.002.A001.

110. Grace Easterly, 'Before 2014: Yemen's Economy Before the War' (Yemen Peace Project, June 16, 2018), https://www.yemenpeaceproject.org/blog-x/2018/7/16/before-2014-yemens-economy-before-the-war.

111. Gerhard Lichtenthaeler, 'Water Conflict and Cooperation in Yemen,' *Middle East Report* 254, no. Spring (March 24, 2010), https://merip.org/2010/03/water-conflict-and-cooperation-in-yemen/.

112. Mona El-Ghobashy, *Bread and Freedom: Egypt's Revolutionary Situation* (Stanford University Press, 2021), 37.

CHAPTER 4. THE SHADOW OF TRANSITION

1.   Laurent Bonnefoy, *Yemen and the World: Beyond Insecurity* (Oxford University Press, 2018), 36.

2.   Tawakkol Karman, for example, who became symbolically significant and was later recognized for her activism with the 2011 Nobel Peace Prize, was known for having organized a weekly protest outside of the Ministry of Justice for years; Karman was a journalist, founder of a civil society organization devoted to press freedoms, and a member of Islah's leadership.

3.   Yadav, 'No Pink Slip for Salih.'

4.   Laura Kasinof, 'Are Yemen's Protests Going to Bring Another Revolution?' *Christian Science Monitor*, January 27, 2011.

5.   Yadav, 'No Pink Slip for Salih.'

6.   'Yemen Politics: Saleh's Turn,' *Economist Intelligence Unit*, January 27, 2011.

7.   From at least 2009, the Washington policy community expressed open concern that Yemen was 'on the brink' or in chaos. Edited volumes and working papers published by prominent think tanks projected Yemen's descent into chaos in the face of interlocking political, economic, and security crises. One such volume unironically used this as its title. See Christopher Boucek and Marina Ottway, eds., *Yemen on the Brink* (Washington, DC: Carnegie Endowment for International Peace, 2010). As Sheila Carapico and I argued, however, 'brinkologists' had been 'forecasting state failure for more than a decade,' contributing to the very insecurity rent-seeking that was central to the regime and deepened the governance crisis. See Yadav and Carapico, 'The Breakdown of the GCC Initiative.' More generally regarding governance aid and insecurity rent-seeking, see Sheila Carapico, *Political Aid and Arab Activism: Democracy Promotion, Justice, and Representation* (Cambridge University Press, 2014); Phillips, *Yemen and the Politics of Permanent Crisis.*

8.   This rhetoric became particularly prominent after regime defections following the massacre of civilian protesters on March 18, as discussed later in this chapter. Jeb Boone, 'Defiant Yemen President Warns

"Mutinous" Military of Long, Bloody Civil War,' *The Independent*, March 23, 2011.

9. Nasser Arrabyee and Sara Shurafa, 'Saleh Will Seek Pardon for Any Mistakes Made,' *Gulf News*, January 25, 2011.

10. 'Yemen Activists Breaking New Ground,' BBC News, February 2, 2011, sec. Middle East, https://www.bbc.com/news/world-middle-east-12344487.

11. Yadav, 'Antecedents of the Revolution: Intersectoral Networks and Post-Partisanship in Yemen.'

12. 'Yemenis Celebrate, Situation Tense as Mubarak Falls,' *Reuters*, February 12, 2011, sec. World News, https://www.reuters.com/article/idINIndia-54845320110212.

13. Ala Qasem, 'Five Barriers to Youth Inclusion, Decision-Making and Leadership in Yemen's Political Parties,' Briefing (SaferWorld, December 2013), 2. https://www.saferworld.org.uk/resources/publications/785-five-barriers-to-youth-engagement-decision-making-and-leadership-in-yemens-political-parties.

14. Interview #57 with author, electronic communication, January 4, 2013.

15. Stacey Philbrick Yadav, 'The "Yemen Model" as a Failure of Political Imagination,' *International Journal of Middle East Studies* 47, no. 1 (2015): 144–7.

16. Lisa Wedeen, *Peripheral Visions: Publics, Power, and Performance in Yemen*, 170.

17. Atiaf Zaid Alwazir, '"Youth" Inclusion in Yemen: A Necessary Element for Success of Political Transition,' *Arab Reform Initiative*, December 24, 2012, 3. https://www.arab-reform.net/publication/youth-inclusion-in-yemen-a-necessary-element-for-success-of-political-transition/.

18. Atiaf Zaid Alwazir, '"Youth" Inclusion in Yemen: A Necessary Element for Success of Political Transition,' *Arab Reform Initiative*, December 24, 2012, 3. https://www.arab-reform.net/publication/youth-inclusion-in-yemen-a-necessary-element-for-success-of-political-transition/.

19. Stephen Zunes, 'The Power of Strategic Nonviolent Action in Arab Revolutions,' Middle East Institute, August 1, 2011, https://www.mei.edu/publications/power-strategic-nonviolent-action-arab-revolutions.

20. This observation is recorded in notes from multiple conversations with and observations of youth activists in 2012 and 2013, but was also confirmed explicitly in ongoing correspondence. Interviews #56 and #57 with author, electronic communication, January 4, 2013.

21. Yadav, 'The "Yemen Model" as a Failure of Political Imagination.'

22. Sarah Phillips, 'Questioning Failure, Stability, and Risk in Yemen,' in *Fragile Politics: Weak States in the Greater Middle East*, ed. Mehran Kamrava (Oxford University Press, 2016), 17.

23. Katherine Hennessey, 'Yemeni Society in the Spotlight: Theater and Film in Yemen Before, During, and After the Arab Spring,' in *Why Yemen Matters: A Society in Transition*, ed. Helen Lackner (London: Saqi Books, 2014), 73.

24. Interview #56 with author, electronic communication, January 4, 2013.

25. SupportYemen and Resonate Yemen, Yemen Enlightenment Debate: 'Foreign Aid to Yemen Caused More Harm than Good,' 2012, https://www.youtube.com/watch?v=G2D8qFkYwWc. This Oxford style debate featured a number of prominent youth activists and was moderated by Ginny Hill for Chatham House. I was present at the recording of a subsequent debate, also moderated by Hill, on the status of shari'a in a civil state. Given the sensitivity of this topic, the organizers declined to record that session and held it under Chatham House rule.

26. Two prominent exceptions to this include the new secular liberal al-Watan, co-founded by the late youth activist, Ibrahim Mothana, who died unexpectedly in 2013, and the *salafi* al-Rashad Union, which sought to distinguish itself from Islah and was among the parties that participated in the National Dialogue Conference. See Laurent Bonnefoy and Judit Kuschnitizki, 'Salafis and the "Arab Spring" in Yemen: Progressive Politicization and Resilient Quietism,' *Arabian Humanities*, no. 4 (January 12, 2015), https://journals.openedition.org/cy/2811#tocto1n2.

27. The most well-known of these is likely #SupportYemen, which borrows its name from a hashtag introduced during the uprising. Members of the #SupportYemen team turned from working as citizen journalists during the early phases of the uprising to producing short films that highlighted the disconnect between national political actors and Yemenis outside of the country's urban centers. The team describes itself as committed to grassroots and participatory storytelling and is composed of members who are 'part of the intersectional movement in Yemen and the world that shares the values and struggle for equality, social justice, and autonomous voices and narratives of people.' https://supportyemen.org/. Members of the collective were also involved in the production of the Oscar-nominated documentary, 'Karama Has No Walls,' which details the events of March 18, 2011.

28. Yadav, 'Antecedents of the Revolution: Intersectoral Networks and Post-Partisanship in Yemen.'

29. Alwazir, '"Youth" Inclusion in Yemen,' 3.

30. Laura Kasinof, *Don't Be Afraid of the Bullets: An Accidental War Correspondent in Yemen* (Arcade Publishing, 2014), 79.

31. Tom Finn, 'Beyond the Walls of Yemen's Revolution,' *The New Yorker*, February 27, 2014, https://www.newyorker.com/culture/culture-desk/beyond-the-walls-of-yemens-revolution. For visual documentation and interviews with survivors, see Sara Ishaq, *Karama Has No Walls*, 2014, https://karamafilm.com/. Finn describes the events of March 18 as the 'bloodiest crackdown in Yemen's history,' while Human Rights Watch describes it as the most violent event of the 2011 uprising; the latter interpretation makes more sense to me in light of limitations on access and documentation of repression in the 2000s, if not earlier. See 'Unpunished Massacre: Yemen's Failed Response to the "Friday of Dignity" Killings' (Human Rights Watch, February 12, 2013), https://www.hrw.org/report/2013/02/12/unpunished-massacre/yemens-failed-response-friday-dignity-killings.

32. 'Unpunished Massacre.'

33. Stephen W. Day, *Regionalism and Rebellion in Yemen: A Troubled National Union*, 282.

34. 'High-Level Defections Weaken Presidential Camp,' *France* 24, March 21, 2011, https://www.france24.com/en/20110321-defects-weaken-president-camp-face-protests-army-saleh-yemen.

35. Hakim Al-Masmari and William Branigin, 'Saleh Suffers String of Major Defections after Protesters Gunned down in Yemen,' *Washington Post*, March 21, 2011, https://www.washingtonpost.com/world/saleh-suffers-string-of-major-defections-after-protesters-gunned-down-in-yemen/2011/03/21/ABhbbJ7_story.html.

36. For an account of both motives and effects of buying time until 'the most effective strongman' to replace Saleh could be identified, see Ginny Hill, *Yemen Endures: Civil War, Saudi Adventurism, and the Future of Arabia*, 238.

37. Hill, *Yemen Endures: Civil War, Saudi Adventurism, and the Future of Arabia*, 239.

38. Robert F. Worth, 'Fighting Intensifies in Yemen as the Government Battles Tribal Groups,' *The New York Times*, May 24, 2011, sec. World, https://www.nytimes.com/2011/05/25/world/middleeast/25yemen.html.

39. Mohammed Ghobari, 'Civil War Fears Chill Traumatised Yemen Neighbourhood,' *Reuters*, August 10, 2011, sec. *World News*,

https://www.reuters.com/article/oukwd-uk-yemen-fighting-idAFTRE7794DP20110810.

40. Kelly McEvers, 'Yemen Tribesmen Protect Anti-Government Protesters,' *Morning Edition* (National Public Radio, August 10, 2011), https://www.npr.org/2011/08/10/139346563/yemen-tribesmen-protect-anti-government-protesters.

41. Bonnefoy and Poirier, 'La Structuration de La Révolution Yéménite,' trans. by Jasper Cooper. *Revue Française de Science Politique* 62, no. 5 (2012): 133.

42. For details of attacks on civilians, see ' No Safe Places": Yemen's Crackdown on Protests in Taizz' (*Human Rights Watch*, February 6, 2012), https://www.hrw.org/report/2012/02/06/no-safe-places/yemens-crackdown-protests-taizz. For discussion of Taiz's reputation and its role in the uprising and a longform interview with Taizi activist, Bushra al-Maqtari, see Robert Worth, 'Yemen on the Brink of Hell,' *New York Times Magazine*, July 20, 2011, https://www.nytimes.com/2011/07/24/magazine/yemen-on-the-brink-of-hell.html.

43. 'Yemen: Protester Killings Show Perils of Immunity Deal' (*Human Rights Watch*, September 20, 2011), https://www.hrw.org/news/2011/09/20/yemen-protester-killings-show-perils-immunity-deal.

44. Hill, *Yemen Endures*, 240.

45. United Nations Security Council, 'Resolution 2014,' October 21, 2011, http://unscr.com/en/resolutions/2014. Note that the Office of the Special Envoy to the Secretary General for Yemen (OSESGY) was not formally established until 2012. Benomar was be the first of four people to fill that role over the course of a decade.

46. 'Agreement/Gulf Cooperation Council (GCC) Initiative' (PA-X: Peace Agreement Database, November 23, 2011), https://www.peaceagreements.org/view/1401.

47. 'Presidential Decree No. 24,' September 12, 2011, https://www.peaceagreements.org/viewmasterdocument/1402.

48. 'Agreement on the Implementation Mechanism for the Transition Process in Yemen in Accordance with the Initiative of the Gulf Cooperation Council,' November 23, 2011, https://www.peaceagreements.org/viewmasterdocument/758.

49. 'GCC Implementation Mechanism,' Article 8, 3.

50. 'GCC Implementation Mechanism,' Article 21f and 21h, 7–8.

51. 'Agreement/Gulf Cooperation Council (GCC) Initiative.'

52. Mohammed Sudam and Mohammed Ghobari, 'Saleh Refuses to Sign Yemen Deal despite Pressure,' *Reuters*, May 22, 2011, sec.

World   News,   https://www.reuters.com/article/us-yemen-idUSTRE73L1PP20110522.

53. 'Yemen: Amnesty Law in Breach of International Law and Yemen's Obligations,' *International Center for Transitional Justice*, January 11, 2012, https://www.ictj.org/news/yemen-amnesty-law-breach-international-law-and-yemen%E2%80%99s-obligations-0.

54. 'No Amnesty for Gross Human Rights Violations in Yemen, Top UN Official Says,' January 6, 2012, https://news.un.org/en/story/2012/01/399912-no-amnesty-gross-human-rights-violations-yemen-top-un-official-says.

55. 'Amnesty International Urges Yemen to Reject Amnesty Law for President Saleh and Aides,' January 10, 2012, https://www.amnestyusa.org/press-releases/amnesty-international-urges-yemen-to-reject-amnesty-law-for-president-saleh-and-aides/.

56. 'Witnesses: Thousands Protest Deal Granting Yemeni President Immunity,' accessed October 20, 2021, http://www.cnn.com/2011/WORLD/meast/04/24/yemen.president.exit/index.html.

57. Ahmed Al-Haj and Ben Hubbard, 'Yemen Immunity Law Sparks Debates over Past Crimes,' *Associated Press*, January 9, 2012.

58. Noha Aboueldahab, *Transitional Justice and the Prosecution of Political Leaders in the Arab Region: A Comparative Study of Egypt, Libya, Tunisia and Yemen* (Bloomsbury Publishing, 2017), 110.

59. Shelagh Weir describes wijah, as a kind of confrontation by demonstration and argues that they are 'essentially exercises in communication and persuasion, not attempts to overcome adversaries by brute force.' Ordered by norms that differ from those governing warfare, she cites an explanation by a Naziri tribeman who explains that 'a wijah is supposed to cause the offending tribe expense and avoid violence' and adds that 'the implicit message might be paraphrased as "we are united behind our shaykh, we are many, and we can afford to take you on."' Shelagh Weir, *A Tribal Order: Politics and Law in the Mountains of Yemen* (University of Texas Press, 2007), 207.

60. Total numbers by the time the Life March reached Sana'a are put at 'thousands' but difficult to disaggregate, since marchers joined those who were continuing to sit-in at Change Square. Video from along the route, including some taken from the hills above the road showing the length of the procession, do support the idea that the crowd grew considerably over the course of 4 days. For a series of such videos, see Noon Arabia, 'Yemen: The Amazing Life March Arrives in Sana'a,' *Global Voices* (blog), December 24, 2011, https://globalvoices.org/2011/12/24/yemen-the-amazing-march-of-life-arrives-in-sanaa/.

61. Noon Arabia, 'Yemen: The Amazing Life March Arrives in Sana'a.'

62. I spent much of that week watching the events unfold via videos shared on Twitter and waiting to see this reflected in news or commentary. What little attention it did receive in Western media fit the model criticized by Murad Alazzany, n40.

63. Murad Alazzany, 'Yemeni Youth March "Shows True Spirit of Revolution,"' *CNN*, January 16, 2012, https://www.cnn.com/2012/01/16/opinion/murad-alazzany-yemen-oped/index.html.

64. 'Seven Shot Dead in Yemen Protests: Medics,' *Agence France Presse*, December 24, 2011.

65. Mohammed Ghobari, 'Truce Called for after Yemen Troops Kill Protesters,' *Reuters*, December 26, 2011.

66. Marie-Christine Heinze and Hafez Albukhari, 'Opportunities for Security Sector Reform in Yemen,' in *Addressing Security Sector Reform in Yemen: Challenges and Opportunities for Intervention During and Post-Conflict* (Center for Applied Research in Partnership with the Orient, 2017), 40–8, https://carpo-bonn.org/wp-content/uploads/2017/12/carpo_policy_report_04_2017.pdf.

67. Ginny Hill, *Yemen Endures: Civil War, Saudi Adventurism, and the Future of Arabia*, 241.

68. Abubakr Al-Shamahi, 'New "parallel Revolution" against Corruption,' *Al Jazeera*, January 2, 2012, https://www.aljazeera.com/opinions/2012/1/2/new-parallel-revolution-against-corruption.

69. An appendix to Gordon's March 2012 account includes a base-by-base list of disruptions from January 2012 to July 2013. Sasha Gordon, 'The Parallel Revolution in Yemen' (American Enterprise Institute, March 6, 2012), https://www.criticalthreats.org/analysis/the-parallel-revolution-in-yemen. Note that I cite this for the list, not the analysis in the article, which reduces the significance of these events to their implications for the containment of Al Qaeda in the Arabian Peninsula as a US counterterrorism priority. The parallel revolution was doubtless of wider significance for Yemenis.

70. Hill, *Yemen Endures*, 260.

71. Tom Finn, 'Yemen's "parallel Revolution" Inspires Street-Level Protests,' *Reuters*, January 27, 2012, https://www.reuters.com/article/us-yemen-strikes/yemens-parallel-revolution-inspires-street-level-protests-idUSTRE80Q0RU20120127.

72. Atiaf Alwazir, 'Yemen's Enduring Resistance: Youth between Politics and Informal Mobilization,' *Mediterranean Politics* 21, no. 1 (2016): 186, https://doi.org/10.1080/13629395.2015.1081446.

73. Qasem, 'Five Barriers to Youth Inclusion, Decision-Making and Leadership in Yemen's Political Parties.'

74. Atiaf Alwazir, 'Yemen's Enduring Resistance: Youth between Politics and Informal Mobilization,' *Mediterranean Politics* 21, no. 1 (2016): 171.

75. Qasem, 'Five Barriers to Youth Inclusion, Decision-Making and Leadership in Yemen's Political Parties,' 1.

76. Given my prior work on Islah, I was contacted by several think-tanks, advocacy organizations, and government agencies for suggestions of Islahi youth who might be available to visit Washington or London during this time period. They were keen to provide 'balanced' representation of Yemeni youth but still approached this through the lens of partisan balance. The two people I most often suggested left the party later in the transitional period to become independents.

77. Qasem, 'Five Barriers to Youth Inclusion, Decision-Making and Leadership in Yemen's Political Parties,' 2.

78. This discussion is based on notes I took at a meeting of youth activists in early 2012 in Madaaba, Jordan, sponsored by Chatham House. It was held under Chatham House rule, so the conversations may be characterized, but not attributed to any individual or group. In other sections of this chapter, I draw on separate interviews with individual participants in the program.

79. National Archives and Records Administration Office of the Federal Register, 'DCPD-201200376 – Executive Order 13611-Blocking Property of Persons Threatening the Peace, Security, or Stability of Yemen,' Government, govinfo.gov (Office of the Federal Register, National Archives and Records Administration, May 16, 2012), https://www.govinfo.gov/app/details/https%3A%2F%2Fwww.govinfo.gov%2Fapp%2Fdetails%2FDCPD-201200376. Emphasis added.

80. Correspondent #67, 'President's Executive Order on Yemen,' electronic communication, May 22, 2012.

81. Tony Capaccio, 'U.S. Military Aid to Yemen Aims to Boost Fight Against Al-Qaeda,' *Bloomberg*, August 25, 2010, https://www.bloomberg.com/news/articles/2010-08-25/military-aid-to-yemen-doubles-as-u-s-aims-to-boost-fight-against-al-qaeda.

82. United States Senate, Committee on Foreign Relations, 'Following the Money in Yemen and Lebanon: Maximizing the Effectiveness of US Security Assistance and International Financial Institution Lending' (Government Printing Office, January 5, 2010), 111–38, S. Prt., https://www.foreign.senate.gov/imo/media/doc/54245.pdf.

83. Sheila Carapico, 'Kill the Messengers: Yemen's 2009 Clampdown on the Press,' Middle East Institute, June 2, 2009, 6–7, https://www.mei.edu/publications/kill-messengers-yemens-2009-clampdown-press.

84. The case of 'Abdulelah Haider Shaea is the most acute illustration of this. Shaea was imprisoned in 2010 on the basis of his reporting on US-Yemeni cooperation in the 2009 drone strike in al-Majalah, in which 20 children and 14 women were killed. Shaea was pardoned by President 'Ali 'Abdallah Saleh in February 2011, as the Yemeni uprising escalated, but he reportedly rescinded the pardon in response to a direct intervention by the United States; his case became an ongoing object of protest by rights organizations in the first year of the transitional period. It also received limited coverage in the United States among organizations following the use of drone strikes in Yemen. Samar Qaed, 'Protesters Increase Demands for Release of Journalist Shaye,' *Yemen Times*, December 6, 2012; Jeremy Scahill, 'Why Is President Obama Keeping a Journalist in Prison in Yemen?,' March 13, 2012, https://www.thenation.com/article/archive/why-president-obama-keeping-journalist-prison-yemen/.

85. Iona Craig and Hugh Tomlinson, 'Saleh Appeals to Saudi Neighbours for Help as Rebellion Gathers Pace,' accessed October 9, 2021, https://www.thetimes.co.uk/article/saleh-appeals-to-saudi-neighbours-for-help-as-rebellion-gathers-pace-93ht596w9mk.

86. Craig and Tomlinson, 'Saleh Appeals to Saudi Neighbours for Help as Rebellion Gathers Pace.'

87. Interview #60 with author, Dubai, June 1, 2012.

88. The full text of the implementation agreement is appended to 'Next Steps in Yemen's Transition,' IFES Briefing Paper (Washington, DC: International Foundation for Electoral Systems, March 2012), 11-19. https://www.ifes.org/publications/next-steps-yemens-transition.

89. Interview #55 with author, electronic communication, January 9, 2012.

90. Aboueldahab, *Transitional Justice and the Prosecution of Political Leaders in the Arab Region*, 106.

91. Charles Schmitz, 'Yemen's National Dialogue,' *MEI Policy Paper* (Middle East Institute, February 2014), https://www.mei.edu/publications/yemens-national-dialogue.

92. Thania Paffenholz and Nick Ross, 'Inclusive Political Settlements: New Insights from Yemen's National Dialogue' (Inclusive Security, March 2016), https://www.inclusivesecurity.org/publication/

inclusive-political-settlements-new-insights-from-yemens-national-dialogue/.

93. Amal al-Ashtal, 'Interview with Amat Al-Alim al-Soswa on Yemen's National Dialogue,' IPI Global Observatory (blog), February 28, 2013, https://theglobalobservatory.org/2013/02/interview-with-amat-al-alim-al-soswa-on-yemens-national-dialogue/.

94. Interview #55 with author, electronic communication, January 9, 2012.

95. Interview #57 with author, electronic communication, January 4, 2013.

96. Yadav, 'The "Yemen Model" as a Failure of Political Imagination.'

97. Mohammed Ghobari, 'Yemeni Government Apologises for Wars Waged by Former President,' *Reuters*, August 21, 2013, sec. World News, https://www.reuters.com/article/uk-yemen-south-apology-idUKBRE97K0TS20130821.

98. Erica Gaston, 'Process Lessons Learned in Yemen's National Dialogue,' Special Report 342 (United States Institute for Peace, February 2014), 3, https://www.usip.org/sites/default/files/SR342_Process-Lessons-Learned-in-Yemens-National-Dialogue.pdf.

99. Erwin van Veen, 'From the Struggle for Citizenship to the Fragmentation of Justice: Yemen from 1990 to 2013' (Clingendael: Netherlands Institute of International Relations, February 2014), 54; Nasser Arrabyee, 'No Alternative But Success' (Carnegie Endowment for International Peace, September 10, 2013), https://carnegieendowment.org/sada/52921.

100. Aboueldahab, *Transitional Justice and the Prosecution of Political Leaders in the Arab Region*, 117–20.

101. 'National Dialogue Conference Outcomes' (PA-X: Peace Agreement Database, January 25, 2014), https://www.peaceagreements.org/viewmasterdocument/1400.

102. Chapter 5 of *Islamists and the State* is primarily concerned with the proliferation of *takfir* and its effects on political dynamics in the 1990s and 2000s. For discussion of *takfir* during the transitional period and in comparison to the same period in Tunisia, see: Ian Hartshorn and Stacey Philbrick Yadav, '(Re)Constituting Community: Takfir and Institutional Design in Tunisia and Yemen,' *Terrorism and Political Violence* 32, no. 5 (2018): 1–18.

103. Interview #75 with author, Zoom, November 18, 2021.

104. Interview #75 with author, Zoom, November 18, 2021.

105. Andrea Carboni, Luca Nevola, and Thanos Petouris, 'Report on the Commission on Land-Related Issues and Commission on the Forcibly

Retired in Southern Yemen' (European Institute of Peace, September 2021).

106. Interview #75 with author, Zoom, November 18, 2021; For more on the apology process, see Ghobari, 'Yemeni Government Apologises for Wars Waged by Former President.'

107. Gaston, 'Process Lessons Learned in Yemen's National Dialogue,' 5.

108. Interview #75 with author, Zoom, November 18, 2021.

109. Tarek Radwan, 'Rethinking Transitional Justice in Yemen,' February 3, 2017, https://www.atlanticcouncil.org/blogs/menasource/rethinking-transitional-justice-in-yemen/.

110. Marta Abrantes Mendes, 'A Passage to Justice: Selected Yemeni Civil Society Views for Transitional Justice and Long Term Accountability in Yemen' (Open Society Foundation, February 2021), https://www.opensocietyfoundations.org/publications/a-passage-to-justice.

111. 'Six-Point Government of Yemen-Houthi Ceasefire Agreement' (PA-X: Peace Agreement Database, December 2, 2010), https://www.peaceagreements.org/viewmasterdocument/1434. For more on Saudi military involvement in the sixth Sa'ada war, see Christopher Boucek, 'War in Sa'ada: From Local Insurrection to National Challenge,' in Yemen on the Brink, 56–7. Brandt points out that Saudi military engagement effected a substantive change in the language of the Six Points, which eventually prioritized non-aggression with the Saudis and the creation of a 10 km buffer zone, neither of which was reflected in the original. Marieke Brandt, *Tribes and Politics in Yemen: A History of the Houthi Conflict* (Hurst, 2017), 323.

112. Brandt, *Tribes and Politics in Yemen*, 326.

113. Luca Nevola, 'Houthis in the Making: Nostalgia, Populism, and the Politicization of Hashemite Descent.'

114. Nevola, 'Houthis in the Making: Nostalgia, Populism, and the Politicization of Hashemite Descent.'

115. Nevola, 'Houthis in the Making: Nostalgia, Populism, and the Politicization of Hashemite Descent.'

116. Nevola uses the expression 'weaponization of nostalgia,' whereas al-Bukhayti's republicanism is discussed in *Brandt, Tribes and Politics in Yemen*, 340. For more on republicanism among Houthi participants in the uprising, see Stacey Philbrick Yadav, 'Sectarianization, Islamist Republicanism, and International Misrecognition in Yemen,' in *Sectarianization: Mapping the New Politics of the Middle East*, ed. Nader Hashemi and Danny Postel (Oxford University Press, 2017), 185–98.

117. Marieke Brandt, *Tribes and Politics in Yemen: A History of the Houthi Conflict* (Hurst, 2017), 338.

118. Brandt, *Tribes and Politics in Yemen*, 340.

119. Maysaa Shuja al-Deen, 'The Houthi–Tribal Conflict in Yemen' (Carnegie Endowment for International Peace, April 23, 2019), https://carnegieendowment.org/sada/78969. Al-Zaakari's prevarications were likewise legible, as he later mended fences with the Houthis when Saleh did, then reversed course after Saleh's death and was himself killed by Houthi forces in 2019.

120. 'Ceasefire between Salafists and Houthis in Dammaj' (PA-X: Peace Agreement Database, January 5, 2014), https://www.peaceagreements.org/viewmasterdocument/2004.

121. Nasser al-Sakkaf, 'Salafis Forced to Flee Dammaj, Government Forces Unable to Protect Them, They Say - Yemen,' *Yemen Times*, January 15, 2014, https://reliefweb.int/report/yemen/salafis-forced-flee-dammaj-government-forces-unable-protect-them-they-say.

122. al-Sakkaf, 'Salafis Forced to Flee Dammaj, Government Forces Unable to Protect Them, They Say - Yemen.'

123. Laurent Bonnefoy, 'Sunni Islamist Dynamics in Context of War: What Happened to al-Islah and the Salafis?,' POMEPS Studies 29 (Project on Middle East Political Science, January 11, 2018), https://pomeps.org/sunni-islamist-dynamics-in-context-of-war-what-happened-to-al-islah-and-the-salafis.

124. Peter Theo Curtis, 'A Militia, a Madrassa, and the Story Behind a Siege in Yemen,' *The New Republic*, January 30, 2012, https://newrepublic.com/article/100214/yemen-shia-militia-sunni-madrassa.

125. Laurent Bonnefoy, 'Sunni Islamist Dynamics in Context of War: What Happened to al-Islah and the Salafis?,' POMEPS Studies (Project on Middle East Political Science, January 11, 2018), https://pomeps.org/sunni-islamist-dynamics-in-context-of-war-what-happened-to-al-islah-and-the-salafis.

126. Peter Salisbury, 'Yemen's Rival Protesters Speak Out,' *Al Jazeera*, August 27, 2014, https://www.aljazeera.com/news/2014/8/27/yemens-rival-protesters-speak-out.

127. Stephen Snyder, 'Yemen's Peace Deal Brings Houthi Rebels into the Government, but Many Problems Remain,' The World from PRX, September 22, 2014, https://www.pri.org/stories/2014-09-22/yemens-peace-deal-brings-houthi-rebels-government-many-problems-remain.

128. April Longley Alley, 'Collapse of the Houthi-Saleh Alliance and the Future of Yemen's War,' POMEPS Studies 29 (Project on Middle East Political Science, January 11, 2018), https://pomeps.org/collapse-of-the-houthi-saleh-alliance-and-the-future-of-yemens-war.

129. Snyder, 'Yemen's Peace Deal Brings Houthi Rebels into the Government, but Many Problems Remain.'

130. van Veen, 'From the Struggle for Citizenship to the Fragmentation of Justice: Yemen from 1990 to 2013,' 49.

131. Robin Simcox, 'Ansar Al-Sharia and Governance in Southern Yemen' (Hudson Institute, December 27, 2012), http://www.hudson.org/research/9779-ansar-al-sharia-and-governance-in-southern-yemen.

132. van Veen, 'From the Struggle for Citizenship to the Fragmentation of Justice: Yemen from 1990 to 2013,' 55.

133. United States Senate, Committee on Foreign Relations, 'Understanding the Threat to the Homeland from AQAP' (Government Printing Office, September 18, 2013), 113–34, S. Prt., https://www.govinfo.gov/content/pkg/CHRG-113hhrg86483/pdf/CHRG-113hhrg86483.pdf.

134. Eleonora Ardemagni, 'Framing AQAP's Intra-Jihadi Hegemony in Yemen: Shifting Patterns of Governance and the Importance of Being Local,' *Sicurezza, Terrorismo e Società* 4, no. 2 (2016): 21–33.

135. 'Fractured Yemen,' *Al Jazeera*, accessed November 8, 2021, https://webapps.aljazeera.net/aje/custom/YemenInteractive/index.html.

136. 'Yemen's al-Qaeda: Expanding the Base,' *Middle East North Africa* (International Crisis Group, February 2, 2017), 6. https://www.crisisgroup.org/middle-east-north-africa/gulf-and-arabian-peninsula/yemen/174-yemen-s-al-qaeda-expanding-base.

137. 'Yemen's al-Qaeda,' 27.

138. Sarah Phillips, 'Questioning Failure, Stability, and Risk in Yemen,' in *Fragile Politics: Weak States in the Greater Middle East*, ed. Mehran Kamrava (Oxford University Press, 2016), 16.

139. Phillips, 'Questioning Failure, Stability, and Risk in Yemen,' 16.

140. Nadwa al-Dawsari, 'The Popular Committees of Abyan, Yemen: A Necessary Evil or an Opportunity for Security Reform?' (Middle East Institute, March 5, 2014), https://www.mei.edu/publications/popular-committees-abyan-yemen-necessary-evil-or-opportunity-security-reform.

141. al-Dawsari, 'The Popular Committees of Abyan, Yemen: A Necessary Evil or an Opportunity for Security Reform?'

142. Jon D. Unruh, 'Mass Claims in Land and Property Following the Arab Spring: Lessons from Yemen,' *Stability: International Journal of Security and Development* 5, no. 1 (2016): 6.

143. Andrea Carboni, Luca Nevola, and Thanos Petouris, 'Report on the Commission on Land-Related Issues and Commission on the Forcibly Retired in Southern Yemen,' 16.

144. Carboni, Nevola, and Petouris, 'Report on the Commission on Land-Related Issues and Commission on the Forcibly Retired in Southern Yemen,' 29.

145. Carboni, Nevola, and Petouris, 'Report on the Commission on Land-Related Issues and Commission on the Forcibly Retired in Southern Yemen,' 31.

146. Carboni, Nevola, and Petouris, 'Report on the Commission on Land-Related Issues and Commission on the Forcibly Retired in Southern Yemen,' 32.

147. Jens Kambeck, 'Returning to Transitional Justice in Yemen: A Backgrounder on the Commission on the Forcibly Retired in the Southern Governorates,' *Peace-Building and State-Building in Yemen* (Center for Applied Research in Partnership with the Orient, July 26, 2016), 22. https://carpo-bonn.org/wp-content/uploads/2016/07/carpo_policy_report_03_2016.pdf.

148. Jens Kambeck, 'Returning to Transitional Justice in Yemen: A Backgrounder on the Commission on the Forcibly Retired in the Southern Governorates,' 11.

149. Andrea Carboni, Luca Nevola, and Thanos Petouris, 'Report on the Commission on Land-Related Issues and Commission on the Forcibly Retired in Southern Yemen,' 6.

150. Carboni, Nevola, and Petouris, 'Report on the Commission on Land-Related Issues and Commission on the Forcibly Retired in Southern Yemen,' 18.

151. Carboni, Nevola, and Petouris, 'Report on the Commission on Land-Related Issues and Commission on the Forcibly Retired in Southern Yemen,' 18. Similarly, on the positive reception of civil judges in adjudicating claims by dismissed military officers, see Kambeck, 'Returning to Transitional Justice in Yemen,' 24.

152. Aboueldahab, *Transitional Justice and the Prosecution of Political Leaders in the Arab Region*, 117.

153. Kambeck, 'Returning to Transitional Justice in Yemen,' 24.

154. Jon D. Unruh, 'Mass Claims in Land and Property Following the Arab Spring: Lessons from Yemen,' 2.

155. Andrea Carboni, Luca Nevola, and Thanos Petouris, 'Report on the Commission on Land-Related Issues and Commission on the Forcibly Retired in Southern Yemen,' 6.

156. Kambeck, 'Returning to Transitional Justice in Yemen,' 24.

157. 'GPC Rejects New Government, Removes Hadi from Party Leadership,' Atlantic Council, MENA Source, November 10, 2014, https://www.atlanticcouncil.org/blogs/menasource/top-

news-gpc-rejects-new-government-removes-hadi-from-party-leadership/.

158. Ashraf Al-Falahi, 'Yemen's Fraught Constitution Drafting Committee' (Carnegie Endowment for International Peace, May 2, 2014), https://carnegieendowment.org/sada/55496.

159. Sheila Carapico, 'Two Resolutions, a Draft Constitution and Late Developments,' *Middle East Report Online*, April 17, 2015, https://merip.org/2015/04/two-resolutions-a-draft-constitution-and-late-developments/.

160. Tobias Thiel, 'Yemen's Imposed Federal Boundaries,' *Middle East Report Online*, July 20, 2015, https://merip.org/2015/07/yemens-imposed-federal-boundaries/.

161. Ghobari, 'Yemeni Government Apologises for Wars Waged by Former President.'

162. Martha C Nussbaum, *Creating Capabilities: The Human Development Approach*, 42–3. Nussbaum develops this concept based on recent work by Jonathan Wolff and Avner De-Shalit.

163. United Nations Office for the Coordination of Humanitarian Affairs, 'Yemen: Food Security Status 2009-2013,' October 30, 2013, https://reliefweb.int/sites/reliefweb.int/files/resources/Food_Security_Status_September_2013.pdf.

CHAPTER 5. IMAGINING JUST FUTURES

1. Tarek Radwan, 'Rethinking Transitional Justice in Yemen,' February 3, 2017. https://www.atlanticcouncil.org/blogs/menasource/rethinking-transitional-justice-in-yemen/.

2. Figure generated using the Armed Conflict Location and Event Data (ACLED) dashboard for January 2015 through December 2021. 'Full Dashboard | ACLED,' Armed Conflict Location and Event Data Project, https://acleddata.com/dashboard/.

3. 'Yemen's al-Qaeda.'

4. Bonnefoy, 'Sunni Islamist Dynamics in Context of War.'

5. United Nations Human Rights Council, 'UN Group of Eminent International and Regional Experts on Yemen Briefs the UN Security Council Urging an End to Impunity, an Expansion of Sanctions, and the Referral by the UN Security Council of the Situation in Yemen to the International Criminal Court,' December 3, 2020, https://www.ohchr.org/EN/HRBodies/HRC/Pages/NewsDetail.aspx?NewsID=26563&LangID=E.

6. Eleonora Ardemagni, '"Two Hadramawts" Emerge in a Fractured Yemen' (Middle East Institute, April 22, 2019), https://www.mei.edu/publications/two-hadramawts-emerge-fractured-yemen; Raiman al-Hamdani and Helen Lackner, 'War and Pieces· Political Divides in Southern Yemen – European Council on Foreign Relations' (European Council on Foreign Relations, January 22, 2020), https://ecfr.eu/publication/war_and_pieces_political_divides_in_southern_yemen/.

7. 'Special Envoy Yemen | Department of Political and Peacebuilding Affairs,' United Nations Department of Political and Peacebuilding Affairs, accessed December 17, 2021, https://dppa.un.org/en/mission/special-envoy-yemen.

8. 'Martin Griffiths: Track II Efforts Complement Official Negotiations, and Lay the Foundation for Peace-Building in Yemen' (Office of the Special Envoy to the Secretary General for Yemen, November 6, 2018), https://osesgy.unmissions.org/martin-griffiths-track-ii-efforts-complement-official-negotiations-and-lay-foundation-peace-building.

9. A succinct summary of the three peace tracks is available via Interpeace, which seeks to combine the three tracks in an integrated Track 6 approach (whereby 1+2+3=6). I will discuss this below when describing efforts to link the peace tracks. 'Our Track 6 Approach,' Interpeace, accessed December 17, 2021, https://www.interpeace.org/our-approach/track-6/.

10. Interview #78, Amman, February 17, 2021.

11. Yadav and Schwedler, 'Toward a Just Peace in Yemen.' This figure is based on data from the Armed Conflict Location and Event Data Project.

12. Ibrahim Jalal, 'Yemen's Joint Declaration: A Bigger Repeat of the Stalled Hodeida Agreement?' (Middle East Institute, March 4, 2021), https://www.mei.edu/publications/yemens-joint-declaration-bigger-repeat-stalled-hodeida-agreement; Hadil Al-Mowafak, 'For Sustainable Peace, Human Rights Must Be Front and Center of Yemen's Peace Process' (Yemen Policy Center, November 15, 2021), https://www.yemenpolicy.org/for-sustainable-peace-human-rights-must-be-front-and-center-of-yemens-peace-process/.

13. Interview #72 with author, electronic communication, November 14, 2021.

14. Ben Hubbard, 'Yemen's Warring Parties Begin First Cease-Fire in 6 Years,' *The New York Times*, April 2, 2022, sec. World, https://www.nytimes.com/2022/04/02/world/middleeast/yemen-cease-fire.

html; 'Hadi Out, Presidential Council Takes Over,' Sana'a Center for Strategic Studies, April 8, 2022, https://sanaacenter.org/publications/analysis/17378.

15. Each of these is detailed among the cascading effects of the war in Stacey Philbrick Yadav and Jillian Schwedler, 'Toward a Just Peace in Yemen,' *Middle East Report* 289 (2018), 4–5, https://merip.org/2019/03/toward-a-just-peace-in-yemen/.

16. Peter Salisbury, 'Bickering While Yemen Burns: Poverty, War, and Political Indifference' (Arab Gulf States Institute in Washington, June 22, 2017), https://agsiw.org/bickering-while-yemen-burns-poverty-war-and-political-indifference/.

17. Sarah Vuylsteke, 'When Aid Goes Awry: How International Humanitarian Response Is Failing Yemen' (Sana'a Center for Strategic Studies, October 2021), https://sanaacenter.org/files/When_Aid_Goes_Awry_00_Executive_Summary_en.pdf.

18. Rim Mugahed, 'The Impact of the COVID-19 Pandemic on Yemeni Women' (Sana'a Center for Strategic Studies, July 20, 2021), https://sanaacenter.org/publications/main-publications/14703.

19. Deborah Avant *et al.*, eds., *Civil Action and the Dynamics of Violence* (Oxford University Press, 2019), 3.

20. United Nations Security Council, 'Resolution 2282,' April 27, 2016, https://www.securitycouncilreport.org/un-documents/document/sres2282.php.

21. Autesserre, *The Frontlines of Peace*; Sharp, *Rethinking Transitional Justice for the Twenty-First Century beyond the End of History*.

22. Interview #80 with author, electronic, November 23, 2021.

23. Autesserre, *The Frontlines of Peace*; Search-Yemen, 'Building Stability in Yemen with Search's Community Dialogue Approach' (Search for Common Ground, August 20, 2021), https://www.sfcg.org/wp-content/uploads/2021/08/CDA-SFCG-Yemen.pdf.

24. Campbell, *Global Governance and Local Peace: Accountability and Performance in International Peacebuilding*.

25. Patrick Heller, 'Democracy, Participatory Politics and Development: Some Comparative Lessons from Brazil, India and South Africa,' *Polity* 44, no. 4 (2012): 643.

26. Erwin van Veen, 'From the Struggle for Citizenship to the Fragmentation of Justice: Yemen from 1990 to 2013' (Clingendael: Netherlands Institute of International Relations, February 2014), 59.

27. This project was commissioned for internal use by Interpeace and was completed in February 2021. Focus groups and interviews for this

report were completed in summer and fall of 2020 and included written responses from 56 peacebuilding CSOs; our team conducted interviews and focus group discussions with dozens of CSO staff in Aden, Taiz, Ibb, Marib, and Hadramawt, as well as supplementary interviews with Track I and Track II actors inside and outside of Yemen. As we note in the report, we relied on one to one interviews in areas under control of Ansar Allah (Houthis) for reasons of security and data privacy; this was a response to the expressed reservations of respondents to participate in focus groups in these areas, as well as our own assessment of security conditions. al-Kholidy, al-Jeddawy, and Yadav, 'Civil Society in Yemen: Identifying Opportunities for Peacebuilding.'

28. Focus group discussion #8, Taiz, December 4, 2020.

29. Marie-Christine Heinze and Stacey Philbrick Yadav, 'For Durable Peace in Yemen, Inclusion Must Mean More than Simply a Voice for Civil Actors,' *Responsible Statecraft*, June 8, 2020, https://responsiblestatecraft.org/2020/06/08/yemen-peace-inclusion-civil-actors/.

30. Interview #72 with author, electronic communication, November 14, 2021.

31. Interview #71 with author, Zoom, June 4, 2021.

32. Interview #72 with author, electronic communication, November 14, 2021.

33. Interview #75 with author, Zoom, November 18, 2021.

34. Gregory D. Johnsen, 'The End of Yemen' (The Brookings Institution, March 25, 2021), https://www.brookings.edu/blog/order-from-chaos/2021/03/25/the-end-of-yemen/.

35. Gregory Johnsen, 'Yemen's Three Wars,' *Lawfare* (blog), September 23, 2018, https://www.lawfareblog.com/yemens-three-wars; Gregory Johnsen, 'Seven Yemens: How Yemen Fractured and Collapsed, and What Comes Next' (Arab Gulf States Institute in Washington, October 8, 2021), https://agsiw.org/seven-yemens-how-yemen-fractured-and-collapsed-and-what-comes-next/.

36. Kathleen Gallagher Cunningham, 'Actor Fragmentation and Civil War Bargaining: How Internal Divisions Generate Civil Conflict,' *American Journal of Political Science* 57, no. 3 (2013): 659–72.

37. Kathleen Gallagher Cunningham, 'Divide and Conquer or Divide and Concede? How Do States Respond to Internally Divided Separatists?,' *American Political Science Review* 105, no. 2 (2011): 275–97; Wendy Pearlman, 'A Composite Actor Approach to Conflict Behavior,' in *Rethinking Violence*, ed. Erica Chenoweth and Adria Lawrence (MIT Press, 2010), 197–220.

38. Fotini Christia, *Alliance Formation and Civil Wars* (Cambridge University Press, 2012).

39. Eleonora Ardemagni, 'Caught in the Gulf Rivalry: Yemen's Al Mahra Avoids the War Despite "Collateral Militarisation,"' *LSE Middle East Center* (blog), December 11, 2020, https://blogs.lse.ac.uk/mec/2020/12/11/caught-in-the-gulf-rivalry-yemens-al-mahra-avoids-the-war-despite-collateral-militarisation/.

40. Adam Baron and Monder Basalma, 'The Case of Hadhramaut: Can Local Efforts Transcend Wartime Divides in Yemen?' (The Century Foundation, April 20, 2021), https://tcf.org/content/report/case-hadhramaut-can-local-efforts-transcend-wartime-divides-yemen/.

41. Ahmed al-Sharjabi, 'Hadi's Days Are Numbered. Only Accountability, Transparency, and Reform Can Stop Yemen's Decline' (Yemen Policy Center, November 18, 2021), https://www.yemenpolicy.org/hadis-days-are-numbered-only-accountability-transparency-and-reform-can-stop-yemens-decline/.

42. Peter Salisbury, 'A New UN Envoy Is an Opportunity for a New Approach in Yemen' (International Crisis Group, June 18, 2021), https://www.crisisgroup.org/middle-east-north-africa/gulf-and-arabian-peninsula/yemen/new-un-envoy-opportunity-new-approach-yemen.

43. al-Sharjabi, 'Hadi's Days Are Numbered. Only Accountability, Transparency, and Reform Can Stop Yemen's Decline.'

44. Jalal, 'Yemen's Joint Declaration'; Al-Mowafak, 'For Sustainable Peace, Human Rights Must Be Front and Center of Yemen's Peace Process.'

45. Michael Keating and Thanos Petouris, 'Southern Inclusivity Is Key to Yemen's Chances for Lasting Peace' (Middle East Institute, August 31, 2021), https://www.mei.edu/publications/southern-inclusivity-key-yemens-chances-lasting-peace; Interview #72 with author, electronic communication, November 14, 2021.

46. al-Gawfi, Zabara, and Yadav, 'The Role of Women in Peacebuilding in Yemen.'

47. Stacey Philbrick Yadav, 'Effective Citizenship, Civil Action, and Prospects for Post-Conflict Justice in Yemen,' *International Journal of Middle East Studies* 52 (2020): 754–8, https://doi.org/10.1017/S0020743820001051.

48. For example, a staff member at an Aden-based peacebuilding CSO explained that her organization has been more successful in Lahj and Abyan than in Hadramawt, given that Hadramawt has reasonably functional institutions. Interview #74 with author, Aden (Zoom), November 18, 2021.

49. 'Yemen's Internet Service Returns after Four-Day Outage Following Air Strike | Reuters,' January 25, 2022, https://www.reuters.com/world/middle-east/yemens-internet-service-returns-after-four-day-outage-following-air-strike-2022-01-25/.

50. Baron and Basalma, 'The Case of Hadhramaut.'

51. Focus group discussion #9, Aden, December 18, 2020.

52. This characterization is a composite portrait based on interviews with men and women working in Ibb, Dhammar, Sana'a, and Hodeidah in late 2020. This climate of fear is a contributing factor in research strategies that rely more heavily on 1:1 interviews in areas under Ansar Allah control.

53. Interview #78, Amman.

54. Progressive political campaigns in North America and Europe have focused narrowly on weapons sales to the Saudi-led coalition. While this is understandable insofar as weapons sales are an accessible point of influence for democratic electorates seeking accountable foreign policy, it has had a painfully reductive effect on understanding of the conflict and has not fundamentally challenged proxy framing. Focus on Saudi airstrikes – while warranted, given investigations by the United Nations Human Rights Council Group of Eminent Experts and others – nonetheless casts too narrow a net and obscures the many ways in which Yemeni actors – Ansar Allah, certainly, and the STC, but also more – are causing civilian harms and violating rights. Such campaigns seem focused on wanting clean hands more than advancing an end to the conflict in Yemen.

55. Adam Baron, 'Yemen,' *The Middle East's New Battle Lines* (European Council on Foreign Relations, May 2018), https://ecfr.eu/special/battle_lines/yemen.

56. Baron, 'Yemen.'

57. I traveled to Muscat in the summer of 2017 and conducted a series of interviews with Omani diplomats and other officials engaged in supporting negotiations between Yemeni parties, as well as some Yemenis who were there. Several of my Omani interlocutors expressed the view that the public pressure on Oman was primarily for domestic Saudi consumption, whereas they had assurances from Saudi counterparts that the kingdom valued having a 'backchannel' through Muscat. They were equally clear that if Oman had to choose between remaining neutral in relation to Qatar or in relation to the war in Yemen, it would not shift its position on Yemen, since this was a more vital arena of national interest. Interview #61 with author, Muscat, July 11, 2017; Interview #65 with author, Muscat, July 3,

2017; Interview #66 with author, Muscat, July 10, 2017. I wrote about Omani neutrality and the relationship between the two conflicts here: Stacey Philbrick Yadav, 'Oman Is a Mediator in Yemen. Can It Play the Same Role in Qatar?,' *Washington Post*, July 22, 2017, https://www.washingtonpost.com/news/monkey-cage/wp/2017/07/22/oman-is-a-mediator-in-yemen-can-it-play-the-same-role-in-qatar/.

58. United Nations Human Rights Council, 'UN GEE Briefs UN Security Council.'

59. Interview #71 with author, Zoom, June 4, 2021.

60. Global Centre for the Responsibility to Protect, 'Yemen: Populations at Risk,' December 1, 2021, https://www.globalr2p.org/countries/yemen/.

61. Stephanie Kirchgaessner, 'Saudis Used 'Incentives and Threats' to Shut down UN Investigation in Yemen,' *The Guardian*, December 1, 2021, sec. World news, https://www.theguardian.com/world/2021/dec/01/saudi-arabia-yemen-un-human-rights-investigation-incentives-and-therats. Bahrain, as well, played a role in advancing the vote. Reuters, '"We Have Failed Yemen" UN Human Rights Council Ends War Crime Probe,' *The Guardian*, October 7, 2021, sec. World news, https://www.theguardian.com/world/2021/oct/07/un-human-rights-council-votes-to-end-yemen-war-crimes-investigation.

62. Reuters, 'We Have Failed Yemen.'

63. Mwatana for Human Rights, 'Civil Society Groups Seek Urgent UN Action on Yemen,' December 2, 2021, https://mwatana.org/en/urgent-action/.

64. Following the dissolution of the GEE, it was revealed that Kamel Jendoubi was a personal target of 'Pegasus Project' surveillance during his time on the GEE, which may have a chilling effect on further documentation efforts. Stephanie Kirchgaessner, 'UN-Backed Investigator into Possible Yemen War Crimes Targeted by Spyware,' *The Guardian*, December 20, 2021, sec. World news, https://www.theguardian.com/world/2021/dec/20/un-backed-investigator-into-possible-yemen-war-crimes-targeted-by-spyware.

65. 'Seven Years of the Saudi-Led Air War in Yemen' (Yemen Data Project, March 24, 2022), https://mailchi.mp/44ee74b497a3/seven-years-of-the-saudi-led-air-war-in-yemen-yemen-data-project-march2022-13474205.

66. Fatima Saleh, Scott Preston, and Mareike Transfeld, 'The Role of the Media in Peacebuilding in Yemen,' CARPO Brief 16 (Center for Applied Research in Partnership with the Orient, April 17, 2020),

https://carpo-bonn.org/wp-content/uploads/2020/04/carpo_brief_16.pdf.

67. Afrah Nasser, 'The Yemen War, Media, and Propaganda' (Atlantic Council, May 3, 2017), https://www.atlanticcouncil.org/blogs/menasource/the-yemen-war-media-and-propaganda/.

68. al-Gawfi, Zabara, and Yadav, 'The Role of Women in Peacebuilding in Yemen.'

69. In a lengthy Twitter thread, cited here by permission, Yemeni activist Rasha Jarhum describes circumstances facing two particularly prominent women working for prisoner releases. Rasha Jarhum رشا جرهوم, '1- CMI Article Created Conflict between Yemenis While Well Intentioned the Use of Mothers of Abductees Is Widely Used for @abducteesmother. I Work with Both @salam_alhajj and @LailaLutf. They Are Both Phenomenal Women. Read the Thread to Know More,' Tweet, @RashaJarhum (blog), November 27, 2021, https://twitter.com/RashaJarhum/status/1464609399520038933.

70. Azal Al-Salafi, 'Yemen's Underground Feminist Movement Forms Shadow Protection Network,' Majlis (Yemen Policy Center, February 2022), https://www.yemenpolicy.org/yemens-underground-feminist-movement-forms-shadow-protection-network/

71. This is documented in the 2020 final report from the UN Panel of experts and also discussed in Peter Salisbury, 'Yemen's Southern Transitional Council: A Delicate Balancing Act' (International Crisis Group, March 30, 2021), https://www.crisisgroup.org/middle-east-north-africa/gulf-and-arabian-peninsula/yemen/yemens-southern-transitional-council-delicate-balancing-act.

72. Panel of Experts on Yemen, 'Final Report of the Panel of Experts on Yemen' (United Nations Security Council, January 27, 2020), 15. https://www.undocs.org/s/2020/326.

73. Bonnefoy, 'Sunni Islamist Dynamics in Context of War.'

74. Panel of Experts on Yemen, 'Final Report of the Panel of Experts on Yemen' (United Nations Security Council, January 25, 2021), 3. https://undocs.org/en/S/2021/79.

75. Luca Nevola, 'Houthis in the Making: Nostalgia, Populism, and the Politicization of Hashemite Descent,' *Arabian Humanities* 13 (2020), https://doi.org/10.4000/cy.5917.

76. Interview #70 with author, electronic correspondence, February 13, 2021.

77. al-Kholidy, al-Jeddawy, and Yadav, 'Civil Society in Yemen: Identifying Opportunities for Peacebuilding.'

78. 'Aid Must Do More Good than Harm' (Sana'a Center for Strategic Studies, November 3, 2021), https://sanaacenter.org/publications/the-yemen-review/15651. In addition to politicizing aid delivery, the UN Panel of Experts also reported that conflict actors engage in 'money-laundering and corruption practices that adversely affect access to adequate food supplies for Yemenis, in violation of the right to food.' Panel of Experts on Yemen, 'Final Report of the Panel of Experts on Yemen,' January 25, 2021, 3.

79. Sarah Vuylsteke, 'When Aid Goes Awry: How International Humanitarian Response Is Failing Yemen' (Sana'a Center for Strategic Studies, October 2021), 9, https://sanaacenter.org/files/When_Aid_Goes_Awry_00_Executive_Summary_en.pdf.

80. Yadav and Mugahed, 'One Hand Does Not Clap.'

81. Interview #70 with author, electronic correspondence, February 13, 2021, 70.

82. al-Kholidy, al-Jeddawy, and Yadav, 'Civil Society in Yemen: Identifying Opportunities for Peacebuilding.'

83. Interview #50, Lahj, September 22, 2021.

84. 'Aid Must Do More Good than Harm' (Sana'a Center for Strategic Studies).

85. 'Aid Must Do More Good than Harm' (Sana'a Center for Strategic Studies).

86. Laurent Bonnefoy, 'Revolution, War, and Regionalizing Yemeni Studies,' *Middle East Report*, Revolutionary Afterlives, 301 (December 2021), https://merip.org/2021/12/revolution-war-and-transformations-in-yemeni-studies/.

87. Interview #79 with author, electronic communication, November 17, 2021.

88. Interview #73 with author, Zoom, November 18, 2021.

89. Interview #79 with author, electronic communication, November 17, 2021.

90. Interview #81 with author, electronic communication, November 23, 2021.

91. Wendy Pearlman, 'Narratives of Fear in Syria,' *Perspectives on Politics* 14, no. 1 (2016): 32.

92. Noha Aboueldahab, 'Writing Atrocities: Syrian Civil Society and Transitional Justice,' *Brookings Doha Center Analysis Paper*, no. 21 (May 2018): 13.

93. Osama 'Ali *et al.*, 'Narratives of (In)Justice in Contemporary Yemeni Novels: Representations of Socio-Political Practices and Normative Constructions' (Center for Applied Research in Partnership with the

Orient, March 22, 2022), https://carpo-bonn.org/wp-content/uploads/2022/03/CARPO_study_11_22-03-22.pdf.

94. Nevens, al-Kholidy, and al-Jeddawy, '"Broken People Can't Heal a Nation": The Role of Arts in Peacebuilding in Yemen.'

95. Rim Mugahed, 'Bus of Hope,' trans. Angela Haddad, January 17, 2022, https://www.yemenpolicy.org/bus-of-hope/.

96. Mugahed and I worked together on a report that drew on the training that she helped administer at the Sana'a Center, where she has also carried out other projects related to gendered dimensions of the conflict This work is described in more detail In a later section. Yadav and Mugahed, '"One Hand Does Not Clap"'; Mugahed, 'The Impact of the COVID-19 Pandemic on Yemeni Women.'

97. Interview #84, electronic communication with author, April 4, 2022.

98. Panel of Experts on Yemen, 'Final Report of the Panel of Experts on Yemen,' January 25, 2021.

99. Interview #82 with author, electronic communication, November 21, 2021.

100. Interview #80 with author, electronic communication, November 23, 2021.

101. Interview #81 with author, electronic communication, November 23, 2021.

102. Sharp, *Rethinking Transitional Justice for the Twenty-First Century beyond the End of History,* 112.

103. Nevens, al-Kholidy, and al-Jeddawy, '"Broken People Can't Heal a Nation': The Role of Arts in Peacebuilding in Yemen.'

104. Interview #74 with author, Aden (Zoom), November 18, 2021.

105. Interview #74 with author, Aden (Zoom), November 18, 2021.

106. Interview #77, Hodeidah, December 3, 2020.

107. Ahmed Nagi, 'Education in Yemen: Turning Pens into Bullets' (Carnegie Endowment for International Peace, November 15, 2021), https://carnegie-mec.org/2021/11/15/education-in-yemen-turning-pens-into-bullets-pub-85777.

108. Interview #79 with author, electronic communication, November 17, 2021.

109. Radwan, 'Rethinking Transitional Justice in Yemen.'

CONCLUSION

1. Yadav and Mugahed, 'One Hand Does Not Clap.'

2. There were exceptions to this, most notably among Nasserist and Islahi women.

3. Mahmoud Rizk, 'Political, Economic and Cultural Factors & the Suffering of the Muhamasheen' (Insaf: Defending Freedoms and Minorities, September 8, 2020), https://insaf-ye.org/archives/2275; Gokh Amin al-Shaif, 'Black and Yemeni: Myths, Genealogies, and Race,' POMEPS Studies 44 (Project on Middle East Political Science, September 16, 2021), https://pomeps.org/black-and-yemeni-myths-genealogies-and-race.

4. Marta Colburn et al., 'Bringing Forth the Voices of Muhammasheen' (Sana'a Center for Strategic Studies, July 13, 2021), https://sanaacenter.org/publications/main-publications/14588.

5. 'Muhamasheen (The Marginalized Group) Between the Reality of Suffering & the Prospects for Change - INSAF,' INSAF: Defending Freedoms and Minorities, July 16, 2020, https://insaf-ye.org/archives/2221.

6. Ibrahim Jalal, 'Century-Old Grievances Continue to Fester in Yemen's Tihama Region' (Middle East Institute, October 14, 2021), https://www.mei.edu/publications/century-old-grievances-continue-fester-yemens-tihama-region.

7. Jalal.

8. Baron and Basalma, 'The Case of Hadhramaut.'

9. Interview #73 with author, Zoom.

10. Sharp, *Rethinking Transitional Justice for the Twenty-First Century beyond the End of History*, 116.

11. Sharp, *Rethinking Transitional Justice for the Twenty-First Century beyond the End of History*, 145.

12. Susanna P. Campbell, 'UN Peacekeeping and Peacebuilding: Progress and Paradox in Local Ownership,' *Ethics & International Affairs* 34, no. 3 (Fall 2020): 319–28.

13. Sharp, *Rethinking Transitional Justice for the Twenty-First Century beyond the End of History*, 139.

14. Amartya Kumar Sen, *Identity and Violence: The Illusion of Destiny* (New York: W.W. Norton, 2007), 77.

15. Campbell, 'UN Peacekeeping and Peacebuilding,' 321. This is an extract from a passage in the UN's own 2015 Review of the United Nation's Peacebuilding Architecture.

16. Abdullahi Ahmed An-Naim, 'From the Neocolonial "Transitional" to Indigenous Formations of Justice,' *International Journal of Transitional Justice* 7, no. 2 (2013): 197–8.

17. Sharp, *Rethinking Transitional Justice for the Twenty-First Century beyond the End of History*, 139.

18. An-Naim, 'From the Neocolonial "Transitional" to Indigenous Formations of Justice,' 198.
19. Bonnefoy, 'Revolution, War, and Regionalizing Yemeni Studies.'
20. Interview #83 with author, WhatsApp, November 30, 2021.
21. A one-page document outlining plans for the conference, sources of donor funding, and intended outcomes was shared with me by planners for the event; it is unpublished.

BIBLIOGRAPHY

Aboueldahab, Noha. *Transitional Justice and the Prosecution of Political Leaders in the Arab Region: A Comparative Study of Egypt, Libya, Tunisia and Yemen.* Bloomsbury Publishing, 2017.

———. 'Writing Atrocities: Syrian Civil Society and Transitional Justice.' *Brookings Doha Center Analysis Paper*, no. 21 (May 2018): 42.

Agence France Presse. 'Yemen Delays Polls to Redesign Political System: MP,' February 25, 2009.

———. 'Seven Shot Dead in Yemen Protests: Medics,' December 24, 2011.

Aiken, Nevin T. *Identity, Reconciliation and Transitional Justice: Overcoming Intractability.* Abingdon: Routledge, 2013.

Alazzany, Murad. 'Yemeni Youth March "Shows True Spirit of Revolution."' *CNN*, January 16, 2012. https://www.cnn.com/2012/01/16/opinion/murad-alazzany-yemen-oped/index.html.

Al-Deen, Maysaa Shuja. 'Media Absent from Yemen's Forgotten War.' *Arab Media and Society*, May 6, 2009. https://www.arabmediasociety.com/media-absent-from-yemens-forgotten-war/.

———. 'Yemen's War-Torn Rivalries for Religious Education - Islamic Institutions in Arab States: Mapping the Dynamics of Control, Co-Option, and Contention.' Accessed September 13, 2021. https://carnegieendowment.org/2021/06/07/yemen-s-war-torn-rivalries-for-religious-education-pub-84651.

Al-Falahi, Ashraf. 'Yemen's Fraught Constitution Drafting Committee.' Carnegie Endowment for International Peace, May 2, 2014. https://carnegieendowment.org/sada/55496.

Al-Haj, Ahmed, and Ben Hubbard. 'Yemen Immunity Law Sparks Debates over Past Crimes.' *Associated Press*, January 9, 2012.

'Ali, Osama, Fadhilah Gubari, Julia Gurol, and Abdulsalam Al-Rubaidi. 'Narratives of (In)Justice in Contemporary Yemeni Novels: Representations of Socio-Political Practices and Normative Constructions.' Center for Applied Research in Partnership with the Orient, March 22, 2022. https://carpo-bonn.org/wp-content/uploads/2022/03/CARPO_study_11_22-03-22.pdf.

Al Jazeera. 'Fractured Yemen.' Accessed November 8, 2021. https://webapps.aljazeera.net/aje/custom/YemenInteractive/index.html.

Alley, April Longley. 'Collapse of the Houthi-Saleh Alliance and the Future of Yemen's War.' POMEPS Studies 29. Project on Middle East Political Science, January 11, 2018. https://pomeps.org/collapse-of-the-houthi-saleh-alliance-and-the-future-of-yemens-war.

Al-Masmari, Hakim, and William Branigin. 'Saleh Suffers String of Major Defections after Protesters Gunned down in Yemen.' *Washington Post*, March 21, 2011. https://www.washingtonpost.com/world/saleh-suffers-string-of-major-defections-after-protesters-gunned-down-in-yemen/2011/03/21/ABhbbJ7_story.html.

Al-Mowafak, Hadil. 'For Sustainable Peace, Human Rights Must Be Front and Center of Yemen's Peace Process.' Yemen Policy Center, November 15, 2021. https://www.yemenpolicy.org/for-sustainable-peace-human-rights-must-be-front-and-center-of-yemens-peace-process/.

Al-Salafi, Azal. 'Yemen's Underground Feminist Movement Forms Shadow Protection Network.' Majlis. Yemen Policy Center, February 2022. https://www.yemenpolicy.org/yemens-underground-feminist-movement-forms-shadow-protection-network/.

Al-Shaif, Gokh Amin. 'On Origin Myths and Geneaological Imagination: The Marginalization of Yemen's Black Community.' Presented at the Crown Center for Middle East Studies, Brandeis University, March 24, 2021.

Al-Shamahi, Abubakr. 'New "parallel Revolution" against Corruption.' *Al Jazeera*, January 2, 2012. https://www.aljazeera.com/opinions/2012/1/2/new-parallel-revolution-against-corruption.

Al-Sharq al-Awsat. 'Yemen After the Sixth War,' March 5, 2010. BBC Monitoring Middle East - Political.

Al-Talei, Rafiah. 'Interview with Dr. Muhammad Abd al-Malik al-Mutawakkil, Assistant Secretary-General of the Federation for Popular Forces.' Arab Reform Bulletin. Carnegie Endowment for International Peace, August 19, 2008.

Alwazir, Atiaf. '"Youth" Inclusion in Yemen: A Necessary Element for Success of Political Transition.' *Arab Reform Initiative*, December 24,

2012. https://www.arab-reform.net/publication/youth-inclusion-in-yemen-a-necessary-element-for-success-of-political-transition/.

———. 'Yemen's Enduring Resistance: Youth between Politics and Informal Mobilization.' *Mediterranean Politics* 21, no. 1 (2016): 170–91. https://doi.org/10.1080/13629395.2015.1081446.

Amnesty International. 'Yemen: Amnesty International Urges Yemen to Complete the Ratification of the Rome Statute,' March 24, 2007. https://www.amnesty.org/download/Documents/68000/mde310042007en.pdf.

———. 'Yemen: Cracking Down Under Pressure.' Amnesty International, August 25, 2010. https://www.amnesty.org/en/documents/MDE31/010/2010/en/.

———. 'Amnesty International Urges Yemen to Reject Amnesty Law for President Saleh and Aides,' January 10, 2012. https://www.amnestyusa.org/press-releases/amnesty-international-urges-yemen-to-reject-amnesty-law-for-president-saleh-and-aides/.

An-Naim, Abdullahi Ahmed. 'From the Neocolonial "Transitional" to Indigenous Formations of Justice.' *International Journal of Transitional Justice* 7, no. 2 (2013): 197–204.

Ansari, Dawud. 'Resource Curse Contagion in the Case of Yemen.' *Resources Policy* 49 (September 2016): 444–54. https://doi.org/10.1016/j.resourpol.2016.08.001.

Ardemagni, Eleonora. 'Framing AQAP's Intra-Jihadi Hegemony in Yemen: Shifting Patterns of Governance and the Importance of Being Local.' *Sicurezza, Terrorismo e Società* 4, no. 2 (2016): 21–33.

———. '"Two Hadramawts" Emerge in a Fractured Yemen.' Middle East Institute, April 22, 2019. https://www.mei.edu/publications/two-hadramawts-emerge-fractured-yemen.

———. 'Caught in the Gulf Rivalry: Yemen's Al Mahra Avoids the War Despite "Collateral Militarisation."' *LSE Middle East Center* (blog), December 11, 2020. https://blogs.lse.ac.uk/mec/2020/12/11/caught-in-the-gulf-rivalry-yemens-al-mahra-avoids-the-war-despite-collateral-militarisation/.

Armed Conflict Location and Event Data Project. 'Full Dashboard | ACLED,' August 28, 2019. https://acleddata.com/dashboard/.

Arrabyee, Nasser. 'No Alternative But Success.' Carnegie Endowment for International Peace, September 10, 2013. https://carnegieendowment.org/sada/52921.

Arrabyee, Nasser, and Sara Shurafa. 'Saleh Will Seek Pardon for Any Mistakes Made.' *Gulf News*. January 25, 2011.

Ashtal, Amal al-. 'Interview with Amat Al-Alim al-Soswa on Yemen's National Dialogue.' *IPI Global Observatory* (blog), February 28, 2013. https://theglobalobservatory.org/2013/02/interview-with-amat-al-alim-al-soswa-on-yemens-national-dialogue/.

Atlantic Council, MENA Source. 'GPC Rejects New Government, Removes Hadi from Party Leadership,' November 10, 2014. https://www.atlanticcouncil.org/blogs/menasource/top-news-gpc-rejects-new-government-removes-hadi-from-party-leadership/.

Autesserre, Séverine. *The Frontlines of Peace: An Insider's Guide to Changing the World*. Oxford University Press, 2021.

Avant, Deborah, Erica Chenoweth, Rachel A. Epstein, Cullen Hendrix, Oliver Kaplan, and Timothy Sisk, eds. *Civil Action and the Dynamics of Violence*. Oxford University Press, 2019.

Balasco L.M. 'Reparative Development: Re-Conceptualising Reparations in Transitional Justice Processes.' *Conf. Secur. Dev. Conflict, Security and Development* 17, no. 1 (2017): 1–20.

Baron, Adam. 'Yemen.' The Middle East's New Battle Lines. European Council on Foreign Relations, May 2018. https://ecfr.eu/special/battle_lines/yemen.

Baron, Adam, and Monder Basalma. 'The Case of Hadhramaut: Can Local Efforts Transcend Wartime Divides in Yemen?' The Century Foundation, April 20, 2021. https://tcf.org/content/report/case-hadhramaut-can-local-efforts-transcend-wartime-divides-yemen/.

Bejan, Teresa M. *Mere Civility*. Harvard University Press, 2017.

Bonnefoy, Laurent. *Salafism in Yemen: Transnationalism and Religious Identity*. Hurst, 2011.

———. 'Sunni Islamist Dynamics in Context of War: What Happened to al-Islah and the Salafis?' POMEPS Studies. Project on Middle East Political Science, January 11, 2018. https://pomeps.org/sunni-islamist-dynamics-in-context-of-war-what-happened-to-al-islah-and-the-salafis.

———. *Yemen and the World: Beyond Insecurity*. Oxford University Press, 2018.

———. 'Revolution, War, and Regionalizing Yemeni Studies.' *Middle East Report*, Revolutionary Afterlives, 301 (December 2021). https://merip.org/2021/12/revolution-war-and-transformations-in-yemeni-studies/

———. 'Revolution, War and Transformations in Yemeni Studies.' *Middle East Report* 301 (2021). https://merip.org/2021/12/revolution-war-and-transformations-in-yemeni-studies/.

Bonnefoy, Laurent, and Judit Kuschnitizki. 'Salafis and the "Arab Spring" in Yemen: Progressive Politicization and Resilient Quietism.' *Arabian*

Humanities, no. 4 (January 12, 2015). https://journals.openedition. org/cy/2811#tocto1n2.

Bonnefoy, Laurent, and Marine Poirier. 'La Structuration de La Révolution Yéménite.' Translated by Jasper Cooper. *Revue Française de Science Politique* 62, no. 5 (2012): 132–49. https://doi.org/DOI 10.3917/ rfsp.625.895.

Boone, Jeb. 'Defiant Yemen President Warns "Mutinous" Military of Long, Bloody Civil War.' *The Independent*, March 23, 2011.

Bou Akar, Hiba. *For the War Yet to Come: Planning Beirut's Frontiers*. Stanford University Press, 2018.

Boucek, Christopher. 'War in Sa'ada: From Local Insurrection to National Challenge.' In *Yemen on the Brink*, edited by Christopher Boucek and Marina Ottaway, 45–59. Carnegie Endowment for International Peace, 2010.

Boucek, Christopher, and Marina Ottway, eds. *Yemen on the Brink*. Washington, DC: Carnegie Endowment for International Peace, 2010.

Bouka, Yolande. 'Collaborative Research as Structural Violence.' *Political Violence at a Glance* (blog), July 12, 2018. https:// politicalviolenceataglance.org/2018/07/12/collaborative-research-as-structural-violence/.

Brandt, Marieke. 'The Irregulars of the Sa'ada War: "Colonel Sheikhs" and "Tribal Militias" in Yemen's Huthi Conflict.' In *Why Yemen Matters: A Society in Transition*, edited by Helen Lackner, 105–22. Saqi Books, 2014.

———. *Tribes and Politics in Yemen: A History of the Houthi Conflict*. Hurst, 2017.

Brehony, Noel. *Yemen Divided: The Story of a Failed State in South Arabia*. London: I.B. Tauris, 2011.

Browers, Michaelle. *Political Ideology in the Arab World: Accommodation and Transformation*. Cambridge University Press, 2009.

Bruck, Gabriele vom. *Islam, Memory, and Morality in Yemen: Ruling Families in Transition*. Palgrave Macmillan, 2005.

Bulutgil, H. Zeynep. 'War, Collaboration, and Endogenous Ethnic Polarization: The Path to Ethnic Cleansing.' In *Rethinking Violence: States and Non-State Actors in Conflict*, edited by Erica Chenoweth and Adria Lawrence, 57–81. Cambridge, MA, MIT Press, 2010.

Burrowes, Robert D. 'Oil Strike and Leadership Struggle in South Yemen: 1986 and Beyond.' *Middle East Journal* 43, no. 3 (1989): 437–54.

Campbell, Leslie. 'Party-Building in the Middle East.' *International Journal* 65, no. 3 (2010): 561–81.

Campbell, Susanna P. *Global Governance and Local Peace: Accountability and Performance in International Peacebuilding*. Cambridge University Press, 2018.

―――. 'UN Peacekeeping and Peacebuilding: Progress and Paradox in Local Ownership.' *Ethics & International Affairs* 34, no. 3 (Fall 2020): 319–28.

Carapico, Sheila. *Civil Society in Yemen: The Political Economy of Activism in Modern Arabia*. Cambridge University Press, 1998.

―――. 'Kill the Messengers: Yemen's 2009 Clampdown on the Press.' Middle East Institute, June 2, 2009. https://www.mei.edu/publications/kill-messengers-yemens-2009-clampdown-press.

―――. *Political Aid and Arab Activism: Democracy Promotion, Justice, and Representation*. Cambridge University Press, 2014.

―――. 'Two Resolutions, a Draft Constitution and Late Developments.' *Middle East Report Online*, April 17, 2015. https://merip.org/2015/04/two-resolutions-a-draft-constitution-and-late-developments/.

―――. ed. *Arabia Incognita: Dispatches from Yemen and the Gulf*. Just World Books, 2016.

―――. 'From Ballot Box to Battlefield: The War of the Two 'Alis.' In *Arabia Incognita: Dispatches from Yemen and the Gulf*, edited by Sheila Carapico. Just World Books, 2016.

―――. 'The Economic Dimensions of Yemeni Unity.' In *Arabia Incognita: Dispatches from Yemen and the Gulf*, edited by Sheila Carapico, 72–81. Just World Books, 2016.

Capaccio, Tony. 'U.S. Military Aid to Yemen Aims to Boost Fight Against Al-Qaeda.' *Bloomberg*, August 25, 2010. https://www.bloomberg.com/news/articles/2010-08-25/military-aid-to-yemen-doubles-as-u-s-aims-to-boost-fight-against-al-qaeda.

Carboni, Andrea, Luca Nevola, and Thanos Petouris. 'Report on the Commission on Land-Related Issues and Commission on the Forcibly Retired in Southern Yemen.' European Institute of Peace, September 2021.

Carothers, Thomas. 'The End of the Transition Paradigm.' *Journal of Democracy* 13, no. 1 (2002): 5–21.

Carpenter, Charli. '"You Talk of Terrible Things So Matter-of-Factly in This Language of Science": Constructing Human Rights in the Academy.' *Perspectives on Politics* 10, no. 2 (2012): 363–83.

Chehayeb, Kareem. 'Anti-Gov't Engineers Hopeful after Lebanon Syndicate Victory.' *Al Jazeera*, July 1, 2021. https://www.aljazeera.com/news/2021/7/1/anti-government-lebanese-engineers-win-syndicate-elections.

Choueiri, Nada, Klaus-Stefan Enders, Yuri V. Sobolev, Jan Walliser, and Sherwyn Williams. *Yemen in the 1990s: From Unification to Economic Reform. Yemen in the 1990s.* International Monetary Fund, 2002. https://www.elibrary.imf.org/view/books/084/08020-9781589060425-en/ch02.xml.

Christia, Fotini. *Alliance Formation and Civil Wars.* Cambridge University Press, 2012.

Clark, Janine A. *Islam, Charity, and Activism: Middle-Class Networks and Social Welfare in Egypt, Jordan, and Yemen.* Bloomington: Indiana University Press, 2010.

Colburn, Marta, Fatima Saleh, Mohammed al-Harbi, and Sumaya Saleem. 'Bringing Forth the Voices of Muhammasheen.' Sana'a Center for Strategic Studies, July 13, 2021. https://sanaacenter.org/publications/main-publications/14588.

Commission on the Measurement of Economic Performance and Social Progress (France), Joseph E Stiglitz, Jean Paul Fitoussi, and Amartya Sen. *Mismeasuring Our Lives: Why GDP Doesn't Add up: The Report by the Commission on the Measurement of Economic Performance and Social Progress.* New York; London: New Press, 2010.

Committee to Protect Journalists. 'Government Seizes Newspaper Offices in Yemen,' May 4, 2009. https://cpj.org/2009/05/government-seizes-newspaper-offices-in-yemen/.

———. 'CPJ Calls on Yemen to End Siege of Independent Newspaper,' January 5, 2010. https://cpj.org/2010/01/cpj-calls-on-yemen-to-end-siege-of-independent-new/.

———. 'Witnesses in Al-Ayyam Case Turn against Prosecution,' January 10, 2012. https://cpj.org/2012/01/witnesses-in-al-ayyam-case-turn-against-yemeni-pro/.

———. 'Courageous Yemeni Editor Undaunted by Harassment.' Accessed August 6, 2021. https://cpj.org/awards/amer/.

Craig, Iona, and Hugh Tomlinson. 'Saleh Appeals to Saudi Neighbours for Help as Rebellion Gathers Pace.' Accessed October 9, 2021. https://www.thetimes.co.uk/article/saleh-appeals-to-saudi-neighbours-for-help-as-rebellion-gathers-pace-93ht596w9mk.

Cunningham, Kathleen Gallagher. 'Divide and Conquer or Divide and Concede? How Do States Respond to Internally Divided Separatists?' *American Political Science Review* 105, no. 2 (2011): 275–97.

———. 'Actor Fragmentation and Civil War Bargaining: How Internal Divisions Generate Civil Conflict.' *American Journal of Political Science* 57, no. 3 (2013): 659–72.

Curtis, Peter Theo. 'A Militia, a Madrassa, and the Story Behind a Siege in Yemen.' *The New Republic*, January 30, 2012. https://newrepublic. com/article/100214/yemen-shia-militia-sunni-madrassa.

Dahlgren, Susanne. *Contesting Realities: The Public Sphere and Morality in Southern Yemen*. Syracuse University Press, 2014.

————. 'The Snake with a Thousand Heads: The Southern Cause in Yemen.' In *Arabia Incognita: Dispatches from Yemen and the Gulf*, edited by Sheila Carapico, 166–72. Just World Books, 2016.

Dawsari, Nadwa al-. 'The Popular Committees of Abyan, Yemen: A Necessary Evil or an Opportunity for Security Reform?' Middle East Institute, March 5, 2014. https://www.mei.edu/publications/ popular-committees-abyan-yemen-necessary-evil-or-opportunity-security-reform.

————. 'Twitter Post,' November 17, 2021. https://twitter.com/ Ndawsari/status/1461048814761041936.

Day, Stephen. 'The Political Challenge of Yemen's Southern Movement.' In *Yemen on the Brink*, edited by Christopher Boucek and Marina Ottaway, 61–74. Carnegie Endowment for International Peace, 2010.

————. *Regionalism and Rebellion in Yemen: A Troubled National Union*. Cambridge University Press, 2012.

Deneulin, Séverine. *Wellbeing, Justice and Development Ethics*. Routledge, 2014.

Dennerlein, Bettina. 'Remembering Violence, Negotiating Change: The Moroccan Equity and Reconciliation Commission and the Politics of Gender.' *Journal of Middle East Women's Studies* 8, no. 1 (2012): 10–36.

Detalle, Renaud, and Joost Hiltermann. 'The Yemeni Elections Up Close.' *Middle East Report*, no. 185 (1993): 8–12. https://doi. org/10.2307/3013194.

Dresch, Paul. *A History of Modern Yemen*. Cambridge University Press, 2000.

Easterly, Grace. 'Before 2014: Yemen's Economy Before the War.' Yemen Peace Project, June 16, 2018. https://www.yemenpeaceproject.org/ blog-x/2018/7/16/before-2014-yemens-economy-before-the-war.

Economist Intelligence Unit. 'Yemen Politics: Saleh's Turn,' January 27, 2011.

El-Ghobashy, Mona. *Bread and Freedom: Egypt's Revolutionary Situation*. Stanford University Press, 2021.

Engstrom, Par. 'Transitional Justice and Ongoing Conflict.' In *Transitional Justice and Peacebuilding on the Ground: Victims and Ex-Combatants*, edited by Chandra Lekha Sriram, Jemima Garcia-Godos, Johanna Herman, and Olga Martin-Ortega, 41–61. Routledge, 2012.

Fakhro, Elham. 'Truth and Fact-Finding in the Arab Monarchies.' In *Transitional Justice in the Middle East and North Africa*, edited by Chandra Lekha Sriram, 161–84. Hurst, 2017.

Fijalkowski, Agata. 'Amnesty.' In *An Introduction to Transitional Justice*, edited by Olivera Simic, 113–36. Routledge, 2017.

Finn, Tom. 'Yemen's "parallel Revolution" Inspires Street-Level Protests.' *Reuters*, January 27, 2012. https://www.reuters.com/article/us-yemen-strikes/yemens-parallel-revolution-inspires-street-level-protests-idUSTRE80Q0RU20120127.

———. 'Beyond the Walls of Yemen's Revolution.' *The New Yorker*, February 27, 2014. https://www.newyorker.com/culture/culture-desk/beyond-the-walls-of-yemens-revolution.

Fraihat, Ibrahim. *Unfinished Revolutions: Yemen, Libya, and Tunisia After the Arab Spring.* Yale University Press, 2016.

Freedom House. 'Freedom in the World Methodology.' Accessed August 11, 2021. https://freedomhouse.org/reports/freedom-world/freedom-world-research-methodology.

Gaston, Erica. 'Process Lessons Learned in Yemen's National Dialogue.' Special Report 342. United States Institute for Peace, February 2014. https://www.usip.org/sites/default/files/SR342_Process-Lessons-Learned-in-Yemens-National-Dialogue.pdf.

Gawfi, Iman al-, Bilkis Zabara, and Stacey Philbrick Yadav. 'The Role of Women in Peacebuilding in Yemen.' CARPO Brief 14, February 27, 2020. https://carpo-bonn.org/wp-content/uploads/2020/02/carpo_brief_14.pdf.

Ghobari, Mohammed. 'Civil War Fears Chill Traumatised Yemen Neighbourhood.' *Reuters*, August 10, 2011, sec. World News. https://www.reuters.com/article/oukwd-uk-yemen-fighting-idAFTRE7794DP20110810.

———. 'Truce Called for after Yemen Troops Kill Protesters.' *Reuters*, December 26, 2011.

———. 'Yemeni Government Apologises for Wars Waged by Former President.' *Reuters*, August 21, 2013, sec. World News. https://www.reuters.com/article/uk-yemen-south-apology-idUKBRE97K0TS20130821.

Global Centre for the Responsibility to Protect. 'Yemen: Populations at Risk,' December 1, 2021. https://www.globalr2p.org/countries/yemen/.

Gordon, Sasha. 'The Parallel Revolution in Yemen.' American Enterprise Institute, March 6, 2012. https://www.criticalthreats.org/analysis/the-parallel-revolution-in-yemen.

Gray, Doris H, Terry C Coonan, and Chandra Lekha Sriram. 'Reframing Gender Narratives through Transitional Justice in the Maghreb.' In *Transitional Justice in the Middle East and North Africa*, 103–22. Routledge, 2017.

Haider, Najam. *Shi'i Islam: An Introduction*. Cambridge University Press, 2014.

Halabi, Fares. 'From 'Overthrowing the Regime' to 'All Means All': An Analysis of the Lebanonisation of Arab Spring Rhetoric.' *Arab Reform Initiative*, December 18, 2019. https://www.arab-reform.net/publication/from-overthrowing-the-regime-to-all-means-all-an-analysis-of-the-lebanonisation-of-arab-spring-rhetoric/.

Halliday, Fred. 'Catastrophe in South Yemen: A Preliminary Assessment.' In *Arabia Incognita*, edited by Sheila Carapico. Just World Books, 2016.

———. 'North Yemen Today.' In *Arabia Incognita*, edited by Sheila Carapico, 50–64. Just World Books, 2016.

Hamdani, Raiman al-, and Helen Lackner. 'War and Pieces: Political Divides in Southern Yemen – European Council on Foreign Relations.' European Council on Foreign Relations, January 22, 2020. https://ecfr.eu/publication/war_and_pieces_political_divides_in_southern_yemen/.

Hamidi, Ayman. 'Inscriptions of Violence in Northern Yemen: Haunting Histories, Unstable Moral Spaces.' *Middle Eastern Studies* 45, no. 2 (2009): 165-87.

Harris, Alistair. 'Exploiting Grievances: Al-Qaeda in the Arabian Peninsula.' In *Yemen on the Brink*, edited by Christopher Boucek and Marina Ottaway, 31–44. Carnegie Endowment for International Peace, 2010.

Hartshorn, Ian, and Stacey Philbrick Yadav. '(Re)Constituting Community: Takfir and Institutional Design in Tunisia and Yemen.' *Terrorism and Political Violence* 32, no. 5 (2018): 1–18.

Hashemi, Nader, and Danny Postel. 'Introduction: The Sectarianization Thesis.' In *Sectarianization: Mapping the New Politics of the Middle East*, edited by Nader Hashemi and Danny Postel, 1–22. Hurst, 2017.

Haykel, Bernard. 'A Zaydi Revival?' *Yemen Update* 36 (Winter/Spring 1995): 20–21.

———. 'Dissembling Descent, or How the Barber Lost His Turban: Identity and Evidence in Eighteenth-Century Zaydī Yemen.' *Islamic Law and Society* 9, no. 2 (2002): 194–230.

Hayner, Priscilla B. *Unspeakable Truths: Transitional Justice and the Challenge of Truth Commissions*. New York: Routledge, 2011. http://site.ebrary.com/id/10422146.

Heinze, Marie-Christine, and Hafez Albukhari. 'Opportunities for Security Sector Reform in Yemen.' In *Addressing Security Sector Reform in Yemen:*

Challenges and Opportunities for Intervention During and Post-Conflict, 40–8. Center for Applied Research in Partnership with the Orient, 2017. https://carpo-bonn.org/wp-content/uploads/2017/12/carpo_policy_report_04_2017.pdf.

Heinze, Marie-Christine, and Stacey Philbrick Yadav. 'For Durable Peace in Yemen, Inclusion Must Mean More than Simply a Voice for Civil Actors.' *Responsible Statecraft*, June 8, 2020. https://responsiblestatecraft.org/2020/06/08/yemen-peace-inclusion-civil-actors/.

Heller, Patrick. 'Democracy, Participatory Politics and Development: Some Comparative Lessons from Brazil, India and South Africa.' *Polity* 44, no. 4 (2012): 643–65.

Hennessey, Katherine. 'Yemeni Society in the Spotlight: Theater and Film in Yemen Before, During, and After the Arab Spring.' In *Why Yemen Matters: A Society in Transition*, edited by Helen Lackner, 68–86. London: Saqi Books, 2014.

Hill, Ginny. *Yemen Endures: Civil War, Saudi Adventurism, and the Future of Arabia*. Oxford University Press, 2017.

Hubbard, Ben. 'Yemen's Warring Parties Begin First Cease-Fire in 6 Years.' *The New York Times*, April 2, 2022, sec. World. https://www.nytimes.com/2022/04/02/world/middleeast/yemen-cease-fire.html.

Human Rights Watch. 'Human Rights Watch World Report 2001: Yemen: Human Rights Developments,' 2001. https://www.hrw.org/legacy/wr2k1/mideast/yemen.html.

———. 'World Report 2009: Rights Trends in Yemen,' January 13, 2009. https://www.hrw.org/world-report/2009/country-chapters/yemen.

———. 'World Report 2009: Taking Back the Initiative from Human Rights Spoilers.' Human Rights Watch. Accessed August 23, 2021. https://www.hrw.org/world-report/2009/country-chapters/yemen.

———. 'Yemen: Protester Killings Show Perils of Immunity Deal.' Human Rights Watch, September 20, 2011. https://www.hrw.org/news/2011/09/20/yemen-protester-killings-show-perils-immunity-deal.

———. '"No Safe Places": Yemen's Crackdown on Protests in Taizz.' Human Rights Watch, February 6, 2012. https://www.hrw.org/report/2012/02/06/no-safe-places/yemens-crackdown-protests-taizz.

———. 'Unpunished Massacre: Yemen's Failed Response to the "Friday of Dignity" Killings.' Human Rights Watch, February 12, 2013. https://www.hrw.org/report/2013/02/12/unpunished-massacre/yemens-failed-response-friday-dignity-killings.

'Yemen's Constitutional Referendum and Local Elections (Human Rights Watch Backgrounder February 2001).' Accessed August 10, 2021. https://www.hrw.org/legacy/backgrounder/mena/yemen-bck-0201.htm.

IFES. 'Next Steps in Yemen's Transition.' IFES Briefing Paper. Washington, DC: International Foundation for Electoral Systems, March 2012. https://www.ifes.org/publications/next-steps-yemens-transition.

IFEX. 'CPJ Protests Conviction of "Al-Ayyam" Journalists,' August 5, 1999. https://ifex.org/cpj-protests-conviction-of-al-ayyam-journalists/.

INSAF: Defending Freedoms and Minorities. 'Muhamasheen (The Marginalized Group) Between the Reality of Suffering & the Prospects for Change • INSAF,' July 16, 2020. https://insaf-ye.org/archives/2221.

International Center for Missing Persons. 'ICMP Welcomes Appointment of Members of the Lebanon National Commission for the Missing and Forcibly Disappeared,' July 17, 2020. https://www.icmp.int/press-releases/icmp-welcomes-appointment-of-members-of-the-lebanon-national-commission-for-the-missing-and-forcibly-disappeared/.

International Center for Transitional Justice. 'The Rabat Report: The Concept and Challenges of Collective Reparations.' International Center for Transitional Justice, 2009. https://www.ictj.org/sites/default/files/ICTJ-Morocco-Reparations-Report-2009-English.pdf.

————. 'Truth and Reconciliation in Morocco,' 2009. https://www.ictj.org/sites/default/files/ICTJ-Morocco-TRC-2009-English.pdf.

————. 'Yemen: Amnesty Law in Breach of International Law and Yemen's Obligations,' January 11, 2012. https://www.ictj.org/news/yemen-amnesty-law-breach-international-law-and-yemen%E2%80%99s-obligations-0.

————. 'The Missing in Lebanon Inputs on the Establishment of the Independent National Commission for the Missing and Forcibly Disappeared in Lebanon,' January 2016. https://www.ictj.org/sites/default/files/ICTJ-Report-Lebanon-CommissionMissing-2016_0.pdf.

————. 'On Solid Ground: Sustainable Development After Massive Human Rights Violations.' Report of the Working Group on Transitional Justice and SDG+16, May 2019.

International Crisis Group. 'Yemen's al-Qaeda: Expanding the Base.' Middle East North Africa. International Crisis Group, February 2, 2017. https://www.crisisgroup.org/middle-east-north-africa/gulf-and-arabian-peninsula/yemen/174-yemen-s-al-qaeda-expanding-base.

International Monetary Fund. 'Republic of Yemen: 2008 Article IV Consultation: Staff Report; Staff Statement and Supplement; Public Information Notice on the Executive Board Discussion; and Statement by the Executive Director for the Republic of Yemen.' *IMF Staff Country Reports* 2009, no. 100 (March 24, 2009). https://doi.org/10.5089/9781451840834.002.A001.

Interparliamentary Union. 'Yemen Parliamentary Chamber: Majlis al-Chura.' Interparliamentary Union, July 5, 1988. Parline-E. http://archive.ipu.org/parline-e/reports/arc/2353_88.htm.

Interpeace. 'Our Track 6 Approach.' Accessed December 17, 2021. https://www.interpeace.org/our-approach/track-6/.

Ishaq, Sara. *Karama Has No Walls*, 2014. https://karamafilm.com/.

Ismail, Sharif. 'Unification in Yemen: Dynamics of Political Integration, 1978-2000.' MPhil, University of Oxford, 2007. https://users.ox.ac.uk/~metheses/Ismail%20Thesis.pdf.

Jalal, Ibrahim. 'Century-Old Grievances Continue to Fester in Yemen's Tihama Region.' Middle East Institute, October 14, 2021. https://www.mei.edu/publications/century-old-grievances-continue-fester-yemens-tihama-region.

———. 'Yemen's Joint Declaration: A Bigger Repeat of the Stalled Hodeida Agreement?' Middle East Institute, March 4, 2021. https://www.mei.edu/publications/yemens-joint-declaration-bigger-repeat-stalled-hodeida-agreement.

Johnsen, Gregory. 'Yemen's Three Wars.' *Lawfare* (blog), September 23, 2018. https://www.lawfareblog.com/yemens-three-wars.

———. 'The End of Yemen.' The Brookings Institution, March 25, 2021. https://www.brookings.edu/blog/order-from-chaos/2021/03/25/the-end-of-yemen/.

———. 'Seven Yemens: How Yemen Fractured and Collapsed, and What Comes Next.' Arab Gulf States Institute in Washington, October 8, 2021. https://agsiw.org/seven-yemens-how-yemen-fractured-and-collapsed-and-what-comes-next/.

Kambeck, Jens. 'Returning to Transitional Justice in Yemen: A Backgrounder on the Commission on the Forcibly Retired in the Southern Governorates.' Peace-Building and State-Building in Yemen. Center for Applied Research in Partnership with the Orient, July 26, 2016. https://carpo-bonn.org/wp-content/uploads/2016/07/carpo_policy_report_03_2016.pdf.

Kasinof, Laura. 'Are Yemen's Protests Going to Bring Another Revolution?' *Christian Science Monitor*, January 27, 2011.

————. *Don't Be Afraid of the Bullets: An Accidental War Correspondent in Yemen*. Arcade Publishing, 2014.

Keating, Michael, and Thanos Petouris. 'Southern Inclusivity Is Key to Yemen's Chances for Lasting Peace.' Middle East Institute, August 31, 2021. https://www.mei.edu/publications/southern-inclusivity-key-yemens-chances-lasting-peace.

Kent, Lia. 'Transitional Justice and Peacebuilding.' In *An Introduction to Transitional Justice*, edited by Olivera Simic, 201–22. Routledge, 2017.

Kholidy, Maged al-, Yazeed al-Jeddawy, and Stacey Philbrick Yadav. 'Civil Society in Yemen: Identifying Opportunities for Peacebuilding.' Internal report. Interpeace, February 2021.

Kirchgaessner, Stephanie. 'Saudis Used 'Incentives and Threats' to Shut down UN Investigation in Yemen.' *The Guardian*, December 1, 2021, sec. World news. https://www.theguardian.com/world/2021/dec/01/saudi-arabia-yemen-un-human-rights-investigation-incentives-and-therats.

————. 'UN-Backed Investigator into Possible Yemen War Crimes Targeted by Spyware.' *The Guardian*, December 20, 2021, sec. World news. https://www.theguardian.com/world/2021/dec/20/un-backed-investigator-into-possible-yemen-war-crimes-targeted-by-spyware.

Lichtenthaeler, Gerhard. 'Water Conflict and Cooperation in Yemen.' *Middle East Report* 254, no. Spring (March 24, 2010). https://merip.org/2010/03/water-conflict-and-cooperation-in-yemen/.

Lieberman, Evan S, and Prerna Singh. 'The Institutional Origins of Ethnic Violence.' *Comppoli Comparative Politics* 45, no. 1 (2012): 1–24.

Lucuta, Gabriela. 'Peacemaking, Peacekeeping, Peacebuilding and Peace Enforcement in the 21st Century.' Peace Insight, April 25, 2014. https://www.peaceinsight.org/en/articles/peacemaking-peacekeeping-peacebuilding-peace-enforcement-21st-century/.

Makdisi, Ussama. *Age of Coexistence: The Ecumenical Frame and the Making of the Modern Arab World*. University of California Press, 2019.

Mamdani, Mahmood. *Neither Settler nor Native: The Making and Unmaking of Permanent Minorities*. Harvard University Press, 2020.

Marzouki, Nadia. 'Whatever Happened to Dignity? The Politics of Citizenship in Post-Revolution Tunisia.' *Middle East Report* 301 (December 15, 2021). https://merip.org/2021/12/whatever-happened-to-dignity-the-politics-of-citizenship-in-post-revolution-tunisia-2/.

McCargo, Duncan. 'Transitional Justice and Its Discontents.' *Journal of Democracy Journal of Democracy* 26, no. 2 (2015): 5–20.

McEvers, Kelly. 'Yemen Tribesmen Protect Anti-Government Protesters.' *Morning Edition*. National Public Radio, August 10, 2011. https://www.npr.org/2011/08/10/139346563/yemen-tribesmen-protect-anti-government-protesters.

Mendes, Marta Abrantes. 'A Passage to Justice: Selected Yemeni Civil Society Views for Transitional Justice and Long Term Accountability in Yemen.' Open Society Foundation, February 2021. https://www.opensocietyfoundations.org/publications/a-passage-to-justice.

Mermier, Franck. 'L'islam Politique Au Yémen Ou La 'Tradition' Contre Les Traditions ?' *Monde Arabe Maghreb Machrek*, 6–19, 155 (1997).

Mihr, Anja. 'An Introduction to Transitional Justice.' In *An Introduction to Transitional Justice*, edited by Olivera Simic, 1–27. Routledge, 2017.

Mugahed, Rim. 'The Impact of the COVID-19 Pandemic on Yemeni Women.' Sana'a Center for Strategic Studies, July 20, 2021. https://sanaacenter.org/publications/main-publications/14703.

———. 'Bus of Hope.' Translated by Angela Haddad, January 17, 2022. https://www.yemenpolicy.org/bus-of-hope/.

Mwatana for Human Rights. 'Civil Society Groups Seek Urgent UN Action on Yemen,' December 2, 2021. https://mwatana.org/en/urgent-action/.

Nagi, Ahmed. 'Education in Yemen: Turning Pens into Bullets.' Carnegie Endowment for International Peace, November 15, 2021. https://carnegie-mec.org/2021/11/15/education-in-yemen-turning-pens-into-bullets-pub-85777.

Nasser, Afrah. 'The Yemen War, Media, and Propaganda.' Atlantic Council, May 3, 2017. https://www.atlanticcouncil.org/blogs/menasource/the-yemen-war-media-and-propaganda/.

National Democratic Institute for International Affairs. 'Promoting Participation in Yemen's 1993 Parliamentary Elections.' National Democratic Institute for International Affairs, 1994. https://www.ndi.org/sites/default/files/331_ye_promoting.pdf.

———. 'The April 27, 2003 Parliamentary Elections in the Republic of Yemen.' National Democratic Institute for International Affairs, 2013. https://www.ndi.org/sites/default/files/1701_yem_elect-rep.pdf.

Nevens, Kate, Maged al-Kholidy, and Yazeed al-Jeddawy. '"Broken People Can't Heal a Nation": The Role of Arts in Peacebuilding in Yemen.' Center for Applied Research in Partnership with the Orient, March 25, 2021. https://carpo-bonn.org/en/category/author/kate-nevens/.

Nevola, Luca. 'Houthis in the Making: Nostalgia, Populism, and the Politicization of Hashemite Descent.' *Arabian Humanities* 13 (2020). https://doi.org/10.4000/cy.5917.

Noon, Arabia. 'Yemen: The Amazing Life March Arrives in Sana'a.' *Global Voices* (blog), December 24, 2011. https://globalvoices.org/2011/12/24/yemen-the-amazing-march-of-life-arrives-in-sanaa/.

Norton, Anne. 'Political Science as a Vocation.' In *Problems and Methods in the Study of Politics*, edited by Ian Shapiro, Rogers Smith, and Tarek E. Masoud, 67–82. Cambridge University Press, 2004.

Nussbaum, Martha C. *Creating Capabilities: The Human Development Approach*. Cambridge, MA, Belknap Press of Harvard University Press, 2013.

Ochoa-Sánchez, Juan Carlos. 'Economic and Social Rights and Transitional Justice: A Framework of Analysis.' *Journal of Human Rights* 18, no. 5 (December 11, 2019): 522–42.

Office of the Federal Register, National Archives and Records Administration. 'DCPD-201200376 - Executive Order 13611-Blocking Property of Persons Threatening the Peace, Security, or Stability of Yemen.' Government. govinfo.gov. Office of the Federal Register, National Archives and Records Administration, May 16, 2012. https://www.govinfo.gov/app/details/https%3A%2F%2Fwww.govinfo.gov%2Fapp%2Fdetails%2FDCPD-201200376.

Office of the Special Envoy to the Secretary General for Yemen. 'Martin Griffiths: Track II Efforts Complement Official Negotiations, and Lay the Foundation for Peace-Building in Yemen.' Office of the Special Envoy to the Secretary General for Yemen, November 6, 2018. https://osesgy.unmissions.org/martin-griffiths-track-ii-efforts-complement-official-negotiations-and-lay-foundation-peace-building.

Orkaby, Asher. 'Benefiting from the Misery of Others.' *Middle East Report Online*, May 26, 2021. https://merip.org/2021/05/benefiting-from-the-misery-of-others/.

Paffenholz, Thania, and Nick Ross. 'Inclusive Political Settlements: New Insights from Yemen's National Dialogue.' Inclusive Security, March 2016. https://www.inclusivesecurity.org/publication/inclusive-political-settlements-new-insights-from-yemens-national-dialogue/.

Panel of Experts on Yemen. 'Final Report of the Panel of Experts on Yemen.' United Nations Security Council, January 27, 2020. https://www.undocs.org/s/2020/326.

———. 'Final Report of the Panel of Experts on Yemen.' United Nations Security Council, January 25, 2021. https://undocs.org/en/S/2021/79.

Parliamentarians for Global Action. 'Yemen and the Rome Statute.' Accessed August 3, 2021. https://www.pgaction.org/ilhr/rome-statute/yemen.html.

PA-X: Peace Agreement Database. 'Agreement/Gulf Cooperation Council (GCC) Initiative.' PA-X: Peace Agreement Database, November 23, 2011. https://www.peaceagreements.org/view/1401.

———. 'Ceasefire between Salafists and Houthis in Dammaj.' PA-X: Peace Agreement Database, January 5, 2014. https://www.peaceagreements.org/viewmasterdocument/2004.

———. 'Six-Point Government of Yemen-Houthi Ceasefire Agreement.' PA-X: Peace Agreement Database, December 2, 2010. https://www.peaceagreements.org/viewmasterdocument/1434.

———. 'National Dialogue Conference Outcomes.' PA-X: Peace Agreement Database, January 25, 2014. https://www.peaceagreements.org/viewmasterdocument/1400.

Pearlman, Wendy. 'A Composite Actor Approach to Conflict Behavior.' In *Rethinking Violence*, edited by Erica Chenoweth and Adria Lawrence, 197–220. MIT Press, 2010.

———. 'Narratives of Fear in Syria.' *Perspectives on Politics* 14, no. 1 (2016): 21–37.

Phillips, Sarah. 'Evaluating Political Reform in Yemen.' Democracy and Rule of Law Program. Carnegie Endowment for International Peace, February 2007. https://carnegieendowment.org/files/cp_80_phillips_yemen_final.pdf.

———. *Yemen and the Politics of Permanent Crisis*. Routledge, 2011.

———. 'Questioning Failure, Stability, and Risk in Yemen.' In *Fragile Politics: Weak States in the Greater Middle East*, edited by Mehran Kamrava. Oxford University Press, 2016.

The Presidency of the Republic of Yemen. 'Presidential Decree No. 24,' September 12, 2011. https://www.peaceagreements.org/viewmasterdocument/1402.

Qaed, Samar. 'Protesters Increase Demands for Release of Journalist Shaye.' *Yemen Times*. December 6, 2012.

Qasem, Ala. 'Five Barriers to Youth Inclusion, Decision-Making and Leadership in Yemen's Political Parties.' Briefing. SaferWorld, December 2013. https://www.saferworld.org.uk/resources/publications/785-five-barriers-to-youth-engagement-decision-making-and-leadership-in-yemens-political-parties.

Radwan, Tarek. 'Rethinking Transitional Justice in Yemen,' February 3, 2017. https://www.atlanticcouncil.org/blogs/menasource/rethinking-transitional-justice-in-yemen/.

Republic of Yemen. 'Law No. 66 of 1991 Governing Parties and Political Organizations,' October 16, 1991. Tab 58. IFES_21. https://www.ifes.org/sites/default/files/el00256.pdf.

Rizk, Mahmoud. 'Political, Economic and Cultural Factors & the Suffering of the Muhamasheen.' Insaf: Defending Freedoms and Minorities, September 8, 2020. https://insaf-ye.org/archives/2275.

Sakkaf, Nasser al-. 'Salafis Forced to Flee Dammaj, Government Forces Unable to Protect Them, They Say – Yemen.' *Yemen Times*, January 15, 2014. https://reliefweb.int/report/yemen/salafis-forced-flee-dammaj-government-forces-unable-protect-them-they-say.

Saleh, Fatima, Scott Preston, and Mareike Transfeld. 'The Role of the Media in Peacebuilding in Yemen.' CARPO Brief 16. Center for Applied Research in Partnership with the Orient, April 17, 2020. https://carpo-bonn.org/wp-content/uploads/2020/04/carpo_brief_16.pdf.

Salehi, Mariam. *Transitional Justice in Process: Plans and Politics in Tunisia.* Manchester University Press, 2021.

Salisbury, Peter. 'Yemen's Rival Protesters Speak Out.' *Al Jazeera*, August 27, 2014. https://www.aljazeera.com/news/2014/8/27/yemens-rival-protesters-speak-out.

———. 'Bickering While Yemen Burns: Poverty, War, and Political Indifference.' Arab Gulf States Institute in Washington, June 22, 2017. https://agsiw.org/bickering-while-yemen-burns-poverty-war-and-political-indifference/.

———. 'Yemen's Southern Powder Keg.' Middle East and North Africa Programme. Chatham House, March 2018. https://www.chathamhouse.org/sites/default/files/publications/research/2018-03-27-yemen-southern-powder-keg-salisbury-final.pdf.

———. 'Yemen's Southern Transitional Council: A Delicate Balancing Act.' International Crisis Group, March 30, 2021. https://www.crisisgroup.org/middle-east-north-africa/gulf-and-arabian-peninsula/yemen/yemens-southern-transitional-council-delicate-balancing-act.

———. 'A New UN Envoy Is an Opportunity for a New Approach in Yemen.' International Crisis Group, June 18, 2021. https://www.crisisgroup.org/middle-east-north-africa/gulf-and-arabian-peninsula/yemen/new-un-envoy-opportunity-new-approach-yemen.

Salloukh, Bassel. 'The Architecture of Sectarianization in Lebanon.' In *Sectarianization: Mapping the New Politics of the Middle East*, edited by Nader Hashemi and Danny Postel, 215–34. Hurst, 2017.

Salmoni, Barak A., Bryce Loidolt, and Madeleine Wells. *Regime and Periphery in Northern Yemen: The Huthi Phenomenon.* RAND National Defense Research Institute, 2010.

Sana'a Center for Strategic Studies. 'Aid Must Do More Good than Harm.' Sana'a Center for Strategic Studies, November 3, 2021. https://sanaacenter.org/publications/the-yemen-review/15651.

———. 'Hadi Out, Presidential Council Takes Over,' April 8, 2022. https://sanaacenter.org/publications/analysis/17378.

Scahill, Jeremy. 'Why Is President Obama Keeping a Journalist in Prison in Yemen?' March 13, 2012. https://www.thenation.com/article/archive/why-president-obama-keeping-journalist-prison-yemen/.

Schmitz, Charles. 'Yemen's National Dialogue.' MEI Policy Paper. Middle East Institute, February 2014. https://www.mei.edu/publications/yemens-national-dialogue.

Schwartz-Shea, Peregrine, and Dvora Yanow. *Interpretive Research Design: Concepts and Processes.* Routledge, 2012.

Schwedler, Jillian. *Faith in Moderation: Islamist Parties in Jordan and Yemen.* Cambridge University Press, 2006.

———. 'Against Methodological Nationalism: Seeing Comparisons as Encompasing Through the Arab Uprisings.' In *Rethinking Comparison: Innovative Methods for Qualitative Political Inquiry*, 172–89. Cambridge University Press, 2021.

Search-Yemen. 'Building Stability in Yemen with Search's Community Dialogue Approach.' Search for Common Ground, August 20, 2021. https://www.sfcg.org/wp-content/uploads/2021/08/CDA-SFCG-Yemen.pdf.

Seitz, Adam C. 'Ties That Bind and Divide: The 'Arab Spring' and Yemeni Civil-Military Relations.' In *Why Yemen Matters: A Society in Transition*, edited by Helen Lackner, 50–67. Saqi Books, 2014.

Sen, Amartya Kumar. *Identity and Violence: The Illusion of Destiny.* New York: W. W. Norton, 2007.

———. *The Idea of Justice.* Cambridge: The Belknap Press of Harvard University Press, 2011.

Shaif, Gokh Amin al-. 'Black and Yemeni: Myths, Genealogies, and Race.' POMEPS Studies 44. Project on Middle East Political Science, September 16, 2021. https://pomeps.org/black-and-yemeni-myths-genealogies-and-race.

Sharjabi, Ahmed al-. 'Hadi's Days Are Numbered. Only Accountability, Transparency, and Reform Can Stop Yemen's Decline.' Yemen Policy Center, November 18, 2021. https://www.yemenpolicy.org/hadis-days-are-numbered-only-accountability-transparency-and-reform-can-stop-yemens-decline/.

Sharp, Dustin N. *Rethinking Transitional Justice for the Twenty-First Century beyond the End of History.* Cambridge University Press, 2019.

Shilliam, Robbie. *Decolonizing Politics: An Introduction*. Polity Press, 2021.

Shuja al-Deen, Maysaa. 'The Houthi–Tribal Conflict in Yemen.' Carnegie Endowment for International Peace, April 23, 2019. https://carnegieendowment.org/sada/78969.

———. 'Presidential Councils in Yemen: Exploring Past Attempts at Power Sharing and Possibilities for the Future.' Sana'a Center for Strategic Studies, April 2021. https://sanaacenter.org/files/Presidential_Councils_in_Yemen_en.pdf.

Simcox, Robin. 'Ansar Al-Sharia and Governance in Southern Yemen.' Hudson Institute, December 27, 2012. http://www.hudson.org/research/9779-ansar-al-sharia-and-governance-in-southern-yemen.

Slyomovic, Susan. 'Morocco's Justice and Reconciliation Commission.' MERIP, April 4, 2005. https://merip.org/2005/04/moroccos-justice-and-reconciliation-commission/.

Snyder, Stephen. 'Yemen's Peace Deal Brings Houthi Rebels into the Government, but Many Problems Remain.' *The World from PRX*, September 22, 2014. https://www.pri.org/stories/2014-09-22/yemens-peace-deal-brings-houthi-rebels-government-many-problems-remain.

Sriram, Chandra Lekha. 'Unfinished Business: Peacebuilding, Accountability, and Rule of Law in Lebanon.' In *Transitional Justice and Peacebuilding on the Ground: Victims and Ex-Combatants*, edited by Chandra Lekha Sriram, Jemima Garcia-Godos, Johanna Herman, and Olga Martin-Ortega, 121–38. Routledge, 2012.

———. ed. *Transitional Justice in the Middle East and North Africa*. Hurst, 2017.

———. 'Beyond Transitional Justice: Peace, Governance, and Rule of Law.' *International Studies Review* 19, no. 1 (2017): 53–69.

Stan, Lavinia. 'Lustration and Vetting.' In *An Introduction to Transitional Justice*, edited by Olivera Simic, 137–55. Routledge, 2017.

Stevenson, Thomas. 'Yemeni Workers Come Home: Reabsorbing One Million Migrants.' In *Arabia Incognita: Dispatches from Yemen and the Gulf*, edited by Sheila Carapico, 87–92. Just World Books, 2016.

Sudam, Mohammed, and Mohammed Ghobari. 'Saleh Refuses to Sign Yemen Deal despite Pressure.' *Reuters*, May 22, 2011, sec. World News. https://www.reuters.com/article/us-yemen-idUSTRE73L1PP20110522.

Support Yemen, and Resonate Yemen. *Yemen Enlightenment Debate: 'Foreign Aid to Yemen Caused More Harm than Good,'* 2012. https://www.youtube.com/watch?v=G2D8qFkYwWc.

Teitel, Ruti G. *Globalizing Transitional Justice*. Oxford University Press, 2015.

Thiel, Tobias. 'Yemen's Imposed Federal Boundaries.' *Middle East Report Online*, July 20, 2015. https://merip.org/2015/07/yemens-imposed-federal-boundaries/.

Transparency International. 'Corruption Perception Index.' Accessed August 11, 2021. https://www.transparency.org/en/cpi/2020/index/nzl.

UMAM. 'Umam D&R.' Accessed July 2, 2021. https://umam-dr.org//about/.

United Nations. 'Agreement Establishing a Union between the State of the Yemen Arab Republic and the State of the People's Democratic Republic of Yemen,' April 22, 1990. https://peacemaker.un.org/sites/peacemaker.un.org/files/YE_900422_AgreementEstablishingUnionYemen.pdf.

———. 'Agreement on the Implementation Mechanism for the Transition Process in Yemen in Accordance with the Initiative of the Gulf Cooperation Council,' November 23, 2011. https://www.peaceagreements.org/viewmasterdocument/758.

United Nations Department of Political and Peacebuilding Affairs. 'Special Envoy Yemen | Department of Political and Peacebuilding Affairs.' Accessed December 17, 2021. https://dppa.un.org/en/mission/special-envoy-yemen. https://foia.state.gov/documents/IntAgreements/0000BA1E.pdf.

United Nations Human Rights Council. 'UN Group of Eminent International and Regional Experts on Yemen Briefs the UN Security Council Urging an End to Impunity, an Expansion of Sanctions, and the Referral by the UN Security Council of the Situation in Yemen to the International Criminal Court,' December 3, 2020. https://www.ohchr.org/EN/HRBodies/HRC/Pages/NewsDetail.aspx?NewsID=26563&LangID=E.

United Nations Office for the Coordination of Humanitarian Affairs. 'Yemen: Food Security Status 2009-2013,' October 30, 2013. https://reliefweb.int/sites/reliefweb.int/files/resources/Food_Security_Status_September_2013.pdf.

United Nations Security Council. 'Resolution 2014,' October 21, 2011. http://unscr.com/en/resolutions/2014.

———. 'Resolution 2282,' April 27, 2016. https://www.securitycouncilreport.org/un-documents/document/sres2282.php.

United States Department of State. '1997 Human Rights Report: Yemen,' January 30, 1998. https://1997-2001.state.gov/www/global/human_rights/1997_hrp_report/yemen.html.

————. 'Diplomatic Note,' December 10, 2003.

United States Institute for Peace. 'Dialogue Versus Debate.' Accessed July 23, 2021. https://www.usip.org/public-education/educators/dialogue-versus-debate.

United States Senate, Committee on Foreign Relations. 'Following the Money in Yemen and Lebanon: Maximizing the Effectiveness of US Security Assistance and International Financial Institution Lending.' Government Printing Office, January 5, 2010. 111–38. S. Prt. https://www.foreign.senate.gov/imo/media/doc/54245.pdf.

————. 'Understanding the Threat to the Homeland from AQAP.' Government Printing Office, September 18, 2013. 113–34. S. Prt. https://www.govinfo.gov/content/pkg/CHRG-113hhrg86483/pdf/CHRG-113hhrg86483.pdf.

Unruh, Jon D. 'Mass Claims in Land and Property Following the Arab Spring: Lessons from Yemen.' *Stability: International Journal of Security and Development* 5, no. 1 (2016): 1–19.

Veen, Erwin van. 'From the Struggle for Citizenship to the Fragmentation of Justice: Yemen from 1990 to 2013.' Clingendael: Netherlands Institute of International Relations, 2014.

Vom Bruck, Gabrielle. 'Regimes of Piety Revisited: Zaydi Political Moralities in Republican Yemen.' *Die Welt des Islam* 50 (2010): 185-223.

Vuylsteke, Sarah. 'When Aid Goes Awry: How International Humanitarian Response Is Failing Yemen.' Sana'a Center for Strategic Studies, October 2021. https://sanaacenter.org/files/When_Aid_Goes_Awry_00_Executive_Summary_en.pdf.

Waldorf, Lars. 'Anticipating the Past: Transitional Justice and Socio-Economic Wrongs.' *Social and Legal Studies* 21, no. 2 (2012): 171–86.

Waltz, Susan E. 'Linking Transitional Justice and Human Rights.' In *Transitional Justice in the Middle East and North Africa*, edited by Chandra Lekha Sriram, 37–60. Routledge, 2017.

Wedeen, Lisa. *Peripheral Visions: Publics, Power, and Performance in Yemen.* Chicago: University of Chicago Press, 2009. http://public.eblib.com/choice/publicfullrecord.aspx?p=448592.

Weir, Shelagh. *A Tribal Order: Politics and Law in the Mountains of Yemen.* University of Texas Press, 2007.

Whitaker, Brian. 'Fragile Union at Mercy of Outside Forces.' *The Guardian*, April 7, 1994.

————. 'Yemen: 1993 Parliamentary Election.' Al-Bab. Accessed August 2, 2021. https://al-bab.com/albab-orig/albab/yemen/pol/election1993.htm.

Willis, John M. *Unmaking North and South Cartographies of the Yemeni Past*. New York: Oxford University Press, 2014.

Worth, Robert. 'Yemen on the Brink of Hell.' *New York Times Magazine*, July 20, 2011. https://www.nytimes.com/2011/07/24/magazine/yemen-on-the-brink-of-hell.html.

————. 'Fighting Intensifies in Yemen as the Government Battles Tribal Groups.' *The New York Times*, May 24, 2011, sec. World. https://www.nytimes.com/2011/05/25/world/middleeast/25yemen.html.

Würth, Anna. 'Mobilizing islam and custom against statutory reform: bayt al-tâ'a in Yemen.' *Égypte/Monde arabe*, no. 1 (June 30, 2005): 277–98.

Yadav, Stacey Philbrick. 'Antecedents of the Revolution: Intersectoral Networks and Post-Partisanship in Yemen.' *Studies in Ethnicity and Nationalism* 11, no. 3 (2011): 550–63.

————. *Islamists and the State: Legitimacy and Institutions in Yemen and Lebanon*. I.B. Tauris, 2013.

————. 'The 'Yemen Model' as a Failure of Political Imagination.' *International Journal of Middle East Studies* 47, no. 1 (2015): 144–7.

————. 'Yemen's Muslim Brotherhood and the Perils of Powersharing.' Rethinking Political Islam. The Brookings Institution, August 2015. https://www.brookings.edu/wp-content/uploads/2016/07/Yemen_Yadav-FINALE.pdf.

————. 'No Pink Slip for Salih: What Yemen's Protests Do (and Do Not) Mean.' In *Arabia Incognita: Dispatches from Yemen and the Gulf*, edited by Sheila Carapico, 173–80. Just World Books, 2016.

————. 'Oman Is a Mediator in Yemen. Can It Play the Same Role in Qatar?' *Washington Post*, July 22, 2017. https://www.washingtonpost.com/news/monkey-cage/wp/2017/07/22/oman-is-a-mediator-in-yemen-can-it-play-the-same-role-in-qatar/.

————. 'Sectarianization, Islamist Republicanism, and International Misrecognition in Yemen.' In *Sectarianization: Mapping the New Politics of the Middle East*, edited by Nader Hashemi and Danny Postel, 185–98. Oxford University Press, 2017.

————. 'Ethnography Is an Option: Learning to Learn in/through Practice.' In *Political Science Research in the Middle East and North Africa: Methodological and Ethical Challenges*, edited by Janine A. Clark and Francesco Cavatorta, 165–74. Oxford University Press, 2018. https://oxford.universitypressscholarship.com/view/10.1093/oso/9780190882969.001.0001/oso-9780190882969-chapter-14.

————. 'Effective Citizenship, Civil Action, and Prospects for Post-Conflict Justice in Yemen.' *International Journal of Middle East Studies* 52 (2020): 754–8. https://doi.org/10.1017/S0020743820001051.

————. 'Civil Action Under Uncivil Conditions in Yemen.' Online Commentary. Institute for Social Justice and Conflict Resolution, May 2021. https://sas.lau.edu.lb/institutes/files/Civil%20Action%20Under%20Uncivil%20Conditions%20in%20Yemen.pdf.

Yadav, Stacey Philbrick, and Sheila Carapico. 'The Breakdown of the GCC Initiative.' *Middle East Report* 273 (2014): 2–6.

Yadav, Stacey Philbrick, and Rim Mugahed. '"One Hand Does Not Clap": The Dual Challenge of Partisan Women's Inclusion in Yemen.' Sana'a Center for Strategic Studies, December 2, 2021. https://sanaacenter.org/publications/analysis/15809.

Yadav, Stacey Philbrick, and Jillian Schwedler. 'Toward a Just Peace in Yemen.' *MERIP* 289 (2018). https://merip.org/2019/03/toward-a-just-peace-in-yemen/.

Yemen Data Project. 'Seven Years of the Saudi-Led Air War in Yemen.' Yemen Data Project, March 24, 2022. https://mailchi.mp/44ee74b497a3/seven-years-of-the-saudi-led-air-war-in-yemen-yemen-data-project-march2022-13474205.

Zunes, Stephen. 'The Power of Strategic Nonviolent Action in Arab Revolutions.' Middle East Institute, August 1, 2011. https://www.mei.edu/publications/power-strategic-nonviolent-action-arab-revolutions.

INDEX

Note: Page numbers followed by '*n*' refer to notes.